GLOBAL CAPITAL, NATIONAL STATE AND THE POLITICS OF MONEY

Also by Werner Bonefeld

OPEN MARXISM, Vol. I: History and Dialectics (*edited with Richard Gunn and Kosmas Psychopedis*)
OPEN MARXISM, Vol. II: Theory and Practice (*edited with Richard Gunn and Kosmas Psychopedis*)
OPEN MARXISM, Vol. III: Emancipating Marx (*edited with Richard Gunn, John Holloway and Kosmas Psychopedis*)
* POST-FORDISM AND SOCIAL FORM (*edited with John Holloway*)
THE RECOMPOSITION OF THE BRITISH STATE DURING THE 1980s

Also by John Holloway

OPEN MARXISM, Vol. III: Emancipating Marx (*edited with Werner Bonefeld, Richard Gunn and Kosmas Psychopedis*)
* POST-FORDISM AND SOCIAL FORM (*edited with Werner Bonefeld*)
STATE AND CAPITAL (*edited with Sol Picciotto*)

* *From the same publishers*

Global Capital, National State and the Politics of Money

Edited by

Werner Bonefeld
Lecturer in Politics
University of Edinburgh

and

John Holloway
Lecturer in Politics, University of Edinburgh, and
Professor, Instituto de Ciencias
Sociales y Humanidades
Universidad Autónoma de Puebla, Mexico

St. Martin's Press

332.041
G562

First published in Great Britain 1995 by
MACMILLAN PRESS LTD
Houndmills, Basingstoke, Hampshire RG21 2XS
and London
Companies and representatives
throughout the world

A catalogue record for this book is available
from the British Library.

ISBN 0–333–61855–6

10   9   8   7   6   5   4   3   2   1
04   03   02   01   00   99   98   97   96   95

Printed in Great Britain by
Ipswich Book Co Ltd
Ipswich, Suffolk

First published in the United States of America 1995 by
Scholarly and Reference Division,
ST. MARTIN'S PRESS, INC.,
175 Fifth Avenue,
New York, N.Y. 10010

ISBN 0–312–12466–X

Library of Congress Cataloging-in-Publication Data
Global capital, national state, and the politics of money / edited by
Werner Bonefeld and John Holloway.
p. cm.
Includes bibliographical references and index.
ISBN 0–312–12466–X
1. Capital.   2. International finance.   3. Marxian economics.
4. National state.   I. Bonefeld, Werner, 1960–   .   II. Holloway,
John. fl. 1978–   .
HB501.G548   1995
332',041—dc20   94–35570
                                                      CIP

Contents

Notes on the Contributors

Werner Bonefeld is a Lecturer in the Department of Politics, University of Edinburgh.

Peter Burnham is a Lecturer in the Department of Politics and International Studies, University of Warwick.

Harry Cleaver is Professor of Economics at the University of Austin, Texas.

John Holloway is Professor/Researcher in the Instituto de Ciencias Sociales y Humanidades of the Universidad Autonoma de Puebla, Mexico, and Lecturer in the Department of Politics, University of Edinburgh.

Christian Marazzi works at the Welfare Department of the Swiss and Italian Government and is a Professor at the Universities of Geneva and Lausanne.

1 Introduction: The Politics of Money

Werner Bonefeld and John Holloway

The neo-liberal retreat from the state which has shaped politics in nearly all countries of the world in recent years implies a change in the form in which power is exercised. The 'retreat from the state' has not, in general, reduced the role of the state or made society less bureaucratic, but it has meant a direct (re-)commodification of many aspects of social life. Many of our social needs which were previously provided by the state (at least in minimal form) are now transformed into objects of exchange. More and more, our access to so many things that previously did not depend entirely on the market – medical care, housing, education, transport, not to mention the 'luxuries' of holidays, food and drink – depends directly on how much money we have. Money has risen to a new prominence in our daily experience.

The rise of money is not merely a question of personal experience. The relation between the productive, commodity and money forms of capital has changed sharply over the last twenty years or so. 'De-industrialisation', a topic of concern in Britain and many other countries over the period, has meant above all the conversion of productive capital into money capital. When a factory is closed, the capital does not simply disappear; nor, usually, does it simply reappear in the construction of a new factory elsewhere. What was previously productive capital becomes money capital which can be moved to wherever in the world it is likely to yield the greatest profit. At the same time, the movement of money has gained in importance in relation to the movement of commodities (trade). In 1979, transactions in the international financial markets represented six times the value of world trade: by 1986 they represented about twenty-five times the value of world trade (see Walter, 1993, p. 197).

The enormous shift of capital into money has important consequences for states and their relation to the international economy. In Britain, Black Wednesday (16 September 1992, when speculation against the pound on the international financial markets forced the Major government to withdraw from the European Exchange Rate

Mechanism and radically to revise its economic policies) did much to bring home to public consciousness the awesome political power of the vast quantities of money (now over $1 trillion) traded each day on the world's financial markets, and to create an awareness of the changing relation between international finance and individual nations states.[1] Events such as this have made it clear that it is not possible to discuss the political development of any state in isolation from the movement of money on the world markets.

One aspect of the rise of money has been the even more spectacular rise in the importance of debt. The possible consequences of the expansion of debt were made clear in the so-called 'debt crisis' caused by the Mexican government's announcement in 1982 that it was having difficulty in meeting its debt repayment obligations. The implications were enormous for the whole world: debt default by Mexico and other leading debtors like Argentina and Brazil could easily have led to the total collapse of the world financial system. In the event, the immediate danger was avoided, partly through the imposition of unprecedented 'austerity' on large parts of the world's population (the 'lost decade' in Latin America, misery and famine in Africa), and partly through the displacement of debt. Debt shifted to the richer and apparently more credit-worthy parts of the world: the US government, by cutting taxes and raising arms expenditure, took over the role of principal debtor (and on a vastly larger scale), and there was a huge increase in personal and company debt throughout the richer countries.[2] The consequence of the huge expansion of private debt were increasingly felt as the credit-based boom of the 1980s turned into the recession of the 1990s, and the offers of easy credit turned into debt enforcement, bankruptcies and house repossessions.[3]

From these few comments on the rise of money and debt, it should be clear that we need to be able to speak of a 'politics of money'. The rise of money means a change in the form in which social relations of power are fought out. Money has always been a dominant form of power relations in capitalist society, but in recent years it has assumed a new quality, acquired a new brazenness. Much that was temporarily hidden from view by the welfare state capitalism of the post-war period has now become obvious: principally, the power of money and (another way of saying the same thing) the inherently global nature of power relations.

Money, then, cannot be treated as an aspect of economics. At one level, certainly, it appears to have a life of its own, to be an economic thing which stands outside and above social conflict. On the other

hand we constantly experience money as a constantly contested relation of power. Every time we go to a shop, every time we pass a
beggar in the street, every time a house is burgled, every time the
rate of interest goes up or the price of shares falls, every time we
hesitate to go to the dentist because of the cost, every time the sheriff
officer (bailiff) makes a call, money is at issue, not as external to
social conflict, not as the framework of conflict, but as the very stuff
of conflict.

This book makes a contribution to the growing field of international political economy. The approach adopted, however, is a specific one. All the authors write from a background in Marxist theory.
However, within the Marxist tradition, as in the non-Marxist tradition, money has too often been treated as an aspect of 'economics',
as an element of the framework within which class struggle takes
place rather than as being a form of class struggle itself. In this book
the focus is on understanding money as class struggle, and on how
the changing role of money is constituted by the antagonistic social
relations of capitalism. This is an area of discussion that has been
largely neglected by Marxists as by others.

The book explores three interrelated aspects of the crisis of capitalist
accumulation. It examines the crisis of Keynesianism and the rise of
monetarism; it analyses the relationship between the global economy
and the national state and the transformation of this relationship
over the last two decades; and it supplies a critique of the politics of
money.

The book is an exploration of money as a form of social relations,
a form of class struggle. All the studies presented here share this
concern: they do not all pursue the same line of argument, but all are
attempts to develop an understanding of the changing significance of
money as class conflict. Central to the whole discussion of money as
a form of class struggle is the understanding that the other side of
monetary instability is the insubordinate power of labour. This issue
is taken up from different perspectives in all our contributions.

Central to the whole discussion is the crisis of Keynesianism (a
form of domination in which many aspects of society are withdrawn
from direct subjection to money) and the rise of monetarism. These
two topics are discussed in Chapters 2 and 3, by John Holloway and
by Werner Bonefeld. Their contributions show that both Keynesianism
and monetarism were political responses to labour's insubordinate
power. Holloway emphasises the importance of the October revolution
of 1917 for the so-called Keynesian revolution and argues that

Keynesianism was a means of making capitalism safe for capital. He
goes on to argue that the class conflict of the late 1960s undermined
the Keynesian notion of a reformed capitalism. Bonefeld argues that
monetarist policies never overcame the crisis of Keynesianism and
that the apparent success of monetarism during the 1980s was a
delusion. Both contributions follow the trajectory of Keynesianism/
monetarism and show that Keynesianism and monetarism are political by virtue of the way in which labour's insubordinate power is
integrated into the capital relation.

   The analysis of the changing relation between national states and
the global movement of money, and of the changing meaning of 'the
state' in relation to world capitalism is developed in Chapters 5 and
6 by John Holloway and by Peter Burnham. Holloway starts by
assessing the so-called 'state derivation' debate of the 1970s and goes
on to examine the territorial organisation of the 'political' in the
form of the national state. Burnham examines the historical development of the capitalist state during so-called primitive accumulation
and shows that the 'capitalist state' always existed in the form of an
'international state system'. He criticises realist approaches to the
study of international relations by analysing the changing relation
between the national state and the global economy during the last
two decades.

   The question of the internal relation between money and class
struggle and of the politics of money in the 1970s and 1980s is developed in Chapters 4, 7 and 8, by Christian Marazzi, by Harry Cleaver
and by Werner Bonefeld. The issue of the relationship of money to
the state is taken up in Bonefeld's Chapter 8. He supplies an interpretation of Marx's writing on money and shows that money exists
contradictorily as command over labour. His interpretation of Marx
shows that the speculative dimension of capitalist accumulation during
the 1980s was not an aberration but that it rather manifested the
most elementary form of capitalist wealth, that is, the expansion of
money through money. At the same time, his contribution also shows
the contradictory character of capitalist speculation. According to
him, money has meaning only when it commands the labour of others.
This speculation, while being the most elementary form of capitalist
accumulation, also deprives capital of its meaning. The result is the
assertion of money as a social power which imposes itself through
force. He summarises Marx's treatment of money by examining
the relation of money to the state. The issue of money as a self-
contradictory social power is analysed in Marazzi's contribution. He

examines the relation of money to exploitation against the background of the breakdown of the system of Bretton Woods and shows that the expansion of money meant that it no longer managed the exploitation of labour. He theorises the crisis of money and examines the politics of austerity in the 1970s, taking as an example the case of New York City. His focus is on money as awesome social power which he addresses in terms of an 'international terrorism of money'. Marazzi shows that the rise of monetarism in the 1970s was a response to the inconvertibility of money into expanded command over labour in production. The contribution by Cleaver shows that the notions of 'Keynesian economics' and 'monetarist economics' are false names given to capitalist strategies to secure the exploitation of labour. He focuses on the failure of monetarist policies in the 1980s and argues that the monetarist regimes of tight money failed to strengthen the link between money and exploitation. For him, the other side of the capitalist failure to use money as a means of managing the exploitation of labour is labour's insubordinate power. He shows that it is this power which lies at the heart of the capitalist crisis. The other side the expansion of credit during the 1980s is the self-activity of the working class which, for him, has become much more socialised and globalised.

The book concludes in Chapter 9 with a joint article by Bonefeld and Holloway, in which we try to draw some of the strands together by suggesting that the development of money can be seen as the movement of the composition, decomposition and recomposition of insubordinate labour. The study draws parallels with the 1930s and argues that the present crisis carries both hope and warning. The warning is that the current fragility of capitalism might be resolved through a slump (or worse) with all its political and human consequences. The hope is that labour's insubordinate power can be made productive and fruitful for a world in which poverty is not the condition of wealth.

From this brief presentation of some of the issues discussed in the studies collected in this book, it might appear that all that is at issue is the definition of concepts and an analysis of the changing relationship between the global economy and the national state with little practical importance. Nothing could be further from the truth.[4]

It is important to remember that the last major crisis of capitalism was resolved only through the destruction of millions of lives, and the possibility of this recurring, but on a far greater scale, is a very real one. 'Crisis', as one of us has argued elsewhere, 'does not simply refer to "hard times", but to turning points. It directs attention to the discontinuities of history, to breaks in the path of development, ruptures in a pattern of movement, variations in the intensity of time' (Holloway, 1992, p. 146). This book contributes to an understanding the dangers and opportunities which the current crisis presents. Crisis does not mean the restructuring of capital, although it may contain the possibility of restructuring. Between crisis-as-rupture and crisis-as-restructuring there is an abyss of possibility. Our hope is that this book will contribute in a small way to the construction of a reasonable society in which humanity exists as a purpose rather than as a resource for the accumulation of money. The critique of capitalist exploitation entails a critique of 'money' and the understanding that the liberation from exploitation means a liberation from money.

Notes

1. 'Central bank reserves are less than the equivalent of two days' turnover in the world's foreign exchange markets, which indicates that one central bank or even a number of central banks intervening together in exchange markets cannot hope to oppose a concerted onslaught on a particular currency or currencies by the exchange markets' (Walter, 1993, p. 199).
2. For example, 'between 1976 and mid-1987, aggregate US debt rose from $2.5 trillion to nearly $8 trillion, and the ratio of total debt to GNP rose from 136% to 178% ... The indebtedness of the private sector in Japan has risen substantially in recent years: the indebtedness of non-financial companies increased from 94% of GDP in 1975 to 135% in 1990, while that of households increased from 45% to 96% of disposable income over the same period' (Walter, 1993, pp. 214–15).
3. For a discussion of the implications of rising personal debt, see Ford (1988).
4. See also the debate between Ticktin and Cleaver (1993).

References

Ford, J. (1988) *The Indebted Society: Credit and Default in the 1980s* (London: Routledge).
Holloway, J. (1992) 'Crisis, Fetishism, Class Composition', in W. Bonefeld, R. Gunn and Psychopedis, K. (eds), *Open Marxism Vol. II: Theory and Practice* (London: Pluto Press).
Ticktin, H. and Cleaver, H. (1993) 'Harry Cleaver debates Hillel Ticktin on Capitalism's present Crisis ... Danger and Opportunity', *Radical Chains*, 4.
Walter, A. (1993) *World Power and World Money* (London: Harvester Wheatsheaf).

2 The Abyss Opens: The Rise and Fall of Keynesianism

John Holloway

I

Keynes lounging in an armchair, comfortable, thoughtful and benign, a pile of books and papers beside him, against the background of a chart showing the dramatic decline in unemployment form the 1930s to the 1960s: the cover of a popular book conveys perfectly the popular image of Keynesianism. For much of the post-war period, Keynesianism was presented simply as a beneficial, rational, scientific advance in the management of the economy, as a theoretical development which provided the basis for overcoming the problem of capitalist crisis and creating a just capitalist society. Even in recent years, when Keynesianism has been so much criticised, the image remains of Keynesianism as a possibly misguided, but certainly well-meaning theoretical development. In the midst of such images, it is sometimes hard to remember that the adoption of Keynesian policies was the culmination of a prolonged conflict, of a violence, horror and bloodiness quite unprecedented in the history of the world.

Keynes was of course an economist. 'Keynesianism' refers strictly to the economic theories which he propounded and to the economic policies associated with his name, which gained influence throughout the world during and after the Second World War. These theories and policies should not, however, be seen in isolation: their adoption formed an important part of the establishment of a new pattern of relations between capital and labour and for that reason the term 'Keynesian' is often used to refer more broadly to the pattern of political and economic relations associated with those theories and policies. It is primarily in this broad sense that the term will be used here.

The central feature of Keynesianism was the acknowledgement of the organisational strength of the working class. Keynesianism made

7

explicit in institutional form the dependence of capital upon labour, the strength of the presence of labour in-and-against capital.

The aim of this chapter is to examine the establishment and the collapse of Keynesianism as a mode of domination, a mode of containing the power of labour.

The power of labour to which Keynesianism responded was most dramatically illustrated in the 'red October' of 1917. The Russian revolution was not an isolated event, but the crest of a wave: the surface of capitalism was broken not only in St Petersburg and Moscow, but, more briefly, in other places too – Berlin, Budapest, Munich, Turin, etc. These revolutionary struggles at the end of the First World War were part of a much broader change: as Woodrow Wilson put it shortly before his death, the Russian revolution was 'the symbol of the discontent of the age' (Schlesinger, 1957, p. 94). The revolutionary movement fed from and fed into a longer-term, less spectacular surge in the power of the working class, expressed in the rise of trade unionism and social democratic parties in all the advanced capitalist countries from the end of the nineteenth century. For all the failings of the organised movement (most notably the collapse of 'socialist internationalism' on the eve of the war), the visible power of the working class had grown enormously in the early years of the century.

Beneath the visible, organised power of labour lay a less visible, more insidious power: the power of the exploited to resist exploitation. The growing organisations derived much of their power from the workers' realisation that, however bad their conditions might be, there were limits to the extent to which they could be exploited. Capital might control their lives, but capital too depended on their work for its survival. Power derived precisely from the condition which defined the working class: labour. This realisation was expressed not only in the withdrawal of labour in strikes, but in the constant, everyday struggle for control of the process of work: the control of how things were done, at what speed. Even the most domineering capitalists were confronted frustratingly with the fact that they did not fully control the work process which was the source of their own profit. As F.W. Taylor recounted of his own experience, 'as was usual then . . . , the shop was really run by the workmen and not by the bosses. The workmen together had carfully planned just how fast each job should be done' (Braverman, 1974, p. 102). Taylor's life work articulated the frustration of capital and was dedicated to overcoming its source, the power of labour to control the labour process.

The extent of the power of the workers to control their own labour varied according to the area, the industry and, most importantly, the type of work involved. It was particularly the more skilled workers who played an indispensable role in the labour process and who were able to exercise most control over their own process of work. The position of the skilled workers gave a particular complexion to the working class movement at the time, reflected in trade union organisation (based mainly on craft lines) and in the ideology of even the more revolutionary sections of the socialist movement, with their vision of socialism in terms of workers' control of the work process. For capital, the skill of the workers turned from being a necessary condition for industrial development into being an obstacle to capital accumulation (Coriat, 1982, p. 12).

From the beginning of the century, capital was increasingly confronted with its own dependence upon labour. This expressed itself both in apprehension of the organised labour movement and in growing difficulty in raising surplus value production sufficiently to offset the rising costs of investment. The imperialist flight of capital to a new workforce, new raw materials and new markets offset the difficulties but also raised inter-capitalist competition to a new level of inter-imperialist rivalry and war.

The impact of the war was double-edged. On the one hand, it split the international labour movement and led to a weakening of the position of the skilled worker within the factory, as established practices were 'diluted' by bringing in women to help with the war effort; on the other, it stirred up a wave of discontent throughout the world that threatened capital as it had never been threatened before.

Capital's response to this threat was complex. From the end of the war, in all the leading capitalist countries, there were voices calling for reform: politicians and theorists of the bourgeoisie who argued that the old capitalism had been discredited and that a radically new social order was necessary. These calls took many different forms and surfaced on many different occasions through the 1920s.

There were three principal issues in the strategic debates of the 1920s: international relations, the role of the state and the control of money.

The first clash between 'progressives' and 'reactionaries' came immediately after the war, in the negotiation of the Versailles peace treaty. Many of the young reformers who were part of their national delegations resigned in disgust when they realised that their leaders were more interested in the 'evil old conspiracy of naked force'

(Schlesinger, 1957, p. 14) than in creating a new era in world history. Among those who resigned was Keynes, who was present as part of the British delegation. One of the key issues was the attitude of the western powers to the new revolutionary government in Russia. For the progressives, the response to the Soviet threat should be conciliatory. In the pamphlet which he wrote to justify his resignation, 'The Economic Consequences of the Peace', Keynes inveighed against the old-style diplomats who 'behave as if foreign policy was of the same genre as a cheap melodrama' (Keynes, 1971, p. 185), and argued that, rather than excluding Russia and taking revenge on Germany, the policy of the victorious powers should aim at reconstructing Germany and reintegrating Russia into world trade: 'whether or not the form of communism represented by the Soviet government proves permanently suited to the Russian temperament, the revival of trade, of the comforts of life and of ordinary economic motives are not likely to promote the extreme forms of those doctrines of violence and tyranny which are the children of war and of despair' (Keynes, 1971, p. 187; cf. also Negri, 1988, p. 16).

The issue of the new international order was quickly settled against the views of the progressives by the Treaty of Versailles. The second issue, the question of the role of the state, remained alive throughout the 1920s. The war had seen an unprecedented expansion in the role of the state, involving extensive control of production (cf. Clarke, 1988, pp. 193ff). In the years after the war, the 'progressives' argued that the development of capitalism made it imperative that the state should maintain an active, interventionist role in the economy. The argument took different forms and rested on different justifications, from acknowledged fear of revolution to charitable concern for the poor to the simple pursuit of economic efficiency, but there were a number of threads that ran through the debate in all countries. The most immediate issue was the role of the state in production. Everywhere, the state had taken over, directly or indirectly, important sections of production and transport during the war. The 'progressives' argued that these should not be returned to private ownership, that the modern state should control certain basic industries in the interests of the national welfare (cf. Schlesinger, 1957, pp. 37ff; Clarke, 1988, p. 200). This argument was lost: the industries taken over during the war were on the whole returned to private hands in the years immediately following. But the argument concerning the role of the state continued. It was argued that the state should be more active in providing social welfare provision for the poor, especially in the case of unemployment. It was argued too that the state should play a more active role in encouraging economic efficiency, especially through the promotion of economic 'rationalisation'. All the functions that are usually associated with the post-1945 'Keynesian' state were already being argued for in the 1920s.

This is true also true of the general conception of the state as being responsible for the management of the economy, particularly through the manipulation of demand. Such ideas were to be found not only in Keynes' early writings, but also, for example, in the work of Foster and Catchings in the United States. In their book, *The Road to Plenty*, published in 1928, they attacked Say's Law, the foundation of orthodox economic theory, which held that total demand for goods must equal total supply, so that the financing of production automatically created enough purchasing power to purchase all the goods produced. Foster and Catchings pointed out that there was no such automatic balance, since the flow of money was constantly interrupted by saving (as indeed Marx had pointed out in Chapter 2 of *Capital* sixty years before). Hence, the only way to maintain prosperity was for the government to maintain an adequate flow of money income to consumers: its policies should be founded on the principles of 'putting more money into consumers' hands when business is falling off, and less money when inflation is under way' (Schlesinger, 1957, p. 135).

Money was central to any discussion of an expanded role for the state. Plans such as that proposed by Foster and Catchings would involve the government running budget deficits in times of recession, and such an idea was abhorrent to the more orthodox politicians and theorists of the day. The issue of financial orthodoxy during this period crystallised around discussions of the gold standard. The reconstruction of the gold standard, under which national currencies are tied to the price of gold, was seen by many as the key to the reconstruction of the international political system after the First World War and was one of the first tasks undertaken by the new League of Nations (Clarke, 1988, p. 204). The significance (both symbolic and real) of the restoration of the gold standard was that it subordinated national currency, and hence the nation state, to the international movement of money, and thereby anchored the minimal role of the state which the conservatives wished to safeguard. It imposed on governments a financial discipline which popular pressures might otherwise lead them to evade. The restoration and maintenance of the gold standard thus became a symbol for the viability of the old liberal world order, which the 'progressives' claimed was doomed to extinction.

The debates of the 1920s on the international order, the role of the state and money, were conducted among policy makers, advisers and critics: the politicians, civil servants and intellectuals of the bourgeoisie. Behind them, however, stood the unspoken (or at least rarely mentioned) subject of all bourgeois theory: the power of the working class. This is not to say that, for example, the idealists who resigned from their national delegations at Versailles were cynically concerned only with a more effective means of suppressing labour, but that the course of the argument was shaped by 'reality' and that the most important feature of that 'reality' was the growing difficulty experienced in dominating and exploiting labour. At issue in the debates of the 1920s was a clash between two strategic responses to the new power symbolised by the October Revolution of 1917.

The subject of the debates occasionally broke through in explicit terms. Far away from the streets of St Petersburg, Berlin or Munich, the US Attorney General, A. Mitchell Palmer, gave colourful expression to the fears of capital everywhere when he said in 1920:

> Like a prairie-fire, the blaze of revolution was sweeping over every American institution of law and order a year ago. It was eating its way into the homes of the American workman, its sharp tongues of revolutionary heat were licking the altars of the churches, leaping into the belfry of the school bell, crawling into the sacred corners of American homes, seeking to replace marriage vows with libertine laws, burning up the foundations of society (Schlesinger, 1957, p. 42).

For politicians of the stamp of Palmer, the response was simple: suppression by force of anything remotely resembling a revolutionary threat, withdrawal of the state from the expanded role assumed during the war, exclusion of trade unionists from the policy making process into which they had been coopted during the fighting, restoration of the power of money over the state. In international affairs, this position was matched by a non-conciliatory approach to the Soviet revolution, first military intervention and then diplomatic isolation. In retrospect, this approach has often been portrayed as simpleminded: it was, however, by and large the strategy which was implemented by all the major governments throughout the 1920s. The 1920s were built on the violent suppression of workers' movements, real and imagined, throughout the world.

The other response was more complex. To speak of it as a single 'strategic response' is, of course, a gross simplification. It was made up of a plethora of policies, policy proposals, managerial innovations and theoretical developments in different parts of the world, with different motivations and different implications. But the common theme everywhere was the assumption of a new role by the state, and the common background everywhere was the wave of discontent symbolised by the Russian revolution. The starting point was an awareness that things had changed. The old balance was broken:

> The idea of the old-world party, that you can, for example, alter the value of money and then leave the consequential adjustments to be brought about by the forces of supply and demand, belongs to the days of fifty or a hundred years ago when trade unions were powerless, and when the economic juggernaut was allowed to crash along the highway of progress without obstruction and even with applause. Half the copybook assumptions of our statesmen is based on assumptions which were at one time true, or partly true, but are now less and less true day by day (Keynes, 1972, p. 305).

The old equilibrium had been broken by the collective power of labour. The assumption that labour power could simply be treated as any other commodity on the market was no longer valid: 'the trade unions are strong enough to interfere with the free play of the forces of supply and demand' (Keynes, 1972, p. 305). As a result, Say's Law had lost its validity: it could no longer be assumed that market forces alone would ensure the most efficient use of resources:

> In the economic field this means, first of all, that we must find new policies and new instruments to adapt and control the working of economic forces, so that they do not intolerably interfere with contemporary ideas as to what is fit and proper in the interests of social stability and social justice (Keynes, 1972, p. 306).

Whereas the 'old-world party' did not recognise, or refused to recognise, the changed balance of forces within society, the progressives argued for a new accommodation with labour. This did not mean taking the side of labour ('I can be influenced by what seems to me to be justice and good sense; but the class war will find me on the side of the educated bourgeoisie', as Keynes declared in the same article, 1972, p. 297), but developing a strategy based on the recognition of the new situation, a strategy that would integrate the working class as a force for development within capitalism (cf. Negri, 1988), a strategy that would not openly defeat, but contain and redefine the power of the working class.

It was not only in discussions of state policy but also in the development of management practices that awareness was growing of a new situation. Taylor had been preaching his gospel of 'scientific management' since the turn of the century: an explicit attack on the power of the skilled worker through the detailed study and the fragmentation of skilled tasks into simple and closely controlled operations. The fragmentation of tasks had been developed further by Henry Ford, who had connected it to the electrically driven conveyor belt to create the assembly line, the detailed steps in the production of the Ford cars being performed at different positions along the line. However, Ford's technological development of scientific management was soon confronted by the fact that cars are produced neither by science nor by technology but by people working. The workers, not surprisingly, found the new organisation of work unbearably boring and rarely stayed long. During the year of 1913, for example, in order to maintain a workforce of 15,000, it was necessary to hire 53,000 workers (Coriat, 1982, p. 56). It was in order to control this chaotic flow of labour that Ford introduced his famous 'five dollars a day' wage contract in 1914.

Five dollars was more than double the previous wage at Ford's factory, but it was not given to everybody. In order to receive such a high wage, it was necessary to be a man, over twenty-one, and to have been working at the factory for at least six months. It was also necessary to show oneself morally worthy of such a high wage. As the director of Ford's newly created department of sociology put it:

> It was easy to foresee that in the hands of certain men, five dollars a day could constitute a serious obstacle on the path of rectitude and of a well-ordered life and could make them a menace to society as a whole; that is why it was established from the beginning that no man could receive this increase who did not know how to use it in a discrete and prudent manner (Lee, 1916, p. 303, quoted by Coriat, 1982, p. 57).

The five-dollar day was extremely successful in reducing the turnover of labour: after 1914 it dropped to less than 0.5% per year (Coriat, 1982, p. 59). This created the basis for a new, more disciplined organisation of production within the factory, an intensification of work which, despite the rise in wage costs, reduced the costs of production of the Model T Ford by about 17% (Beynon, 1973, p. 24; Coriat, 1982, p. 59). In addition, it also created a new group of relatively prosperous workers, who then provided a new market for the mass-produced Model T.

The striking feature of the Ford contract is the trade-off between the acceptance of disciplined, soul-destroying monotony during the day and a relatively comfortable consumption after hours, the rigid separation between the death of alienated labour and the 'life' of consumption. What needs to be emphasised, however, is not simply the oppressive nature of Fordist production, but that the Ford contract was a striking acknowledgement of the dependence of capital upon labour, and the attempt to reformulate the power of labour (ultimately, the power not to labour) as monetary demand for commodities. It was the innovatory acknowledgement-and-redefinition of the power of labour that made Ford an important figure in this period, 'the most influential of all business leaders' (Schlesinger, 1959, p. 73).

It was not just Ford and his followers who were introducing new styles of management. There were other voices of managerial change during the 1920s as management sought to deal with the problems of high turnover and the informal resistance of the workers: many of the large corporations began to experiment during this period with more 'liberal' ways of organising work and more systematic methods of organising production (Gordon *et al.*, 1982, pp. 172ff). All these methods sought ways of channelling the discontent of the workers into a form that would serve the interests of capital.

The changes at managerial level and the new views on the way that the state should develop were quite uncoordinated, although there were those who argued that what was needed was 'a Taylor . . . for the economic system as a whole' (Tugwell, quoted in Schlesinger, 1959, p. 194), and others who saw connections between Taylor and Keynes (Schlesinger, 1959, p. 201).

In the 1920s, however, the changes in management were still only beginning to spread and 'the old-world party' still reigned supreme in politics. In retrospect, the views of the conservatives are generally portrayed as simply reactionary and out of touch with the new reality of the post-war world. It can be argued, however, that the time had not yet come for the new strategy of domination. The old balance was broken, but it is not clear that the conditions yet existed for the establishment of any new equilibrium. In the immediate post-war world, the threat of revolution still loomed large in many parts of the world. It was only after the revolutionary wave of struggles had been violently suppressed that the strategy of reformulating working class power became credible. It was only after the defeat of the General Strike in Great Britain in 1926, for example, that there developed a new institutionalisation of working class struggle, which would later provide the counterpart of Keynesian policy initiatives.

After the working class had been defeated on the streets and the immediate threat of revolution had receded, the conditions were more favourable for the institutional integration of working class power, but the urgency of change was less obvious. Only after the crash of 1929 and the ensuing crisis did the pressure for change gain a new force.

The crash of 1929 was the final crash of the old order, the final breakdown of the established mode of domination. That the crash was a turning point in historical development is generally undisputed, but it is usually presented as an economic event external to the development of class relations. The immediate cause of the crash is generally seen as an overaccumulation of capital in relation to a limited market (cf., e.g., Clarke, 1988, p. 217). The boom in the US economy during the 1920s had been based on the rapid expansion of the new consumer durables industry, but the market was narrow, being limited essentially to the middle class. An expansion of credit allowed accumulation to continue after the market had been exhausted, but this took the form of stock market speculation. The barrier of the limited market finally asserted itself in the stock market collapse of 1929.

The crash was more than that, however: it was the other face of the October Revolution of 1917. On the surface there is no connection between the two events: 'it would seem obvious that the events of 1917 had no bearing on those of 1929', as Negri points out (1988, p. 22). In fact, the two dates mark important aspects of the same crisis. The revolution of 1917 had been the loudest declaration by the working class that the old relation between capital and labour was at breaking point. The crash of 1929 brought home to capital that this was indeed the case, despite all its attempts to recreate the pre-war world.

But then why is the 'inner connection' between 1917 and 1929 not more obvious? If the crash of 1929 was the vindication of the claims made by socialists about the intensity of the contradictions of capital and the immanence of breakdown, why did it come too late, long after the revolutionary tide had already receded? If the crash of 1929 was simply the most dramatic expression of the breakdown of the old pattern of relations between capital and labour, if 'the crisis of 1929 was actually a continuation of the unresolved economic crisis preceding World War I', as Mattick puts it (1978, p. 116), then why did it not occur when the power of labour was at its greatest? What was the connection between the power of the working class, seen at its most dramatic in 1917, and the collapse of capitalism twelve years later? If crisis is the expression of the power of labour in-and-against capital, then why did crisis come when, on the face of it, labour had been decisively beaten?

Credit is the key to understanding the distance between 1917 and 1929, the key to the dislocation of the two faces of the crisis. The power of labour is refracted through the forms of the capital relation, especially through money and credit. As the prevailing pattern of exploitation comes up against its limits, as capital's pursuit of profit is obstructed by the established positions of labour, there is an expansion both in the demand for and in the provision of credit. On the one hand, capitals seek loans to tide them over what they see as temporary difficulties. On the other, capital which finds it difficult to find profits in production seeks to expand through the financial markets. Built into the existence of money as a form distinct from value is the possibility (or inevitability) of a temporal dislocation between the breakdown of the relation between capital and labour and its manifestation in the form of a fall in capitalist profitability.

Credit is always a gamble on the future. In borrowing, capital commits a portion of surplus value not yet produced. If the required surplus value is not produced, the capital will fall. If the conditions of production can be altered sufficiently to expand the production of surplus value by the requisite amount, then the gamble will have succeeded. Credit expansion, by postponing a fall in profitability, makes the restructuring of production relations objectively more urgent than ever. It also makes it more difficult, by maintaining the conditions in which the power of labour has developed.

This is essentially what happened in the 1920s. The restocking boom which was the immediate aftermath of the war was over in Europe by 1921 (Clarke, 1988, p. 197). In the United States, however, the boom continued through the 1920s, sustained at first by the restructuring of production that had taken place during the war (Mattick, 1978, p. 116) and the development of the new automobile and consumer durable industries, and then increasingly through an enormous expansion of credit, both in the form of bank loans and through the creation of fictitious capital on the stock market (Mattick, 1978, p. 119). Productivity rose sharply in the United States during the 1920s, but not sharply enough to produce the surplus value required to sustain profitability. Eventually the gap between the surplus value actually produced and that which was being gambled upon in the stock market manifested itself in the crash of October 1929: 'finally America, too, succumbed to the post-war realities', as Mattick puts it (1978, p. 116).

Even after the crash, however, there was no immediate recognition of the need for a new order, certainly at the political level. In the United States, in Britain and elsewhere, the government response was retrenchment. Pressure on the state to play a more active role in stimulating the economy and in providing welfare relief for the millions thrown out of work was answered by financial orthodoxy. The balanced budget became the symbol of the political defence of a world which no longer existed.

In the sphere of individual capitals change was forced more quickly. The collapse in profitability forced capitals to reorganise their relation with labour in order to survive. The new systems of management that had slowly been making ground in the 1920s soon became a precondition for survival:

> Two effects of the Depression immediately focussed attention on the need for new systems of labour management. First, the collapse of profits itself pressured corporations to consider whatever methods were available which might restore profitability and improve their control over the labour process. Second, the Depression led fairly quickly to worker dissatisfaction – and ultimately, of course, to the emergence of industrial unions. The industrial union movement constituted a new force with which large employers had to contend, directly challenging some of the most important elements of both the drive system and the early explorations of more sophisticated policies (Gordon *et al.*, 1982, p. 176).

It was this new thrust of the power of labour that at last gave shape to capital's changing form of domination. In the United States, the dissatisfaction of labour, the protest against the power of money symbolised by the balanced budget, had brought the defeat of Hoover in the elections of 1932 and the triumph of Roosevelt with his commitment to a 'new deal'. The original new deal was, however, vague and self-contradictory: it was only under the pressure of the industrial struggles of the 1930s and the rise of the new industrial unionism organised in the CIO that it acquired the shape that we associate with it today.

The new industrial unionism grew out of the new relations at work. The spread of Fordism meant the spread of a new type of mass, unskilled worker working in large factories. The Fordist deal, the trade-off between boredom and pay, had made the wage the focus of struggle more clearly than ever before. When Ford announced his 'five dollars a day' in 1915, it had been a unilateral act to stem the flight from intolerable working conditions. But once the wage had been made the focal point of the relation to such an exclusive extent, the workers were unlikely to wait for the fiat of management. Pressure for collective wage bargaining led to the mushrooming of a new industrial unionism in the early 1930s. The demand for recognition of the new unions as the representatives of labour in collective bargaining was accepted by more and more companies throughout the 1930s. This was not without resistance, but there was also recognition by capital that the channelling of discontent into the wage demand was an important component in establishing a more orderly relation with labour. This was dramatically captured by the posters for the recruitment drive of the CIO: 'President Roosevelt wants you to join the union.' As Tronti points out:

> The password 'organise the unorganised' was acceptable to both modern capitalism and the new union. In recent history there are these moments of elective affinity between the two classes when, each in its own camp, [they] find themselves internally divided and must simultaneously resolve problems of strategic location and of organisational restructuring (1976, p. 117).

It was this drive of labour that led to the labour policies of the Roosevelt administration and the enactment of the Wagner Act of 1935. Under immense social pressure and against often strong resistance from important sections of capital, a new relationship between capital and labour was forged in the United States in the 1930s, focussed on the recognition and attempted integration of the power of labour. The 'New Deal' 'implied the beginning of a fresh game but with the same players' (Mattick, 1978, p. 129). The 'fresh game' was what later became known as Keynesianism: 'Lord Keynes', in Tronti's striking phrase, 'is actually an American economist' (1976, p. 115).

In the mid-1930s, however, the fresh game was still far from being established. For one thing, there were alternative, competing models of what the new game should look like. In Germany, the crisis of the old pattern and the drive of labour had met with a different response. Here the violent suppression of the post-war revolutionary currents was not so cleanly separated from the institutional incorporation of the working class movement, so that the new corporatism took a particularly bloody form. In Russia too, the enormous power of labour's thrust in 1917 had given a very different form to the eventual containment of that power under Stalin.

It was not simply the existence of competing models that prevented the firm establishment of the new game. More crucial was the fact that the conditions had not yet been established for a firm restoration of capitalist profitability. The economic recovery of the early New Deal years proved to be short-lived. At the end of 1937, there was a new slump. Steel production, for example, declined from 80% of capacity to 19%. Despite the subsequent revival, there were still 10 million unemployed in the United States in 1939 and private investments were still one-third below the level of 1929 (Mattick, 1978, pp. 138–9). Although the practices of the New Deal were given a new theoretical coherence by the publication of Keynes' *General Theory* in 1936, neither theoretical coherence nor government policies were sufficient to achieve the restructuring that was required to re-establish capitalism on a firm footing.

That restructuring was achieved through war. 'Death, the greatest of all the Keynesians, now ruled the world once more' (Mattick, 1978, p. 142). War succeeded where the New Deal, Naziism and Stalinism had shown only possible lines of development. The war achieved a destruction and devaluation of constant capital even greater than that associated with the bankruptcies and depreciations of the Great Depression. At work, the managerial changes introduced after the crash of 1929 were carried further, but in a new atmosphere of discipline: in the United States, for example, 'many employers used the advantage of wartime discipline after 1941 to seek to regain some of the initiative and control they had surrendered to industrial unions at the end of the Depression' (Gordon *et al.*, 1982, p. 182). In this, employers in all the major countries were helped considerably by the trade unions, which preached the subordination of class antagonism to the common goal of winning the war (cf., e.g., Gordon *et al.*, 1982, p. 183; Middlemas, 1979, pp. 266ff). The changes in relations at work were accompanied by rapid change in the technology of production as governments poured resources into areas of technological development considered to be strategically important, so that there was rapid progress in areas such as electronics and petrochemicals. Unemployment was solved through the enlisting and killing of millions of people: a massive 'scrapping of labour power' (Bonefeld, 1988, p. 56).

The war was the culmination of the restructuring efforts of the inter-war years. In an article in 1918, John Dewey, already one of the intellectual leaders of American liberalism, had pointed to 'the social possibilities of war' – the use of technology for communal purposes, the subordination of production for profit to production for use, the organisation of the means for public control (Dewey 1918, cited in Schlesinger, 1957, p. 39). The Taylorisation of society which Roosevelt's adviser, Tugwell, had looked for in the New Deal was given a new degree of reality in the war. The expansion of the state which New Dealers and Keynesians had long sought was realised to an unprecedented extent. The balanced budget so fiercely defended by the 'old-world party' was forgotten. And with the end of the war and the establishment of one clearly hegemonic power, the United States, state intervention and monetary regulation could attain an international dimension quite impossible in the inter-war period. Now at last, capital could deal again and, over the bodies of twenty million people, a fresh game could start.

For the first time in almost fifty years, the imminent collapse of capitalism, which had for so long been a preoccupation of both socialist and bourgeois thought, was no longer on the immediate agenda. From the turn of the century, the issue of the breakdown of capitalism had been at the centre of Marxist discussion: debate centred around the inevitability or otherwise of the breakdown, but for all concerned the question was one of immediate importance. For bourgeois thought, too, the war, the revolutionary wave, the crash and the Great Depression, fascism, rearmament and renewed war, shock upon shock to any notion of capitalist stability, had made failure, collapse and revolution the dominant preoccupations of thirty years.

The hopes and fears of revolution did not immediately disappear with the ending of the war in 1945. On the contrary, the immediate post-war period was a time of great ferment. But the balance of things had shifted. For the first time in nearly fifty years, capital had a basis on which it could pursue accumulation and exploitation with vigour, a basis on which it could build a new appearance of stability, hiding in a mist of amnesia and poppies the millions who had been slaughtered on the way.

II

The new game was broken up in the late 1960s and early 1970s. It had never been played without interruptions. Even after the turbulence of the immediate post-war period had been contained, even after the clear establishment of 'Marshallism' in Europe and of US domination throughout the world, anti-colonial and revolutionary movements and industrial unrest rumbled throughout the 1950s and early 1960s. However, it was not until the late 1960s that the pattern of relations between capital and labour which had been established after the war began to disintegrate.

The 'crisis of Keynesianism', as it is often referred to, is not simply a crisis of economic theory, or of economic policy making: these are manifestations of a crisis in the relation between capital and labour, a crisis in the particular pattern of the containment of the power of labour. Put like that, it is clear that the crisis can be understood neither in terms of the failure of the objective structures (or the working of the 'objective laws of capital'), nor simply in terms of the subjective drive of labour, nor, even more clearly, in terms of tensions between capitalists, or national capital groups. It was the relationship between capital and labour that broke down: there was a swelling and bursting of the tensions present in the relationship from the beginning. The antagonism contained by Keynesianism could be contained no longer.

The post-war pattern of domination had as its precondition the effective exploitation of labour. Fordist methods of mass production had become widely established not only in the United States but in Europe in the aftermath of the war. These brought a sharp rise in labour productivity, but at a cost. Fordist production rested on an implicit trade-off between a high degree of alienation and boredom at work and rising consumption after hours: dissatisfaction was transformed into demand and regulated through annual pay bargaining. As this became established as the dominant pattern, its contradictions became clearer.

The fundamental contradiction of all capitalist production is that expressed in the category of alienation, the contradiction between the potential of human creativity in the production of use-values and the form imposed on that creativity under capitalism, the creation of value under the control of another: in short, the reduction of concrete work to abstract labour. Under Fordist production methods, with their unprecedented degree of unskilled repetitive labour, this contradiction reached a new level of intensity. Increasingly, it expressed itself not as a struggle against the abstraction of work (and for workers' control) but as a rebellion against labour as such. The deadening boredom of Fordist labour was met by revolts of all sorts which aimed primarily at breaking the deadly repetition of meaningless tasks: there was a rise in sabotage, absenteeism, short 'wildcat' stoppages, and so on. These began to have a much more serious impact on productivity and profitability than the more widely publicised strikes over pay.

The revolt against labour was all the more effective for being embedded in a peculiarly rigid work organisation. The attack against the power of the skilled worker led by Taylor and subsequently by Ford, directed as it was against the flexibility and judgement of skill, had resulted in a very inflexible organisation of production. The fragmentation of work into minute, finely timed tasks and the subsequent integration of those tasks with the working of machinery dedicated to a specific process, the same rigid fragmentation which initially served to break the power of the skilled worker, became through struggle both a weapon in the revolt against labour and a limit on capital's right to command. The rigidity magnified the effect of any disruption of the flow of the labour process, since the non-performance of one fragment of the process often made the performance of other fragments impossible: not just within a particular factory or company, but between chains of suppliers and manufacturers. The rigidity also created defined positions which often became positions of power for the workers, from which they could fight to increase wages. Thus, the work-to-rule and the demarcation dispute became common forms of industrial conflict, as workers used or defended the rigidities originally imposed by capital.

In the face of rigidity and revolt, money was the great lubricant. Wage-bargaining became the focus of both managerial change and worker discontent. Raising wages (or granting special bonuses) became the principal means by which management overcame its own rigidities and introduced changes in working practices: 'payment for change' became established as a principle of trade union bargaining, at least in the better organised industries. Wage negotiations also became the principal focus of organised working class protest; the trade unions became increasingly the 'managers of discontent', in C. Wright Mills' phrase, channelling conflict into the form of a monetary demand to be fought over in the ritual process of pay-bargaining.

The monetisation of conflict became more and more problematic as the productive power of labour expressed itself in higher living standards. As the revolt against labour grew, the channelling of discontent became both less effective and more costly. On the one hand, rising real wages were often insufficient incentive to establish effective managerial control over the labour process. Complaints about loss of managerial control over the workplace became more and more common throughout the late 1960s and early 1970s (cf. Holloway, 1987). At the same time, the difficulties in establishing effective control and the power of the resistance to the imposition of new working practices expressed themselves in growing wage demands, often accompanied by threatened or actual strike action to enforce them (cf. Armstrong *et al.*, 1984). Wage control and the curbing of what was seen as trade union power became a dominant preoccupation of the period.

As the revolt against exploitation grew, both in its monetised and non-monetised forms, the extraction of surplus value became more and more difficult for capital. However, it is important not to overstate this. Despite the undoubted effectiveness of working class struggle, the rate of exploitation did not decline: on the contrary, it continued to increase, as the growing mechanisation of the production process made labour more productive, so that the surplus value appropriated by capital continued to grow. What changed was not that the rate of exploitation declined, but that exploitation became more costly for capital: in order to exploit a worker effectively, capital required to invest an ever-increasing amount in machinery and raw materials. This is indicated, for example, by the slowing in the growth of productivity in all the major economies between 1968 and 1973, despite growing investment in mechanisation (Armstrong *et al.*, 1984, p. 249). Thus, the rate of profit (the rate of return on total capital invested) declined in spite of the increasing rate of exploitation.

The key to the decline in the rate of profit (documented, for example, by Glyn and Sutcliffe, 1972 and Armstrong *et al.*, 1984) was thus the fact that exploitation was becoming more and more costly for capital. The rise in the costs of exploitation is what Marx referred to as a rise in the organic composition of capital: as capitalist production develops, there is a tendency for constant capital (the part of capital corresponding to dead labour embodied in machinery and raw materials) to rise in relation to variable capital (the part of capital corresponding to living labour power). Often the emphasis on the organic composition of capital is counterposed to explanations of the crisis in terms of the struggles of the working class (as in the debates

between 'Fundamentalists' and 'Neo-Ricardians', for example). However, if the rising organic composition of capital is seen not as an
economic law external to class struggle, but as an expression of the
rising costs of exploitation, the polarity between class struggle and
the laws of capitalist development dissolves.

Why did it become more and more costly for capital to exploit
labour effectively? The revolt against labour and the struggles for
higher wages had an immediate effect, both in restraining and dis-
rupting exploitation and in raising the costs. They also had a less
immediate effect in prompting capital to circumvent the 'refractory
hand of labour' by introducing machinery to replace the unruly and
unreliable workers. In this sense, the response of capital to the particular impetus of these struggles was simply part of its more general
unceasing struggle to consolidate and intensify its domination by
appropriating the products of labour and converting them as dead
labour into means for intensifying the exploitation of living labour.
Capital lives by turning the productive power of labour against itself
(cf. Bonefeld, 1990). Although the need to mechanise is imposed on
individual capitals in the form of the economic pressure of competition, mechanisation is not an 'economic tendency' separate from
class struggle, but part of the unceasing struggle of capital to survive:
the rising costs of exploitation express the difficulties of capitalist
reproduction.

A historically new feature of the crisis of the rising costs of exploitation in the 1960s was the role played by what might be called
the 'indirect costs of exploitation'. The expansion of the state, which
was such a central feature of constructing an environment after the
war in which capital accumulation could continue, brought with it
major new costs for capital. Although changes in taxation form a
significant part of the constant struggle by capital to reduce the costs
of exploitation, state expenditure is in general paid for by capital,
whatever the form of taxation, in the sense that it constitutes a de-
duction from the surplus value available for accumulation (cf. Bullock and Yaffe, 1975). The development of the Keynesian welfare
state after the war contributed much both to the effectiveness and
the stability of exploitation, but it did so at a cost.

The costs of creating a stable state environment for accumulation
increased as its effectiveness decreased. In the same way as the wage
became less and less effective as a means of channelling the revolt
against labour, the state became less and less effective as a means of
channelling social discontent. The socialisation of capital which was

involved in the expansion of the state after the war brought with it an intensification of alienation in society. Just as Fordist production heightened the contradiction between the potential of human creativity and the alien form imposed on that creativity in capitalist value production, so the expansion of the state as welfare state heightened the contradiction between the potential for conscious social organisation and the form imposed on that potential under capitalism, the state. As the state penetrated more and more aspects of social life, there was a growing awareness of the contrast between social control and state control. The revolt against labour was complemented by a revolt against the state, often expressed quite simply in vandalism and crime, but also in the conscious pursuit of struggles in forms that were not easily integrated by the state: struggles over housing, education, health, transport and so on (cf., e.g., Cockburn, 1977; LEWRG, 1979). The interpenetration of factory struggles and struggles in society, dramatically illustrated by the May events in France in 1968 or Italy's 'hot autumn' of 1969, was an important feature of the late 1960s and early 1970s in very many countries: this is what Negri (1988) refers to as the recomposition of the working class as social mass worker (operaio sociale).

The increasing difficulty of containing protest within the established channels of state conciliation expressed itself in the rising cost of 'demand management'. The institutionalisation of protest which was central to the Keynesian state was not simply based on bureaucratisation through the trade unions, social democratic parties and institutions of the welfare state: its material support was the ability to grant limited but significant concessions to the pressures contained. As the pressures on the state grew, the costs of containing the pressures grew too, and with them taxation and the indirect costs of exploitation.

By the late 1960s, it was becoming clear that the relatively stable expansion of the post-war years was coming to an end. Profits were declining in all the leading capitalist countries (cf. Armstrong *et al.*, 1984, pp. 245ff) and social unrest was increasing. Rising costs, particularly wage costs, were blamed for the fall in profits and increasing efforts were devoted to controlling the rise in wages, while increasing productivity. Initially, however, the basic post-war pattern of relations between capital and labour was not questioned. It was assumed that the attempt to control wages and raise productivity could be achieved only through the existing framework, that is, through the institutionalised recognition of the power of labour, through the trade unions.

The efforts to control wages and raise productivity brought the trade unions even more crucially to the centre of the whole system of rule. This was true at the level of the company, where often significant changes in working practices or in technology could be achieved only through agreement with the trade unions (cf. Holloway, 1987). It was equally true where the state sought to control the rise in wages through some sort of incomes policy. It soon became clear that the only way in which a state incomes policy could succeed was with the active cooperation of the trade unions. Keynesianism-in-crisis made very explicit what underlay the whole post-war pattern of relations between capital and labour: the recognition and institutionalisation of the power of labour, and hence the central role of the trade unions.

The attempt to control wages made clear the contradictory position of the trade unions. While they could be drawn sufficiently into the state to make them the means of restraining wage demands, the only way in which the unions could at the same time retain the support of their members was by bargaining for other state concessions (on planning, employment policy or improvements in welfare state benefits) in return for wage restraint. The more the unions were drawn into the state, the more the state system rested on the granting of concessions: for capital, the restraint of the direct costs of exploitation (wages) had to be paid for by an increase in the indirect costs (rising state expenditure). The growing entrenchment of the unions at the heart of the system made everything more rigid: it was increasingly difficult to bring about major changes either in the organisation of production or in the organisation of the state.

The increasing integration of the unions into the state made them appear more powerful. But their power was the institutionalised power of labour, and, as institutions, they increasingly stood outside and opposed to the power which they represented. The more powerful they appeared in terms of influence within the state, the less effective they became in either representing or restraining their members. Their power was increasingly a hollow power, an institutional power without substance. The same applied, in different degree, to social democratic parties. The central role of the trade unions in channelling the power of labour under the post-war mode of capitalist domination often gave a privileged position in the political system to those parties which had close links with the trade unions. Especially as the difficulties of accumulation became more obvious from the mid-to-late 1960s, social democratic parties were often favoured, even by organisations representing capital, as the only parties capable of controlling the demands of labour: a striking example was the 'leaked' revelation by the Confederation of British Industry (CBI) just before the February 1974 election that they favoured a Labour victory. However, as the contradictory position of the trade unions became more evident, the contradictions within social democratic parties also became more intense, with increasingly sharp conflict between 'left' and 'right' wings, and increasing loss of contact with the class which they claimed to represent.

The growing difficulties of accumulation expressed themselves in a growing crisis of the institutional structures of Keynesianism, both at the level of the individual firm and at the level of the state. However, the predominant response of capital, even as the crisis deepened, still did not take the form of an outright attack on the established pattern of social relations. There was increasing emphasis on wage control, restraint on the expansion of public expenditure and repression of non-institutionalised expressions of the power of labour; but the assumptions of Keynesianism were still widely accepted as the framework for economic and political development. The growing contradictions of the whole post-war pattern of domination and struggle were contained through the expansion of money.

The 'old-world party' had of course warned of the dangers of inflation long before the war. When the Roosevelt administration took the United States off the gold standard in 1933, Bernard Baruch, a leading Democrat had protested:

> It can't be defended except as mob rule. Maybe the country doesn't know it yet, but I think we may find that we've been in a revolution more drastic than the French Revolution. The crowd has seized the seat of government and is trying to seize the wealth. Respect for law and order is gone (quoted in Schlesinger, 1959, p. 202).

There was a sense in which Baruch was right. Roosevelt's decision to abandon the gold standard was a move to unhinge the management of the national economy from the constraints of the world market in order to be able to respond to intense social pressure. But this was not an abandonment of the rule of money. On the contrary, the only way of saving the rule of money from the 'mob' was through financial nationalism, unhinging national currencies from the international flow of value. 'Sauve qui peut' became the motto of capital, faced in the different nation states with demands that could not be reconciled with the free operation of the international market. Abandoning the gold standard did not mean relinquishing the rule of money: it meant simply that the rule of money could respond more flexibly to social pressures in each national financial area.

The unhinging of the national currencies was not, of course, total. The international flow of capital continued, in the form both of international finance and of international trade, but less freely than before. Some degree of order was restored through the establishment of different currency areas and the Tripartite Agreement of 1936 between France, Britain and the United States, under which the authorities agreed to intervene to maintain fixed exchange rates between the three major currency areas. However, it was not until after the war that a new international monetary order was established by the Bretton Woods agreement of 1944, which came into effective operation in 1947.

The Bretton Woods system sought to reconcile the rule of international money with the recognition of the power of labour. It did so by establishing a system built around the recognition of the dollar as the key international currency. This was made possible by the overwhelming strength of US capital, clearly established by the end of the war. The dollar and gold were to be used interchangeably as international money, the dollar being convertible into gold at a fixed parity. National currencies were tied to the dollar by fixed exchange rates, which could be altered only in the case of fundamental disequilibrium; the new International Monetary Fund (IMF) was to provide money to overcome short-term imbalances (Burnham, 1990; Bonefeld, 1993a).

One effect of this system was to introduce the inflationary flexibility of the dollar into the international flow of money. As Mandel puts it, 'at Bretton Woods the victorious imperialist powers of World War Two established an international monetary system which was designed to provide the basis for an international version of the inflationary credit expansion which had by now gained acceptance on the national scale' (1975, p. 462). The power of the 'mob', which had forced Roosevelt to come off the Gold Standard in 1933, was now integrated into the international flow of capital. The Marshall Plan and other dollar-aid programmes after the war sought to achieve the Keynesian solution at an international level: the transformation of protest into demand through the creation of money (cf. Mandel, 1975, p. 463).

A second element of the Bretton Woods system was the conservation of a degree of protection of national economies from the world market. The force of social pressures in the crisis of the 1930s had forced national governments to insulate their national economies from the destructive power of the world market by abandoning the gold standard and erecting tariff barriers. Some degree of insulation was preserved by the establishment of fixed exchange rates, which protected national currencies from short-term movements of money on the world market. The effect was not to isolate national economies from the international flow of capital, but to create a series of valves designed to regulate that flow and preserve some degree of short-term protection. Just as abandoning the gold standard was an essential part of Roosevelt's New Deal, the preservation of these valves was an essential part of the Keynesian conception of active state intervention.

Both through the role of the dollar and the system of fixed exchange rates, the power of 'the mob' was integrated into the international monetary system, where it reappeared as instability.

At the core of this instability was the expansion of credit, which has been a crucial element in the accumulation of capital since the war. The new international monetary order gave more scope to the expansion of credit at the national level and ensured, through the dual role of the dollar as national and as international currency, that credit inflation in the United States would enter into the international system as an element of instability.

The expansion of credit to maintain demand, forced upon national governments by the intensity of social pressure during the 1930s, had been given theoretical justification by Keynes as a permanent feature of economic policy. In practice, however, the main source of credit creation in the post-war period was not deficit financing by the state but the expansion of bank overdrafts granted by the banks to the private sector: both production credit to companies and consumer credit given to individuals, mainly for the purchase of houses and consumer durables. Mandel points out that in the United States, private indebtedness rose from 73.6% to 140.0% of the annual GNP between the years 1946 and 1974, while the public debt actually fell proportionally (Mandel, 1975, p. 418). In other words, national governments exercised only indirect control over much of the expansion of credit, which was driven forward by the demand for credit both by productive capital and by consumers seeking a better standard of living, and by the supply of loanable capital seeking a more secure return than that which could be obtained from direct investment in production.

The lack of state control over the expansion of credit was greatly exacerbated by the development of a market in dollars outside the United States, the so-called 'Eurodollar' market. This resulted from the position of the dollar as international currency. The recovery of the capitalist economies in other countries after the war gradually led to a relative decline in the superiority of the US economy. The dollars which flooded the world markets, and which were initially used to buy commodities exported from the United States, were increasingly transformed into reserves in European banks (Bonefeld, 1993a). Increasingly, these reserves were then used as a source of credit both for public authorities and for private capital. Beginning in the early 1960s, there was the growth of an international financial market which existed outside all state control, and which existed alongside the national, regulated markets. By 1969, other capitalist countries held $40 billion dollars (as compared with $11 billion in 1964), a figure which far exceeded the gold held in the US reserves (Bonefeld, 1990). Under those circumstances, the convertibility of the dollar into gold began to appear more and more fragile.

The fragility of the international monetary system became more apparent as the growing costs of exploiting labour effectively expressed themselves in falling profits and increasing social tension. The demand for credit increased as states sought to respond to social pressures and to maintain declining demand, and as companies sought loans as a way of tiding them over what they hoped would be temporary difficulties. The supply of credit also increased as capital sought outlets that were more profitable and more secure than productive investment.

An additional source of instability came from the changing position of national currencies, which were related to the dollar through fixed exchange rates under the Bretton Woods system. The fixed exchange rates insulated the national currencies from short-term speculation on the international money markets, but at the cost of possibly chronic balance of payments problems and then intensified speculation as the necessity of a change in the fixed rates became apparent. The link between the world market and the national economy then asserted itself in the form of a sharp currency crisis. This was the fate of sterling, when the decline of the British economy expressed itself in balance of payments problems, speculation and finally the devaluation of the pound in 1967.

The devaluation of the pound, which was still an important currency in international transactions, further increased the fragility of the position of the dollar, already stretched by the expansion of the

Eurodollar market and the huge increase in public debt as a result of the vain attempt to quell the revolution in Vietnam. The impossibility of containing social tension, nationally and internationally, other than by the expansion of credit, expressed itself in growing monetary instability. Holders of dollars increasingly sought security by converting their dollars into gold. Faced with the enormous disparity between the number of dollars and the US gold reserve, the Nixon administration announced in August 1971 that the convertibility of the dollar into gold was to be suspended indefinitely. A new system of fixed exchange rates was established by the Smithsonian Agreement of December 1971, but this too was subjected to severe speculative pressure and in March 1973 the principle of fixed exchange rates was abandoned (Bonefeld, 1993a; Armstrong *et al.*, 1984, p. 293).

To the extent that the system of fixed exchange rates had insulated national economies from the short-term speculative movement of capital, the final demise of the Bretton Woods system meant that that insulation no longer existed. State policies were again subordinated directly to the flow of money on the international markets. As Bonefeld (1993b, pp. 58–9) puts it, 'The ultimate sanction for a domestically engineered management of accumulation that was in some way "incompatible" with global accumulation was speculative pressure on its national currency. This pressure restricted national authority over money and credit-expansion and subordinated national policies to the international movement of money'. This was not, however, a return to the gold standard, the realm of seemingly secure power so staunchly defended by the old-world party against Roosevelt and the Keynesians, against the depradations of the 'mob'. International money was no longer represented by gold but by the dollar, and its movement was now much faster and more volatile than it had ever been in the days of the gold standard.

The pressures on the old post-war pattern of social relations were mounting on all sides. Falling profits and mounting social unrest made a mockery of Keynesian claims to reconcile social conflict and ensure the harmonious, crisis-free development of capitalism. The breakdown of the international monetary system removed the insulation from the world market which was an essential element of the Keynesian conception of state intervention. These tensions found expression in the sharp recession of 1974–5: production fell sharply in all the leading countries, inflation and unemployment soared (Mandel, 1978, p. 14) and the flood of 'petrodollars' into the Eurodollar markets increased the volatility of the world monetary system.

From all sides, the death of Keynesianism was proclaimed. In the debates of economists, Keynesianism rapidly lost ground to the newly fashionable monetarist economic theory. Conservative politicians, in Britain, the United States and elsewhere, increasingly attacked the expansion of the state, the position of the trade unions and the 'politics of consensus', and turned to theorists such as Friedmann and Hayek to justify their positions. Even social democratic parties, whose own position in the political system depended upon the recognition of the power of labour, began to denounce Keynesian solutions as no longer realistic. As the British Prime Minister, James Callaghan, put it at the Labour Party Conference in 1976:

> We used to think that you could spend your way out of a recession and increase employment by cutting taxes and boosting government spending. I tell you in all candour that that option no longer exists and that so far as it ever did exist, it only worked on each occasion since the war by injecting a bigger dose of inflation into the economy, followed by a higher level of unemployment at the next step.

The New Deal was over, the game was finished. Or so it seemed. But so far only one of the players had stood up from the table. The social forces that had imposed the recognition of the power of labour upon capital still existed, stronger than ever, and could not be abolished simply by the declarations of politicians. And if the Keynesian game was over, what were the new rules to be? Keynesianism had taken over thirty years of struggle and the deaths of millions of people to establish. After nearly thirty years of relative stability, capitalism was again in chaos. Could a new order be established simply by the will of the politicians, or would it again require the world to pass through destruction and misery? The abyss stood open.

References

Armstrong, P., Glyn, A. and Harrison, J. (1984) *Capitalism since World War II* (London: Fontana).
Beynon, H. (1973) *Working for Ford*, (Harmondsworth: Penguin).
Bonefeld, W. (1988) 'Class Struggle and the Permanence of Primitive Accumulation', *Common Sense*, 6.
Bonefeld, W. (1990) 'The State Form and the Development of the State under Monetarism', Ph.D. thesis, University of Edinburgh.

Bonefeld, W. (1993a) *The Recomposition of the British State During the 1980s* (Aldershot: Dartmouth).

Bonefeld, W. (1993b) 'The Global Money Power of Capital and the Crisis of Keynesianism', *Common Sense*, 13.

Braverman, H. (1974) *Labour and Monopoly Capital* (New York: Monthly Review Press).

Bullock, P. and Yaffe, D. (1975) 'Inflation, the Crisis and the Post-War Boom, *Revolutionary Communist*, 3/4.

Burnham, P. (1990) *The Political Economy of Postwar Reconstruction* (London: Macmillan).

Clarke, S. (1988) *Keynesianism, Monetarism and the Crisis of the State* (Aldershot: Edward Elgar).

Cockburn, C. (1977) *The Local State* (London: Pluto Press).

Coriat, B. (1982) *El Taller y el Cronometro* (Madrid: Siglo XXI).

Foster, W.T. and Catchings, W. (1928) *The Road to Plenty* (New York: Popular Edition).

Glyn, A. and Sutcliffe, B. (1972) *British Capitalism, Workers and the Profit Squeeze* (Harmondsworth: Penguin).

Gordon, D., Edwards, R. and Reich, M. (1982) *Segmented Work, Divided Workers: The Historical Transformation of Labour in the US* (Cambridge: Cambridge University Press).

Holloway, J. (1987) 'The Red Rose of Nissan', *Capital & Class*, 32.

Keynes, J.M. (1936) *General Theory of Employment, Interest and Money* (London: Macmillan).

Keynes, J.M. (1971) 'The Economic Consequences of Peace', Vol. II of *Collected Writings* (London: Macmillan).

Keynes, J.M. (1972) 'Am I a Liberal?', Vol. IX of *Collected Writings* (London: Macmillan).

Lee, J.R. (1916) 'The so-called profit sharing system in the Ford plant', *Annals of the Academy of Political Science*, LXV.

London Edinburgh Weekend Return Group (LEWRG) (1979): *In and Against the State* (London: CSE Books).

Mandel, E. (1975) *Late Capitalism* (London: New Left Books).

Mandel, E. (1978) *The Second Slump* (London: New Left Books).

Mattick, P. (1978) *Economics, Politics and the Age of Inflation* (London : Merlin).

Middlemas, K. (1979) *Politics in Industrial Society* (London: André Deutsch).

Negri, A. (1988) *Revolution Retrieved: Selected Writings on Marx, Keynes, Capitalist Crisis and New Social Subjects 1967–1983* (London: Red Notes).

Schlesinger, A. (1957) *The Age of Roosevelt: the Crisis of the Old Order*, 1919–1933 (Cambridge, Mass.: The Riverside Press).

Schlesinger, A. (1959) *The Age of Roosevelt: The Coming of the New Deal* (Cambridge, Mass.: The Riverside Press).

Tronti, M. (1976) 'Workers and Capital', in *The Labour Process and Class Strategies*, CSE Pamphlet 1 (London: Stage 1).

3 Monetarism and Crisis

Werner Bonefeld

INTRODUCTION

Keynesianism appeared to be a spent force by the mid-1970s. The spectre of a socially reformed and economically vibrant capitalism stood shamefaced when confronted with mass unemployment, hyperinflation, balance of payments deficits, depressed rates of profit and sluggish economic growth. Keynesian 'economic planning' stumbled when called upon in the 1970s. As indicated by Holloway,[1] the abandonment of the Bretton Woods[2] system signalled the breakdown of the cornerstone of Keynesianism after the Second World War. The Bretton Woods system regulated the international deficit financing of demand on the world market on the basis of an inflationary supply of dollars to the rest of the world. The international framework of inflationary demand management was built around the recognition of the dollar as the dominant international currency. The dollar was defined in *parity* to *gold*. National currency was subordinated to the dollar which performed the dual function of international and national currency. National currency was tied to the dollar by fixed exchange rates, which could be altered only in the case of fundamental disequilibrium. However, the dual function of the dollar implied that the stability of Bretton Woods depended on a US trade surplus compensating for balance of payments imbalances. As long as the US maintained a large trade balance, the dollar functioned as credit that was supplied to other countries as a means of exchange for US-produced commodities. These dollars did not perform as a means of payment but as credit whose realisation as means of payment existed in the form of a claim on the future exploitation of labour. The Bretton Woods system established the connection between the exploitation of labour and the realisation of surplus value in circulation on the basis of a global expansion of the money supply.

The abandonment of the Bretton Woods system in 1971–3 was a response to the enormous increase in money capital divorced from the exploitation of labour. In the late 1960s and early 1970s credit expansion boosted the world economy and so helped to integrate labour into the capital relation through full-employment guarantees as well as an inflationary erosion of real wages. Faced with working class unrest in the late 1960s, falling rates of profit, decreasing rates of growth and readily available credit, capital not only started to run all over the world in search of profitable returns in 'bloody Fordism' (cf. Lipietz, 1982, 1984). It also started to gamble with the future exploitation of labour (see Holloway, 1990). The expansionary response to the class conflict accelerated the liberation of money from production and, as a consequence, aided the monetarist offensive which gathered strength by the mid-1970s.

During the 1920s and 1930s, monetarists like Hayek and von Mises had repeatedly warned about the dangers inherent in a reformed capitalism. Keynes and Hayek had argued for different responses to the slump. This battle was lost by Hayek. The slump of 1929 and the underlying 'labour question' (cf. Holloway's 'The Abyss Opens', Chapter 2 in this volume) led to a development in which 'crude capitalism' was to be modified in terms of a 'self-interested adjustment to the potentially revolutionary threats from below' (Keegan, 1993, p. 22). By the 1960s Keynesianism was celebrated and Keynes hailed as a saviour. The *Age of Keynes* was announced. However, soon after the breakdown of Bretton Woods, Keynesianism became castigated as a destructive doctrine and the *End of the Keynesian Era*[3] was proclaimed. Monetarism 'succeeded' Keynesianism not because of its intellectual cunning. Monetarism took over by default. The practical importance of monetarism did not arise from its coherence as a doctrine. What gave monetarism its practical importance was the deregulation of global financial relations in the early 1970s.

During the 1970s, the monetarism of the New Right articulated the new capitalist offensive of deflation. Capitalism was 'living beyond its means' and monetarism sought to make that good by making workers pay the costs through the intensification of exploitation, lower direct and indirect wages, cuts in services, and a tight control of the relationship between public expenditure and wages. Monetarism provided a radical response to the crisis of capitalist reproduction: as full-employment growth guarantees became a danger to 'domestic' accumulation, monetarism declared the destruction of employment guarantees to be a condition for economic recovery; as the amount of public expenditure triggered a financial crisis of the state, monetarism declared the abolition of the Keynesian relation between public expenditure and wages;[4] as the corporatist strategy of social integration failed to secure social peace, monetarism declared trade unions to be undesirable; as unemployment increased dramatically, monetarism declared in favour of market freedom and a natural rate of unemployment. Market freedom was declared as the basis of all democratic and economic freedom.

While Keynesianism was concerned with the future of capitalism, monetarism is preoccupied with the preservation of the present. Rather than mortgaging the future exploitation of labour through deficit spending, monetarism called in the receiver. The importance of monetarism is the rejection of the commitment to a policy of full employment in favour of the subordination of social relations to so-called market freedom. The concerted attempt by monetarism to bring back the ideology of the market to the centre of the political stage involved, fundamentally, the imposition of so-called economic freedom on the working class. The role of the state is to secure economic freedom of equal exchange on the market as opposed to the so-called coercion of market forces through collective provision of resources. Monetarism attacked the institutional forms that under-pin the political strength of labour to command a living standard 'incompatible' with the limits of the market. The imposition of monetary austerity upon social relations involves two things. First, any attachment to any values other than those of material gain are ruthlessly penalised. Secondly, for those who already possess it, money is the means of freedom and prosperity. For those who do not have money their lack of money defines their poverty and also their exist-ence as a labouring commodity. As with any other market agent, the proprietors of labour power have to conform their expectation to the limits of the market, without the state meddling in the market through policies designed to guarantee employment and income.

Since the mid-1970s, the commitment to full-employment policies as the primary aim of economic, financial and welfare policy has been abandoned. The reconstitution of social relations on the basis of economic freedom implies the destruction of the way in which labour had been politically integrated since the Second World War. The regaining of control over the money supply involved, funda-mentally, the destruction of the Keynesian relation between public expenditure and wages, i.e. an integration of labour on the basis of social reform and material concessions. Since the late 1970s, the at-tempt to cut back on credit has meant an attack on the entire way in which social relations had been constituted since the war: pushing the trade unions out of the state, cutting back on social welfare expenditure, deregulating wage protection and making the unemployed work for their benefits, and making the whole state more repressive through bureaucratic forms of control with which to enforce the imposition of tight money upon social relations.

But something went wrong. In the beginning, monetarism promised a 'return to basics': you cannot spend what you have not earned. However, when, in 1982, Mexico threatened to default, monetarist orthodoxy was relegated to the dustbins of history. Rather than 'engendering' the capitalist world through the repayment of debt, as well as prudent government inactivity, the new orthodoxy was to spend and spend and spend. During the 1980s, rather than cutting back on credit, credit expanded to a degree unprecedented in modern history. However, monetarist policies were retained insofar as social relations were held responsible for the increase in debt. While the governments of the New Right privatised public corporations in order to balance their books, debt was socialised through fiscal reforms, rescue of banks, the use of public expenditure as a means of imposing the discipline of poverty, and the encouragement of credit-based private consumption. There was an unholy alliance between mass unemployment and sluggish productive investment, on the one hand, and growing public and private indebtedness, on the other. This alliance did not last. The crash of 1987 is intrinsically connected with the eruption of the debt crisis in 1982. The western world had responded to the events of 1982 with expansionary policies which were not checked by the creation of assets against which to balance the debt. In other words, the dissociation of money from production continued unabated during the 1980s. The market, helped by the deregulation of credit controls, took the freedom to liberate money from labour and toil. Monetarist regimes indulged in an expansion of credit *during* the boom. When the shock arrived in the early 1990s there was a widespread fear of a credit crunch. The recession of the 1990s showed that the economic miracle of the 1980s was, in fact, an illusion. However, it would be wrong to see monetarism as a sinful doctrine. It did not preach monetary tightness only to practice profligacy in debt. Monetarism was, in the 1970s at least, an ideology of hope in increased productivity and thus an evangelist of a stronger link between money and exploitation.

This chapter looks at monetarism's fate. It will be argued that monetarism has not overcome the crisis of Keynesianism.

IN THE BEGINNING WAS HARMONY

In the late 1960s and early 1970s, class conflict had forced political authorities 'to hold back from encouraging aggressive employers for fear of the destabilising political impact of such class confrontation' (Clarke, 1988, p. 281). In response to the tremendous social unrest at that time, expansionary policies were invoked as a means of transforming protest into demand and full employment guarantees. Deficit financing of accumulation and accelerated inflation were thus constituted as means of pacifying social conflict.

The breathing space created by credit expansion gave the illusion of restored accumulation which, in fact, was sustained in an increasingly speculative dimension. The proliferation of speculative investment decreased the strength of the link between money and exploitation at the same time as the Keynesian consensus reached its peak. The expansionary response supported the boom between 1970 and 1972 which was the 'fastest two-year period of expansion since 1950-1 in the aggregate GDP of the advanced capitalist countries' (Maddison, quoted in Keegan, 1993, p. 48). It seemed, at the time, that the Keynesian consensus of the post-war period was beyond reproach. The expansionary response to the crisis was based on, and boosted by, the 'collapse of the Bretton Woods exchange rate system and the subsequent easing of demand management constraints' (Maddison, quoted in Keegan, 1993, p. 48). In other words, the pacification of the class conflict through policies of social reform were boosted by the abandonment of the system which was 'designed' to cope with balance of payments deficits. As Cleaver (1989, p. 22) indicates, the abandonment of Bretton Woods 'constituted the *de facto* admission on the part of national governments that they had no longer the power to manage accumulation internally in ways compatible with global accumulation'. Originally, Keynesians viewed the deregulation of international money as a liberation from the constraints on domestic management imposed by Bretton Woods. 'The floating of exchange-rates was celebrated as successful in making Keynesian policy universally more elastic by removing the restrictions of the international balance of payments' (Itoh, 1978, p. 1; see also Mandel, 1987). Expansionary policies were a pragmatic response to class struggle. However, there was a price to be paid: the Keynesian consensus was threatened in its entirety.

Credit-sustained expansion postponed economic recession until shortly after the official abandonment of Bretton Woods in 1971–3. Following upon the quadrupling of oil prices at the end of 1973, which in its effect coincided with a downturn of accumulation, output stagnated or fell in most industrial countries. By 1974, the recession had hit all advanced capitalist countries. The chain of bankruptcies and defaults was not confined to productive capital, but included the banking system. When the crisis struck, the banking system was overextended. The most serious international aspect of the crisis was in the unregulated Eurodollar markets[5] where some banks failed and where many banks came within a hair's breadth of default[6].

DEMAND MANAGEMENT, MONEY AND THE FUTURE

The expansionary response to the events of the late 1960s presented an attempt to avoid a direct confrontation with labour in the present, and to seek a solution to the labour question in the future. In other words, the expansion of the money supply created a massive claim on the future exploitation of labour. The flight from the present into the future presented thus, as Suzanne de Brunhoff (1978, p. 47) put it, 'a quest for future capitalist production in order to escape the possibilities of overproduction in the present'. This flight from the present lies at the heart of Keynesian demand management (see Negri, 1988b). The link between the future and the present is constituted by credit expansion, an expansion which is underwritten by the state through its reserves and fiscal power. However, the guarantee of the future, that is the guarantee of the future settlement of credit obligations depends on the exploitation of labour in the present. Growing indebtedness which is not matched by an expansive exploitation of labour, i.e. capital growth, sooner or later becomes intolerable as interest charges absorb a growing proportion of the surplus value and make productive investment increasingly unprofitable. At the same time speculative pressures on currencies intensify because of inflationary devaluation and an accumulation of deficits which is not 'validated' by the exploitation of labour. In order to maintain credit as a claim on the future, the exploitation of labour has to provide a real resource transfer with which to service the interest on the credit and if possible repay debt. In other words, credit-sustained accumulation calls for an effective exploitation of labour so as to provide the resources with which to service debt. In the absence of an effective exploitation of labour, the ratio of debt to surplus value will continue to increase, undermining profitability and future accumulation of capital, and so creating bad debt and financial crisis.

Deficit Financing, Floating and Monetarism

The inflationary growth of globally unregulated credit redefined the 'power of money'.[7] The movement of money capital on globally unregulated markets integrated nation states through a synchronisation of falling rates of profits, of balance of payment problems and of the business cycle. These developments undermined attempts to 'control the cycle in one country' (O'Connor, 1984, p. 2). After the breakdown of Bretton Woods, capital movements within the international economy began to dominate balance of payment and exchange rate considerations. Under conditions of high inflation and little economic growth the spectrum of economic activity about which decisions have to be made shifted to a much quicker and more unstable regime, led by the exchange rates. The crisis of accumulation manifested itself to the state in the form of adverse effects of the floating of exchange rates. The breakdown of Bretton Woods involved the abandonment of currency relations in a fixed relation to the dollar and the deregulation of currency relations. This deregulation is referred to as the floating of exchange rates. Floating established multi-currency standards with flexible rates between them. Floating exchange rates established a market for currency speculation by money capital. The integration of the multiplicity of states on the basis of floating rates imposed monetary discipline over the national organisation of money through the destabilising movements of speculative money capital against national currency. While the deficit financing of employment sustained, in particular, weaker capitals, the inflationary devaluation of national currency made it harder to 'protect domestic accumulation' against adverse effects of floating exchange rates.

The implications for the national organisation of money are fundamental. The deregulation of global credit relations replaced the formalised structures of currency adjustment between states with an imposition of money upon states. The dissociation of money from exploitation involved a gamble with the future, a gamble which was 'policed' by the movement of speculative capital. The movement of this capital imposed global monetary tightness upon expansionary solutions to the 'labour question'. The deregulation of money involved 'speculative capital' performing the role of an international policeman.

If any given nation state was having difficulties in imposing tight money upon social relations and in guaranteeing the value of its currency through effective exploitation of labour, massive movements of funds out of that country or out of its currency would reinforce its financial crisis. The ultimate sanction for a domestically engineered management of accumulation (expansive policy) that is in some way 'incompatible' with global accumulation is speculative pressure on its national currency. This pressure restricts national authority over money and credit expansion and subordinates national policies to the international 'terrorism of money' (cf. Marazzi's 'Money in the World Crisis', Chapter 4 in this volume).

Expansionary policies maintained producers at the cost of increasing inflation and indebtedness on a global scale (see Mandel, 1987). The 1970s were characterised by stagnation. In this context, deficit financing meant that borrowing from unregulated dollar markets was not matched by an effective exploitation of labour. Rather, the validity of credit was backed by the states as lenders of last resort. Additionally the state finances balance of payment deficits by credit from Eurodollar banks. The state incurs thereby an accumulation of debt. At the same time at which the exploitation of labour is sustained by credit, the validity of the credit depends on the capacity of the state to guarantee the convertibility of credit into central bank money. The Keynesian integration of labour became more speculative the more capitalist reproduction was sustained by an inflationary growth of credit divorced from production. The crisis of the capitalist integration of labour came to a head in the form of inflation and a fiscal crisis of the state.[8] The barrier to sustained economic reproduction appeared in the form of limited supply of official reserves with which to support national currency in the face of speculative movement of money capital. Floating currencies increased the demand for international reserves because of the greater difficulty in stabilising exchange rates. 'This meant that national authorities needed larger, not smaller, reserves to defend floating currencies, while the latitude to pursue domestic policies independently of external considerations was reduced, not increased' (Clarke, 1988, p. 344). Larger reserves provide the security to sustain the formal exchange equality of international money. Failure to secure acceptance by international money holders of the political guarantee of convertibility of money into central bank money involves, firstly, speculative pressure on currency, prompting a diversion of the global flow of money and threatening to undermine the integration of 'domestic production' in the world market. It involves, secondly, a destabilisation of international credit relations as creditors demand cash payment, threatening to undermine the reproduction of all social relations which rest on credit. Expansionary policies changed from being the answer to the labour question to being the main problem confronting capital's integration of labour.

During the 1970s the capacity of states to underpin the credit system gradually eroded as the guarantee of money by central bank reserves was increasingly in question. Following upon the bank crashes of 1974, banks became, by 1976 and 1977, increasingly worried about the security of their loans to countries such as Argentine, Turkey, Peru and Indonesia, all of whom had asked for the postponement of payments. Fears about a renewed financial crisis were not limited to these countries: the British 'IMF crisis' of 1975, the pound sterling crisis of 1976, the dollar crisis of 1977 and the 'near' insolvency of Italy in 1976 (see Mandel, 1987) were stark reminders that labour's integration into the capital relation was achieved by borrowing from the future.

The financial difficulties of states indicated that expansionary responses to the 'labour question' were faltering. This made it harder for governments to resist pressures to deregulate existing guarantees of income, employment, and welfare. Higher unemployment was the price to be paid for lower inflation. The contradiction of the containment of labour on the basis of deficit financing is that credit expansion is not guaranteed by an effective exploitation of labour but by the state through its reserves and its revenues. Credit-sustained accumulation depended on the capacity of the state to guarantee the convertibility of credit into cash payment. The implication of unregulated global credit relations is that the state transforms from redistributor of wealth in the last instance to lender of last resort in the last instance. This development made the balance of payments and budget deficits important variables for the ability of nation states to guarantee formal exchange equality on the world market.

Since the early 1970s, rapid monetary accumulation has coincided with depressed rates of profit and sluggish productive accumulation. The net creditors on financial markets were productive capitals (Altvater, 1985).[9] At the same time as productive capital placed earned profits on financial markets, it financed productive investment by credit. The growing indebtedness of functioning capital manifested itself in the form of a decreasing importance of boom lending and a growing importance of what Hilferding (1910/1981) called 'circulation credit', or what Altvater (1985) refers to as 'recycling credit'.[10] Recycling credit does not finance expansive accumulation but, rather, alleviates illiquidity by enabling producers to service debt without defaulting. This form of credit is purely speculative as it is supplied to debtors to enable them to meet difficulties in servicing interest on credit, so preventing insolvency. The increasing use of such credit indicated the difficulty of turning credit into effective command over labour, a command which guarantees credit growth through the surplus value extorted from the worker.

For capitalists receiving this kind of credit, it exists not as means of purchase, but as means of payment or, in the face of insolvency, as a means of deferring liquidation and, hence, postponing credit default. The speculative dimension of this credit maintains solvency on an ever-more fictitious basis, calling for an ever more drastic imposition of exploitation in production so as to maintain financial solvency. However, recycling credit does not really leave the banks as it exists as interest payment. At the same time, the burden of debt increases for the debtor and the anticipated exploitation of labour produces inflationary pressure through a 'pseudo-social validation of private labour' (cf. De Brunhoff, 1978). Against the background of an accumulation of monetary claims on not-yet existing surplus value, credit came to function largely as a means of preserving the social relations of production on an increasingly speculative basis.

During the 1970s, economic growth, though it recovered by 1976, remained slow in comparison with the rates achieved in the 1960s. Labour was integrated into the capital relations on the basis of a speculative deferral of capital liquidation. The attempt to sustain accumulation through an inflationary erosion of wages and expansionary policies came into conflict with the results it produced. There was no breakthrough in productivity and the cost of exploiting labour increased through the effects of 'deflationary inflation' (cf. Mattick, 1980). The inflationary growth of credit will reduce profits for productive investment as the ratio of debt to surplus value increases. Besides, inflation will devalue money capital, leading to outward flows of capital and downwards pressure on the exchange rate. The speculative deferral of insolvency came up 'against the real impossibility of using inflation to finance future investments' (see Marazzi's 'Money in the World Crisis', Chapter 4 in this volume).

Against this background capitalist reproduction depended on a deflationary integration of labour into the capital relation so as to reduce the ratio of debt to surplus value through an effective exploitation of labour. In other words, money has to command labour for the purpose of exploitation rather than keeping unproductive producers afloat through an inflationary expansion of credit. The eradication of debt entails a shift from inflationary demand management to a policy of sound money so as to improve the reserves. The regaining of control over the money supply involves a deflationary attack on social relations through the intensification of work and a reduction in public spending that put money into the hand of workers. The containment of labour within austerity was articulated by monetarism's assertion that 'poverty is not unfreedom' (cf. Joseph and Sumption, 1979) and by its demand that 'you cannot spend what you have not earned'.

The notion that poverty is not unfreedom lies at the heart of monetarist orthodoxy. Monetarism is a theory of hope in that it has faith in unfettered market freedom. Rather than borrowing from the future and thereby mortgaging the future exploitation of labour, monetarism calls for the collection of unpaid debt. During the 1970s, the monetarism of the New Right developed as a response to the dissociation between money and exploitation. Behind the deregulation of the global flow of money and the detachment of the dollar from gold lay the pressure to deflate. Monetarism called in the receiver: in order to repay and service interest on credit, it called upon patriotic sentiments according to which one has to live on less than that which 'the nation has produced' and earned in order to achieve the capitalism's golden formula of equilibrium between demand and supply.

By the mid-1970s, monetarism's call for a return of the market was apt. The proposal for a capitalism of 'value for money' encapsulates the notion of a closer relationship between money and exploitation. Rather than allowing for deficits and an accumulation of potentially worthless debt, it promised monetary tightness and a leaner and fitter economy. Strengthening the link between money and exploitation depended upon the decomposition of the working class into a profitable labour force. As von Mises (1949, p. 591), puts it, 'as far as there are wages, labour is dealt with like any material factor of production and bought and sold on the market'. Like any other factor of production, labour will be thrown on the scrap-heap if it is no longer needed or if its productive potentials have been exhausted in production. Instead of income guarantees, people are asked to price themselves into jobs; instead of full-employment guarantees, unemployment is seen as 'natural'; instead of providing welfare guarantees, the use of public expenditure provides poverty level wages as a means of encouraging enterprise and of forcing people into poverty, tax, as well as debt traps. During the 1970s, governments of all persuasions espoused the monetarist sermon of hope in market freedom with almost indecent haste. Governments banked on the disciplining role of mass unemployment and debt. There was a belief that a policy of tight money would encourage employers to reassert their right to manage so as to stay in business through an effective exploitation of labour. The idea was that this reassertion would integrate labour into the capital relation on the basis of profitability rather than credit-sustained postponement of bankruptcy.

The target of the subordination of social relations to tight money was the political power of the working class, as well as the trade unions and their ability to bargain effectively. The imposition of non-coerced exchanges on the market represented an attempt to create an effective role for money in managing the accumulation of capital through the encouragement of greater wage flexibility, the liberation of the market from the 'rigidities' of collective bargaining, legally enforceable minimum labour standards and protective social legislation. The monetarist attempt to strengthen the link between money and exploitation acknowledged the circumstance that money must command labour.

MONETARISM AND DEBT

The focus of international credit relations was the dollar and American banks. The stability of international currency and credit relations depended on the stability of the dollar which started to deteriorate in 1977. In the face of a balance of payment deficit of $20 billion, and a rise in inflation from 6.8% in 1977 to 9% in 1978, Carter let the dollar depreciate. 'From late 1977 the dollar was allowed to float down on the foreign exchange market, but this turned to a rout in Autumn 1978 as short-term capital cut and fled' (Evans, 1985, p. 116). In an attempt to alleviate pressure on its reserves, Carter introduced deflationary measures so as to push up interest rates and stem the flow and borrowed on international currency markets. High interest rates in the United States restored confidence in the dollar, marked by appreciation of the dollar relative to other currencies. However, this step turned the overliquidity of money into a scarcity of money. The dollar crisis and the restoration of the dollar through high interest rates was merely a first tremor, foreshadowing worse. The transformation of overliquidity into monetary scarcity signalled that accumulation was heading for a renewed recession by the end of the 1970s.

Monetarist policies had been adopted in all western capitalist countries by the mid-1970s. However, the political strength of the working class had been recognised in corporatist forms of class collaboration. The debate of the late 1970s on neo-corporatism, the crisis of Modell Deutschland, and on the crisis of the crisis state (see Panitch, 1986; Esser and Fach, 1981; Hirsch, 1980; Negri, 1988c, 1988d; London, 1980, among others) indicates that the imposition of 'austerity by consent' (cf. Bologna, 1977/1994) was faced with grave problems. Carter's deflationary policies paved the way for the much more rigorous monetarism of the New Right which was led by Thatcher in the UK and Reagan in the United States.

Monetarist regimes supported the recession of the early 1980s through pro-cyclical policies. They sought to tighten the money supply, to squeeze 'credit' through high interest rates and to reduce the ratio of debt to GDP through public expenditure cuts. Rather than supporting productive capital through easy credit, low interest rates, and deficit spending, deflationary policies reinforced the difficulties of hard pressed producers through a monetary squeeze on their solvency. Tight money attacked, in the face of a deep recession, working class wages directly by increasing unemployment and indirectly through increased job insecurity. Control of the money supply was based on the formidable idea that mass unemployment and poverty would support the decomposition of the working class into a profitable labour force.

The deep recession of the early 1980s brought to the fore the contradictions of credit-sustained accumulation. When the crisis struck, costly and scarce money reinforced mass insolvency and liquidation of functioning capital as well as mass unemployment. More advanced producers faced intense financial pressure because the introduction of new methods of production at the end of the 1970s was largely financed by credit, permitting a prevalidation of the productive potentials of fixed capital at a time of a looming recession. Further, by clamping down on credit the anticipated profitability of new investment programmes fell below the rate of interest, so permitting a continued transfer of earned profits into money markets. Upon credit default, banks invested new recycling credits (see Mandel, 1987, pp. 210–11). The spillover of capital into speculative channels continued, precipitated by high interest rates and a lack of profitable opportunities in productive investment. Capital continued to speculate on its own future while profits that were indeed produced declined so reducing the base from which the interest could be lopped off. Although high interest rates prevented banks from defaulting in the early 1980s, the effects of restoring the confidence of money capital through a policy of tight money threatened to bring about a severe financial crisis as the default of productive activity involved a massive default of credit which threatened the stability of banks because of the overextension of credit (Guttmann, 1989). Further, the rapid deterioration and devaluation of reproductive capital left gaping holes in the share-holders' dividend. At the same time as functioning capitals went into receivership, slashed investment and devalued productive capacity, the money supply, far from contracting, exploded as companies bor-rowed heavily from global credit markets so as to maintain solvency and cash flow (Sutcliffe, 1983; Clarke, 1988).

During the recession political authorities were not able to inflict substantial damage on the relation between public expenditure and wages. The tendency in public expenditure was upward (Mullard, 1987; Friedman, 1989; Malabre, 1988). High interest rates made addi-tional means of payment for financing public expenditure more ex-pensive. Further, the destruction of productive activity aggravated the fiscal crisis of the state and balance of payment problems, putting pressure on national reserves. At the same time, banks sought to augment their reserves by discounting bills of exchange with the central bank (Guttmann, 1989). The synchronisation of balance of payment difficulties and debt problems threatened to undermine the attempt to maintain formal exchange equality through a policy of state austerity.

The tightening of the money supply substantially raised the cost of servicing debt for so-called debtor countries. During the 1970s, real interest rates had been negative because inflation rates had been higher than nominal interest rates: 'In those days every time a Third World country borrowed to pay obligations instead of dipping into reserves, inflation meant it got the goods or services for less in the end' (George, 1988, p. 28). However, when interest rates began to rise rapidly, these countries were left holding the baby. The tightening of the international money supply called into question the ability of so-called debtor countries to turn credit into means of payment, precipitating a threat to the stability of global credit relations. On average, between 1973 and 1982, debt increased by 20% annually in the debtor countries, as compared with a 16% annual increase in net exports and a 12% annual increase in GNP. External debt increased from \$11 billion in 1972 to almost \$800 billion in 1982 (Altvater and Hübner, 1987, p. 21). High interest rates turned credit into the source of an acute liquidity crisis in those countries.

The imposition of tight money escalated the crisis of money to a crisis of the state. As credit was called upon as means of payment, growing international demand for cash in the face of faltering repayment of credit increased the vulnerability of the international system of finance and credit. The compulsion to export under any circumstances in order to repay debt, and growing social tension, forced Poland (1981), Argentina (1982) and Mexico (1982) to declare insolvency. The debtor crisis fed back into metropolitan countries through the international flow of money and pressure on banks. Monetarism was faced with the real possibility that money would turn its power against itself.

The attempt to contain social reproduction within the limits of its capitalist form through a policy of state austerity had come into conflict with the results it produced. When Mexico came within a hairbreadth of default in 1982, global credit relations ruptured to such an extent that the political authorities in metropolitan countries, especially the United States, reduced interest rates sharply and abnegated monetarist 'economic' policies and reinvoked credit expansion. The danger of a major slump was averted by a huge reflation package which had restored pseudovalidation on a global scale by 1982.

The monetarist attempt to reimpose the limits of the market precipitated a potential destruction of the market itself. Monetarism, while it was made politically strong and credible through the failure of Keynesianism, reproduced the contradiction between monetary and productive accumulation in an intensive form. The failure to convert credit into effective command over labour indicates labour's productive and disruptive power which capital had sought to contain by imposing tight money upon social relations. The shift from a policy of state austerity to a policy of deficit financing reintroduced an integration of labour on the basis of deficit financing of demand. The failure to impose control through a policy of tight money, and the reassertion of command over labour in the form of mass unemployment and mass liquidation of productive capacity, undermined claims on future exploitation to such an extent that the international financial system was severely shaken. The transfer of debt to the United States was a response not to the possible collapse of international credit relations *simpliciter*, but to the crisis of capitalist domination over the productive power of labour that made itself felt in the possible collapse of international credit relations. Rather than improving the strength of the relation between money and exploitation, the imposition of tight money undermined exploitation and therewith money itself. The imposition of tight money threatened to destroy money's own precondition, that is, labour's productive activity. A massive claim on surplus value defaulted. The limits of accumulation asserted themselves in the form of a scarcity of the credit with which labour's productive power had been contained on the basis of a speculative deferral of overaccumulation. In the face of a looming collapse of international credit relations, monetarism as an economic policy was dropped and replaced by a policy of fiscal redistribution and credit expansion, containing labour through a renewed speculative deferral of overaccumulation and crisis. The unmitigated failure to contain labour through a contraction of the money supply led to the reintroduction of those policies the New Right officially proclaimed against, that is, the fiscal and credit expansionism of Keynesianism.

Monetarism and Credit Expansion

Western capitalist countries responded to the crisis of 1980–2 with Keynesian deficit demand management on a world scale. The driving force of the recovery was the United States which supported the boom through two spectacular deficits: the budget deficit and the trade deficit. Demand management particularly in the area of military expenditure paved the way. As Mandel (1988) put it, the most committed Conservatives became the most ardent Keynesians. Their monetarist rhetoric notwithstanding, they supported the boom with huge deficits.[11] This support was not dissimilar to Keynes's 'deficit spending', i.e. the creation of debt, the inflation of the money supply, and the spending of money which prevalidates the exploitation of labour. The budget deficit of the United States grew enormously. During the 1980s, 'interest on the debt and the cost of defence account for nearly 40% of all federal expenditures' (Malabre, 1988, p. 110). The average budget deficit for 'the six years 1982–7 was $184 billion' (Friedman, 1989, p. 19). By 1986 the United States had accumulated over $250 billion foreign debt: 'This $250 billion is only the foreign debt: as of 1986, the US government owed an additional $1,750 billion to American purchasers of government securities, so its total public debt was actually $2 trillion' (George, 1988, p. 25).[12] The financing of the United States trade and budget deficits through capital imports transformed the United States from the biggest creditor to the biggest debtor in the world. The dollar was sustained by the inflow of speculative capital and debt bondage forced upon so-called debtor countries: 'It's clear that the Third World can't pay – and yet it does! For Latin America alone, new capital inflow (both aid and investment) came to under $38 billion between 1982 and 1985, while it paid back $144 billion in debt service. Net transfer from the poor to rich: $106 billion' (George, 1988, p. 63). Reagan's attempt to make the United States politically and economically strong again by 'living beyond its means' turned the supply-side policy into a policy of importing speculative capital. The money flow into the United States was made possible by high interest rates in the United States. High interest rates did not prove an effective brake on the inflationary expansion of credit. Creditors were shielded from the full burden of outstanding debt (see George, 1992) while debtors were shielded from the debt burden through fiscal relief. Embarrassed creditors, like the big banks, were refinanced upon their gambling losses (Mandel, 1987). Banks received tax relief on 'bad debt' and sold 'bad debt' to public institutions. While indebted countries were, during the 1980s, not allowed to grow out of debt, the banks were able to socialise their debt problems. As George (1992, p. 106) put it, 'during the 1980s, the only thing that was socialised rather than privatised was debt itself'. In the United States, tax cuts laid the basis for the fiscal absorption of high interest rates. In the United Kingdom, tax cuts were implemented on the basis of public expenditure restraint and earnings from privatisation. The failure to decompose the working class into a profitable labour force would have implied, as indeed it did, a progressive dissociation between money and exploitation expressed in higher rates of inflation, financial instability and depressed rate of growth in productive activity. During the boom there was a record number of bank failures. In scale these failures far exceeded the 1930s (see Mandel, 1987, p. 300; Dziobek, 1987). Many of the surviving banks were themselves for a time 'technically bankrupt' (cf. Keegan, 1993, p. 185).

The expansionary response to the debtor crisis acknowledged the circumstance that the only consistent way to contain labour within the capital relation is expanded accumulation. However, the expansionary response did not mean that monetarism was simply abandoned. Indeed, monetarist policies continued. There was a 'juxtaposition' of two different policies. On the one hand, we find policies of monetary expansion (relaxation of credit and controls and fiscal expansionism) and, on the other, an imposition of austerity upon social relations. The former policy acknowledged the circumstance that the deregulated global credit relations had meant the liberation of 'domestic' monetary targets. The latter policy comprises an attempt at monetary adjustment, i.e. at guaranteeing credit expansion through the control of public expenditure. After 1982 monetarism's policy of market freedom focused on the control of that part of public expenditure which supported policies of social reform. The imposition of tight money upon social relations involved an attempt to strengthen the link between consumption and work. The idea was that by controlling public expenditure, economic growth would translate into a fall in the share of public expenditure relative to GDP. This would fend off speculative pressure on the exchange rate because the convertibility of debt into real money was guaranteed by state revenue. This would allow tax cuts designed to offset the pressure of credit costs on debtors and to provide incentives for enterprise. In other words, accumulation was sustained by a relaxation of credit constraints as well as a massive redistribution of national wealth to capital through fiscal policies.

The expansionary response to the 'crisis of 1982' and the attack on the Keynesian relation between public expenditure and wages went together. The adjustment between credit expansion and the control of the money supply focused on the working class. As Gamble (1988, p. 122) put it, 'Keynesian techniques continued to be used, only now the objective was to restore financial stability rather than to preserve high levels of employment and growth'. The retention of tight monetary policies aimed at reducing wage costs and living standards through restrictive monetary policies that discriminated against the working class, and through divisive fiscal policies which increased the overall tax burden while favouring capital through fiscal incentives. It also meant that the welfare state was used not as a means of alleviating the effects of unemployment but as a means of administering social control by the imposition of economic and financial insecurity as well as forced labour.[13] In order to contain the class struggle through the only consistent way of imposing the wage relation, i.e. sustained accumulation, political authorities relaxed monetary policies and sought to contain the fictitious – or speculative – integration of labour into the capital relation through restraint in public expenditure and the imposition of 'market freedom' upon the working class through the weakening of trade union bargaining power, unemployment, deregulation of wage protection, segmentation of labour markets, tax and poverty traps, and use of the welfare state as a means of keeping people in poverty and debt and of making people work for their benefits. In this context, the shift to expansionary policies made impossible the restoration of a Keynesian-inspired collaboration with trade unions. Instead, social peace was to be imposed rather than negotiated in an attempt to make the social environment stable without thereby making extensive monetary concessions to the working class. Under the impact of relaxed credit controls and Reagan's 'military Keynesianism' (Clarke, 1988; Gamble, 1988; Harman, 1993; Mandel, 1987), monetarist policies attacked those institutions associated with an integration of labour through social reform.[14]

During the 1980s, the global liberalisation of financial markets and the deregulation of credit controls made possible an orgy of speculation; the breeding of profits by speculative capital through unproductive investment in money markets. Under the impact of financial deregulation, 'consumer expenditure surged forward, financed by a fall in personal savings as inflation moderated and by a rapid growth of consumer credit' (Clarke, 1988, p. 336). In the United States, savings fell dramatically from about 6% of personal income in the 1970s to 2.9% in 1985 (Guttmann, 1989, p. 42; for the United Kingdom see Keegan, 1989). The unregulated and uncontrolled banking system made it possible for a great number of people to maintain, in the face of a policy of state austerity, living standards through access to private credit. In the United Kingdom, the decline in the saving ratio was reinforced by an increase in personal financial liabilities of individuals. These liabilities 'rose from 45 per cent of pre-tax incomes at the beginning of the Eighties to 81.3 per cent at the end of 1987' (Keegan, 1989, p. 209). For many people, the only way to sustain living standards was to incur debt. Monetarist policies developed, after 1982, in two ways: credit-sustained accumulation and the unrestricted and unregulated expansion of credit on the one hand, and the integration of private debt through austerity policies with an abrasive law and order control of social relations on the other. The ballooning of global deficit financing of demand indicates that the New Right had lost faith in their own gospel when confronted with the realities of a major slump in the early 1980s. Their transformation into unbelieving Keynesians mortgaged the future exploitation of labour at the same time as law and order spending of all kind increased dramatically.

The 'extremely Keynesian politics of the Reagan administration' (cf. Wolf, 1988) was a Keynesianism dressed in new clothes. While

Keynesians emphasise the anti-cyclical dimension of deficit spending, the Keynesianism of the New Right sustained the boom through a pro-cyclical credit expansion. The deficit financing of aggregate demand took place not during the recession but during the boom. Further, the pro-cyclical deficit spending of the 1980s did not reduce the level of unemployment. The Keynesian commitment to redistribution of income and employment was abandoned at the same time as governments pursued expansionary policies associated with Keynesianism. In other words, the erstwhile monetarists remained anti-Keynesian *not* because Keynesian policies were expansionary but because they were redistributive. Since the 'crisis of 1982', Keynesian policies of credit expansion were used pro-cyclically, favouring those who have and imposing austerity upon those upon whose exploitation capitalist reproduction rests. Expansionary policies and state policies of austerity coincided. Welfare provisions were dismantled in favour of discipline by austerity; fiscal policies were used to discipline people through tax and poverty traps; draconian measures were instituted against trade unions. The idea was to make people pay for the increase in credit through worsening conditions, intensification of work and lower wages. Expansionary policies were thus to be checked by poverty and credit was to be guaranteed through a stronger link between consumption and work. Worsening conditions and any increase in poverty was the mirror image of the boom of the 1980s.

However, the coexistence of mass unemployment, deficit spending and growing indebtedness defined the speculative character of the boom. Growing indebtedness was in no way matched by an expanded exploitation of labour. Indeed, during the boom the investment in money increased enormously while investment in direct exploitation of labour lagged behind dramatically (see Glyn, 1992; Mandel, 1987). Keynesian deficit financing provided financial investment opportunities. Earned profits were financialised rather than invested productively. While it might be argued that indebtedness was induced as a means of delaying a much deeper recession than the one of the early 1980s, or possibly even of delaying a slump of the proportion of 1929–32 (see Mandel, 1987, 1988), the result was the accumulation of increasingly irredeemable debt. No surprisingly the *Economist* reported in May 1987 that American economists were wondering what lay ahead that year, continued growth or slump? The Keynesianism of the New Right was a desperate measure of crisis management. Rather than tightening the relation between money and exploitation, the link between the two declined progressively. While monetarism proclaimed in favour of the virtues of market freedom, capital made money out of money in a desperate attempt to accumulate as much as possible without getting dirty in the contested terrain of production.[15]

The boom of the 1980s rested on intensification of work and increase in productivity. The increase in productivity was based, to a great extent, on the liquidation of unproductive producers in the early 1980s. Also, productivity increased because unemployment rose as output fell (see Glyn, 1992; Nolan, 1989). The boom was a boom in 'money' as money was transformed into a saleable thing. Despite downward pressures on wages and the decomposition of class relations through unemployment, and despite the recomposition of working practices, and an increase in the rate of exploitation (see Harman, 1993), ongoing resistance to industrial restructuring prevented either a sufficient rise in profit rates on productive investment or the generation of state surpluses to induce or finance a new cycle of investment. The recovery of accumulation was consumption-led -- a return to an integration of labour into the capital relation on the basis of the deficit financing of demand. Capital has opted for monetary over productive investment, fuelling property bubbles, takeover mania and the esoteric art of speculation – because of the tremendous opportunities offered in these investments. However, all these investments represent a considerable avoidance of real investment, an aversion to precisely the supply-side launching of accumulation which the deficit financing of demand had tried to induce.[16] The credit-sustained boom of the 1980s was a response to the failure to decompose the working class into a profitable labour force. During the boom the dissociation between monetary and productive accumulation accelerated, a dissociation which fuelled the boom and which led to the crash in 1987 and the recession of the 1990s. Capital, when confronted with the possibility of a major slump in the early 1980s, started to gamble and the affluence of the 1980s was the affluence of a gambler. Monetarist politicians which had preached that government should get off the back of people, had forgotten their erstwhile predictions which von Mises (1944, p. 21) had summarised long ago: 'Credit expansion can bring about a temporary boom. But such a fictitious prosperity must end in a general depression of trade, a slump'.

The crash of 1987 signalled the failure of the Keynesianism of the New Right.[17] The crash, while bringing home dramatically how precarious were the foundations of the boom, did not result in an entire meltdown of the stockmarket. This was prevented by a huge reflation package which included the lowering of interest rates, the relaxation of controls on the money supply, and financial support for banks and other financial institutions. The reflation package helped to sustain the credit-sustained boom. Samuel Brittan's advice was well observed: 'When a slump is threatening, we need helicopters dropping currency notes from the sky. This means easier bank lending policies and, if that is not enough, some mixture of lower taxes and higher government spending' (quoted in Harman, 1993, p. 15). The crash led to the abandonment of the monetarist rhetoric which surrounded the Keynesianism of the New Right. As the *Economist* stated after the crash: 'The immediate task is a Keynesian one: to support demand at a time when the stock market crash threatens to shrink it' (quoted in Harman, 1993, p. 15). Keynesianism was thus officially resurrected and hailed again, even by its erstwhile critics, as a saviour.

The credit-sustained boom lasted until 1990. By the late 1980s inflation began to rise on a global scale. The recession of the 1990s has been the longest and deepest since the end of the Second World War. There were more bankruptcies than during the previous recessions since the 1960s (see Harman, 1993). The property market crashed in the United States, the United Kingdom and Japan, and Germany is in its deepest recession since Weimar.[18] Unemployment increased dramatically and corporate default on debt caused banks to write off bad debt on an enormous scale. The consumer boom collapsed. Credit was not only squeezed: credit expansion came to a crunching halt.

The divorce of monetary accumulation from the exploitation of labour in production impinged on the state in the form of a disunity as between the so-called 'overheating of the economy' and speculative pressure on currency. By the early 1990s the credit expansion with which the impact of the crash of 1987 had been smothered was increasingly 'incompatible' with the global limits of credit markets. The expansionary response to the crash led to a development in which the composition of social capital looks more than ever like an upside-down pyramid: 'Phantom credits' accumulated in the form of a speculative betting on the future of capitalism's ailing life-blood, that is, the integration of labour as the variable component of expanded exploitation. However, the increase in the ratio of debt to surplus value meant that the exploitation of labour looked less and less likely to support shareholders' dividends. Big firms such as Pan Am and Maxwell Communications went bust. Everywhere profits dived. Against this background it became not only increasingly 'unprofitable' to make money out of the growing ratio of debt to surplus value; it became also more dangerous. Against the background of the Savings & Loans and property crises, the junk bond market collapsed in the late 1980s. Investors were confronted with a huge amount of non-recoverable debt and the rapid increase in bankruptcies meant that banks ended up with bad debt problems. Credit became more expensive to get and banks called in debt so as to protect their reserves. The precarious financial situation of producers intensified at the same time as credit-based consumer spending came to a halt. By the early 1990s, there was growing concern that a global credit crunch was imminent. Many industries had been swamped with debt and more than a few of these companies lacked the means with which to pay off their debt. Just as rampant speculation fed into itself for years, so too did the new scepticism. Investors began to run for the exits.

National states are not insulated from the rest of the world[19] but integrated through the exchange rate mechanism and their containment of labour within global accumulation is 'policed' through speculative capital movements. While governments might have been tempted to inflate the debt away and thereby to reduce the burden of debt on many firms as well as devalue real wages and erode standards of living, speculative runs on currency would result in a liquidity crisis, reinforcing the fiscal crisis of the state and making it difficult to finance balance of payments deficits. Against the background of the Savings & Loans crisis of the late 1980s and speculative pressure on currencies, governments responded with tighter monetary policies increasing interest rates so as to fend off speculative pressure and to make it possible for banks and other financial institutions to compensate for debt defaults and speculative losses. By 1988–9 employers had to concede higher wages as unemployment fell from its previous height and as workers demanded financial compensation for the growth in manufacturing productivity during the 1980s (see Harman, 1993). Unit labour costs accelerated (see *Financial Times*, 14 October 1989). By the late 1980s, there was growing concern that the increase in profitability during the 1980s was no longer sufficient to maintain expanding investment. The fall in profits triggered a vicious circle as companies were forced to borrow so as to overcome difficulties. High interest rates cut into profits at the same time as the life-blood of the boom, i.e. credit, changed, by the early 1990s, into a forcible collection of unpaid debt which is the backbone of the policy of state austerity. The irony of a Keynesian policy in a monetarist framework was that when the recession came in 1990 there was not much leeway for a Keynesian anti-cyclical policy of deficit spending. Monetary policies tightened because of the danger of rampant speculation on the future direction of policy, the liquidity of national states, the ability of companies to honour credit obligations, and the stability of the property market.

In the United Kingdom inflation moved almost into double figures in 1990. Against the background of the London poll tax riot of April 1990 and worries in the international financial markets about the economic and political situation in Britain, the then Thatcher government joined the ERM in an attempt to anchor monetary policy and so to insulate speculative betting on domestic policies (see Smith, 1992). As in the early 1980s, monetary policy was tightened at the start of recession. The aim was to externalise the responsibility for the deflationary consequences of a policy of high interest rates and to gather support for sterling from other European states. Against the background of huge balance of payments deficits and budget deficits,[20] the monetary constraints of the ERM meant that interest rates which had been raised to 15% by 1989 were only reduced to 14% prior to entry and fell to 10% in the summer of 1992 (see Stewart, 1993, pp. 62–3). However, there was no fall in real interest rates 'because meanwhile the inflation rate fell from around 10 per cent to around 4 per cent' (Stewart, 1993, p. 63). The defence of sterling against speculative runs was initially successful in that unemployment started to rise from less than 6% in 1990 to 9% in 1991 and over 10% in 1992 (Stewart, 1993; McKie, 1993). The number of bankruptcies as well as company liquidations increased dramatically by 1990 and continued to rise (see Smith, 1992, p. 257). Additionally companies slashed investment. There was a massive devaluation of capital. Wage demands subsided and strikes fell to a very low level (see McKie, 1993). High interest rates had originally been regarded as a means of deflating the economy without seriously undermining big companies. Their profits were seen to be high enough to protect them. Initially, high interest rates forced smaller business into bankruptcy and attacked social relations through consumer debt default, including mortgages. The British government hoped for a soft landing by making social relations pay for inflationary pressure. The socialisation of the debt problem meant a dramatic increase in homelessness, repossessions, personal bankruptcies, and unemployment. However, the socialisation of debt through the imposition of poverty did not check the downturn.

In response to the breakdown in consumer spending, retailers were hit by debt deflation. Retailing capacity became redundant, causing the property market, against the background of mortgage default and closure of offices, first to bubble and then to burst. The crisis in the property market fed back into the financial system causing debt default at the same time as bad debt problems caused by company failure mounted. Bigger companies were not shielded through their profits for long. Corporate indebtedness had increased dramatically during the 1980s. The debt burden was at around 20% of the capital stock compared with 8% in 1980–1 (see Smith, 1992, p. 193). Manufacturing investment fell sharply by 1990–1 (Smith, 1992, p. 193). Profits did not withstand high interest rates and so started to 'dip seriously. The banking system was on the 'brink of collapse under the weight of corporate failures and personal bankruptcies' (Smith, 1992, p. 244). Banks sought to support their accounts by higher bad debt provisions and to socialise their debt problems through redundancies, higher fees, and wider interest rate margins on loans. Credit became more expensive and more difficult to obtain. At the same time, 'consumers' and 'companies' were reluctant to borrow and endeavoured to service their debt (see Stewart, 1993, p. 102).

The level of lending decreased on a global scale. For example, in the United States, business borrowing fell: 'Previously the pattern was for firms to increase their borrowing in recessions: total bank loans rose by 12.2 per cent in 1973, by 3.5 per cent in 1980s and 5.4 per cent in 1981. But in 1990 total loans *fell* by 3.6 per cent' (Harman, 1993, p. 42). However, the availability of money was not in question. There was a lack of profitable opportunities to spend it (Harman, 1993, p. 44). There was thus a lack of lending and a global shortage of capital at the same time as companies required additional credit to maintain solvency. While credit was hard to come by, past debts fell due. As Harman (1993, p. 45) indicates, 'the discussion about the "credit crunch" is an indication that the system has reached an impasse'.

During the recession, the ratio of debt to GDP rose allowing for a growing share of interest payments in government budgets (see *Financial Times*, 27 September 1993). With government becoming increasingly vulnerable to a sharp rise in interest rates, public spending pressure increased as unemployment rose. High interest rates, persistently slow economic growth, public spending pressure and loss of revenue tightened the fiscal crisis of the state. Budget deficits increased at the same time as the guarantee of global credit relations through the reserves and state revenue decreased in strength. As a consequence speculative policing of domestic attempts to safeguard currencies through deflationary control of social relations increased, reinforcing the fiscal crisis of the state through runs on currency and thus through a drain on the reserves. Against the background of both huge balance of payments deficits and budget deficits, as well as sluggish economic growth and a stumbling banking system, the pound sterling became a target of market rule. The pound sterling crisis of 1992, when its membership in the ERM was suspended and sterling devalued, and the near suspension of the ERM in 1993, indicated that the recession had reached an impasse. In 1993, the decision to increase the fluctuation margins in the ERM to 15% either side of the central rates amounted to an admission on the part of governments that tight monetary policy had not succeeded in controlling social relations through austerity and that they thus could not fend off speculative pressures.

Against the background of reduced rates of inflation, mass unemployment, and the turmoil on the currency markets, budget deficits everywhere were at a high level in 1992: 'The average for the main OECD countries had risen to 43.6 per cent, from 22.7 per cent in 1979, and by the end of 1993 all the European Community countries were expected to be outside the Maastricht target for government debt of 3 per cent of GDP' (Harman, 1993, p. 49). Will the debt crisis which beset the Third World in the 1980s move north? There is a renewed Keynesian stimulus to demand as deficits increase and as the first green shoots of recovery are visible due to wage restraint, a massive devaluation of capital, as well as the socialisation of bad debt problems: 'Keynesianism does seem to be making a comeback' (Gamble, 1993, p. 80). What, however, does that mean? Keynesian policies of deficit financing on a global scale have 'already been used up to support the cyclical expansion of the 1980s, leaving in its wake a tremendous overhang of government debt whose servicing takes up a larger and larger share of Federal outlays' (Burkett, 1994, p. 12). In the wake of the Los Angeles riots, Clinton announced a 'war on poverty' and, in Britain, Major promised, against the background of the abandonment of the poll tax, to create a 'classless society'. Should we indeed see the return of the so-called 'affluent society' which captured the imagination of so many during the late 1950s and early 1960s? The image of prosperity is seductive especially against the background of mass unemployment, growing poverty and increasing homelessness. However before we let ourselves be seduced we will first have to return to basics: 'The weakness of the present upturn signifies the reemergence of a long-run crisis having the same basic character as in the 1930s' (Burkett, 1994, p. 9).

Keynesianism in the 1990s is expensive. Governments all over the world are preaching the gospel of rising productivity and competitiveness. The promise is thus that fewer and less paid workers will produce more. As Burkett (1994, p. 13) puts it, 'under current conditions, rising productivity translates primarily into higher unemployment'. In other words, a rise in the productive power of labour makes it very difficult for capital to regard the unemployed as a variable component for the purpose of expanded exploitation. Against the background of consumer debt and recent attempts by governments to balance their books by further cuts in the welfare state, targeting, for example, single mothers and pensioners, and higher tax burdens for those who do-not-have, the attempt to avoid a slump by boosting the exploitation of labour through deficits is not without its problems. As the *Financial Times* (9 September 1993) points out: 'Governments know that if policy ceases to be credible, international markets will simply switch off the financial tap.' Without an effective exploitation of social labour power accumulation will remain a speculative gamble: 'Little wonder the IMF privately fears that the debt threat is moving north. These days it is the build-up of first world debt, not Africa's lingering crisis, that haunts the sleep of the IMF officials' (E. Balls in *Financial Times*, 27 September 1993). Clinton's promise of a 'war on poverty' should be taken seriously. Political regimes in so-called debtor countries supply not only ample evidence of a monetarism in crisis, but also present the more likely future of a capitalism which continues to invest in the future because it can not redeem itself in in the present.

MONETARISM: A CONCLUSION

Since the late 1960s, depressed rates of productive accumulation have coincided with a rapid monetary accumulation. There has been a dramatic dissociation between money and exploitation. Credit has not been transformed into command over labour for the purpose of expanded surplus value production. Capital has opted for speculation rather than the generation of surplus value. The significance of monetary speculation lies in the avoidance of a direct relationship with the working class. Speculation does not meet with the same resistance that capital encounters in the factory. Since the mid-1970s, the attempt to rebuild profitability without enduring a slump on the scale of the 1930s has been associated with a policy of deflation, and the sacrifice of the commitment to full employment and a policy of social reform.

The breakdown of Bretton Woods and the deregulation of international credit and money markets proved to be the single most important event of the class struggle in-and-against the form of the capitalist state. Behind the deregulation of international money lay the strategy of austerity as a means of decomposing class relationships through the ruthless impartiality of monetary intervention and the intensification of work. However, the rule of money exists only through the reproduction of this command's precondition: the harnessing of labour into expanded profitable reproduction. Keynesian and monetarist policies depend on sustained accumulation so as to contain labour through the fragmenting imposition of the wage relation. Both policies accentuate different moments of the contradictory unity of surplus value production, stimulating a breakdown of both, money and production, through the sacrificing of one moment of the contradiction in favour of the other. The dissociation of monetary accumulation from productive accumulation constituted the contradictory unity of surplus value production in the form of a crisis-ridden disunity between functioning capital and the credit system. Both of these poles of the contradiction exist as different moments of the circuit of social capital, a crisis-ridden contradiction which entails the crisis of domination over labour. It has been emphasised that neither Keynesianism nor monetarism succeeded in containing labour and in solving the 'labour question'. The attack on the working class during the 1980s and 1990s radicalised established trends. This radicalisation was confined and precipitated by the crisis of Keynesianism. Monetarist policies responded to the crisis of Keynesianism without overcoming it.

During the 1980s, Keynesian economic policies continued to be used while the attack on the welfare state did not weaken the relation between wages and public expenditure. The increase in private debt contradicted the attempt to strengthen the connection between consumption and work. The result was the deepening of the crisis of Keynesian policies of state austerity. The recession of the 1990s expresses the failure of the Keynesianism of the New Right.

During the 1980s, the class struggle over credit and monetary policies involved the struggle over the imposition of monetary austerity upon social relations in and through unemployment, deflationary attack, imposition of poverty, and the intensification of work and law and order control. However, the intensification of work, the shedding of labour and the microchip revolution did not result in a profitable integration of labour into the capital relation. The circuit of social capital was based on a renewed speculative deferral of overaccumulation and crisis, precipitated by renewed global deficit financing of demand. Labour was integrated into the capital relation on the basis of debt.

The speculative accumulation of the 1980s stretched the limits of the market through credit and the ultimate barrier to accumulation appeared to be the availability of credit. However, the availability of credit is the availability of money capital that reasserts the limits to capitalist accumulation in the form of speculation and (eventually, as in 1987) a financial crisis. The debt crisis of the 1980s, the crash in 1987, and the recession of the 1990s, expressed the crisis of capitalist domination over labour for the purpose of exploitation. Within the context of the persistence of crisis, and the failure of past policy measures to achieve a solution, money asserted itself in a repressive rather than a creative way. The imposition of tight money upon social relations has not been matched by a recomposition of class relations capable of relaunching a new cycle of accumulation. Far from stimulating investment, employment and output, the result of credit expansion in a tight monetary framework was the deterioration of conditions and mass unemployment. There was no breakthrough in investment. Credit expansion was used for speculation rather than for the generation of surplus value. The reconstitution of the circuit of social capital does not just require, as during the 1980s, a divisive and fragmenting decomposition of class relations in terms of the property owner and citizen. Rather, it involves the imposition of valorisation upon the labour process. Such an imposition implies not just the intensification of work and the repressive exclusion from production of those whom capital is forced to disregard as a variable for exploitation. Rather, it entails the transformation of money into truly productive capital, that is, a capital which exploits labour on an expanding scale. This transformation presupposes the recomposition of the relation between necessary and surplus labour. The recomposition of this relation is still beyond the horizon.[21]

By the early 1990s, the weakness of productive activity and the instability of the financial system presents the failure of neo-liberalism to secure the future exploitation of labour in the present. Against the background of the deep and prolonged recession of the early 1990s, there is nostalgia for Keynesianism. There is a growing number of studies which, after so many years of deficit spending, argue for a return to Keynesian policies. These studies emphasise that market economies are not self-stabilising and so in need of some sort of Keynesian intervention (see Stewart, 1993; Keegan, 1993). Keynesianism is seen, again, as a means of making capitalism safe for capitalists. In the 1990s it has become old fashioned to demand from government that it should get off the backs of people and provide greater scope for market forces. There is a demand for a new consensus. Old style Keynesianism is criticised for its excessive interventionism while monetarism is rejected for its excessive deflationary zeal and its religious belief in market self-regulation. Excessive deflation as well as excessive encouragement of expansion is damaging (cf. Keegan, 1993). One cannot rely on market forces but it is not advisable to return to full-blown state intervention (see Stewart, 1993). There is a demand for a new 'realism': market and state have to cooperate (cf. Mitchell, 1989, p. 51). Would the 'fine tuning' of this relationship involve also a return to a 'social capitalism' (cf. Keegan, 1993), i.e. a capitalism of social reform? There are proposals for a reformed Keynesianism and a 'market socialism'.[22] As in the past, the reformist left proposes to defend market forces against their inherent disruptive constitution. They wish to humanise the inhumane.[23] The so-called Keynesian era did not start in the 1930s but developed through the experience of fascism and war.

Notes

1. See Holloway's 'The Abyss Opens', Chapter 2 in this volume.
2. On this system see Burnham (1990) and Burnham's 'Capital, Crisis and the International State System', Chapter 5 in this volume; see also Bonefeld (1993a, 1993b) as well as Brett (1983) and Pilbeam (1992).
3. Skidelsky (1977); Lekachman (1966). This part is indebted to Gamble (1993, p. 42).
4. See Callaghan, quoted in Holloway's 'The Abyss Opens', Chapter 2 in this volume.
5. On these markets see Holloway's 'The Abyss Opens', Chapter 2 in this volume; see also Cleaver's 'The Subversion of Money as Command', Chapter 7 in this volume, as well as Bonefeld (1993a) and Wachtel (1990).
6. See Itoh (1978); Mandel (1987); Wolf (1988); see also Sampson (1983).
7. On the redefinition of the 'power of money' see Marazzi's 'Money in

the World Crisis', Chapter 4 in this volume; see also Bonefeld's 'Money, Equality and Exploitation', Chapter 8 in this volume.

8. On the fiscal crisis see: O'Connor (1973); Gough (1975), Hirsch (1978a, 1978b). See also Offe's (1984) work on the crisis of the welfare state. For an assessment of these approaches, see Clarke (1991, 1992, 1988).

9. OPEC countries contributed also to the growth of the Eurodollar market (see Wachtel, 1990). However, the so-called petrodollar represented a small proportion of the rise of the volume of money placed on this market (Schubert 1985). See also Altvater and Hübner (1987).

10. The following quote by Marx (1966, p. 515) might help to clarify the argument:

> The demand for loanable capital is demand for means of payment and nothing else; it is by no means demand for money as a means of purchase. [This] demand for means of payment is a mere demand for convertibility into *money*, so far as merchants and producers have good securities to offer; it is a demand for *money-capital* whenever there is no collateral, so that an advance of means of payment gives them not only the *form of money* but also the *equivalent* they lack, whatever its form, with which to make payment.

11. The following is close to Mandel (1988, p. 105).

12. On the debt in other western capitalist countries see Mandel (1988, 1987), Wolf (1988). In the United Kingdom budget deficits and the trade deficit improved during the 1980s due to the earnings of North Sea oil (Keegan, 1984, 1989), privatisation (Gamble, 1988); a higher tax burden (Rowthorn, 1992), and drastic cuts in that public expenditure which supported policies of social reform. See also Clarke (1988); Bonefeld (1993a); and the contributions in Michie (1992).

13. See the workfare programmes in the United States and training programmes in the United Kingdom.

14. After the abandonment of the 'monetarist economics', the British Prime Minister Thatcher promised to 'kill Socialism in Britain' (see Bonefeld, 1993a) and fought the miners in 1984–5. The miners were branded as the 'enemy within' and defeated with the help of paramilitary policing (see Bonefeld, 1993a; Fine and Millar, 1985).

15. See Cleaver's 'The Subversion of Money-as-Command', Chapter 7 in this volume.

16. See n. 15 above.

17. On the crash see the contributions to *Capital & Class*, 34; Harman (1993); Mandel and Wolf (1988); see also Bonefeld (1993a).

18. See Harman (1993) on the recession in Germany and Japan.

19. see Holloway's 'Global Capital and the National State', and Burnham's 'Capital, Crisis and the International State System', Chapters 5 and 6 in this volume. See also Bonefeld (1992) and Burnham (1990, 1993).

20. The balance of payments was in the red from 1987 onwards and has, since then, increased steadily (see Stewart, 1993). The PSBR was negative from 1987–8 to 1990–1 and deteriorated sharply in 1991–2 and increased dramatically in 1992–3 to 36.5 billion compared with a budget surplus of 0.5 billion in 1990–1 (see McKie), 1993.

21.   On the relation between 'money', on the one hand, and necessary
       labour and surplus labour, on the other, see Negri (1984, Lesson Two);
       see also Marazzi's 'Money in the World Crisis', and Bonefeld's 'Money,
       Equality and Exploitation', Chapters 4 and 8 in this volume.
22.   See McNally (1993) for a critique of market socialism.
23.   See Agnoli (1990) on reformism's affirmative critique and acceptance
       of the *status quo*.

References

Agnoli, J. (1990) *Die Transformation der Demokratie und andere Schriften
    zur Kritik der Politik* (Freiburg: Ca-Ira).
Altvater, E. (1985) 'Kredit und Hegemonie', in M. Jänicke (ed.), *Vor uns die
    goldenen fünfziger Jahre* (Munich: Piper).
Altvater, E. and Hübner, K. (1987) 'Ursachen und Verlauf der internationalen
    Verschuldungskrise', in E. Altvater *et al.*, *Die Armut der Nationen* (Berlin:
    Rotbuch).
Bologna, S. (1977/1994) 'The Tribe of Moles', forthcoming in S. Bologna,
    Selected Writings by Sergio Bologna (London: Red Notes).
Bonefeld, W. (1992) 'Social Constitution and the Form of the Capitalist
    State', in W. Bonefeld, R. Gunn and K. Psychopedis (eds), *Open Marxism
    Vol I: History and Dialectics* (London: Pluto Press).
Bonefeld, W. (1993a) *The Recomposition of the British State During the
    1980s* (Aldershot: Dartmouth).
Bonefeld, W. (1993b) 'The Global Money Power of Capital and the Crisis of
    Keynesianism', *Common Sense*, 13.
Brett, E.A. (1983) *International Money and Capitalist Crisis* (London:
    Heinemann).
Burkett, P. (1994) 'The strange US Economic Recovery and Clintonomics
    historically Considered', *Capital & Class*, 52.
Burnham, P. (1990) *The Political Economy of Postwar Reconstruction*
    (London: Macmillan).
Burnham, P. (1993) 'Marxism, Neo-Realism and International Relations',
    Common Sense, 14.
Clarke, S. (1988) *Keynesianism, Monetarism and the Crisis of the State*
    (Aldershot: Edward Elgar).
Clarke, S. (1991) 'The State Debate', in S. Clarke (ed.), *The State Debate*
    (London: Macmillan).
Clarke, S. (1992) 'Global Accumulation of Capital and the Periodisation of
    the Capitalist State Form', in W. Bonefeld, R. Gunn and K. Psychopedis
    (eds), *Open Marxism Vol. I: History and Dialectics* (London: Pluto Press).
Cleaver, H. (1989) 'Close the IMF, Abolish Debt and End Development',
    Capital & Class, 39.
De Brunhoff, S. (1978) *The State, Capital and Economic Theory* (London:
    Pluto Press).
Dziobek, C. (1987) 'Die verschuldete westliche Welt', in E. Altvater *et al.*,
    Die Armut der Nationen (Berlin: Rotbuch Verlag).
Esser, J. and Fach, W. (1981) 'Korporative Krisenregulierung', in U.v. Aleman
    (ed.), *Neo-Korporatismus* (Frankfurt: Campus Verlag).

Evans, T. (1985) 'Money Makes the World Go Round', *Capital & Class*, 24.
Fine, B. and Millar, R. (eds) (1985) *Policing the Miners' Strike* (London: Lawrence & Wishart).
Friedman, B.M. (1989) *Day of Reckoning* (New York: Vintage).
Gamble, A. (1988) *The Free Economy and the Strong State* (London: Macmillan).
Gamble, A. (1993) 'The Decline of Corporatism', in D. Crabree and A.P. Thirwall (eds) *Keynes and the Role of the State* (London: Macmillan).
George, S. (1988) *A Fate Worse Than Debt* (London: Penguin).
George, S. (1992) *The Debt Boomerang* (London: Pluto Press).
Glyn, A. (1992) 'The "Productivity Miracle", Profits and Investment', in J. Michie (ed.), *The Economic Legacy 1979–1992* (London: Academic Press).
Gough, I. (1975) 'State Expenditure in Advanced Capitalism', *New Left Review*, 92.
Guttmann, R. (1989) 'Der Strukturwandel des amerikanischen Finanzkapitals', *PROKLA*, 74.
Harman, Ch. (1993) 'Where is Capitalism Going', *International Socialism*, 58.
Hilferding, R. (1910/1981) *Finance Capital* (London: Routledge & Kegan Paul).
Hirsch, J. (1978a) 'The Crisis of Mass Integration', *International Journal of Urban and Regional Research*, 2 (ii).
Hirsch, J. (1978b) 'Was heißt eigentlich "Krise der Staatsfinanzen"', *Leviathan Sonderheft*, 1/78.
Hirsch, J. (1980) *Der Sicherheitsstaat*, VSA, Hamburg.
Holloway, J. (1990) 'The Politics of Debt', *Common Sense*, 9.
Itoh, M. (1978) 'The Inflational Crisis of Capitalism', *Capital & Class*, 4.
Joseph, K. and Sumption, J. (1979) *Equality* (London: John Murray).
Keegan, W. (1984) *Mrs. Thatcher's Economic Experiment* (London: Penguin).
Keegan, W. (1989) *Mr Lawson's Gamble* (London: Hodder & Stoughton).
Keegan, W. (1993) *The Spectre of Capitalism* (London: Vintage).
Lekachman, R. (1966) *The Age of Keynes* (New York: McGraw-Hill).
Lipietz, A. (1982) 'Towards Global Fordism', *New Left Review*, 151.
Lipietz, A. (1984) 'Imperialism or the Beast of Apocalypse', *Capital & Class*, 22.
London (1980) London Edinburgh Weekend Return Group, *In and Against the State* (London: Pluto Press).
Malabre, A.L. (1988) *Beyond Our Means* (New York: Vintage).
Mandel, E. (1987) *Die Krise 1974–1986* (Hamburg: Konkret Literatur Verlag).
Mandel, E. (1988) 'Der Börsenkrach. Dreizehn Fragen', in E. Mandel and W. Wolf, *Börsenkrach und Wirtschaftskrise* (Frankfurt: Internationale Sozialistische Publikationen).
Mandel, E. and Wolf, W. (1988) *Börsenkrach & Wirtschaftskrise* (Frankfurt: Internationale Sozialistische Publikationen).
Marx, K. (1966) *Capital Vol. III* (London: Lawrence & Wishart).
Mattick, P. (1980) *Economic Politics and the Age of Inflation* (London: Merlin).
McKie, D. (ed.) (1993) *The Guardian Political Almanac 1993/4* (London: Fourth Estate).

McNally, D. (1993) *Against the Market* (London: Verso).

Michie, J. (ed.) (1992) *The Economic Legacy 1979–1992* (London: Academic Press).

Mitchell, A. (1989) *Competitive Socialism* (London: Unwin).

Mullard, M. (1987) *The Politics of Public Expenditure* (London: Croom Helm).

Negri, A. (1984) *Marx Beyond Marx: Lessons on the Grundrisse* (South Hadley, Mass.: Bergin & Garvey Publishers).

Negri , A. (1988a) *Revolution Retrieved: Selected Writings on Marx, Keynes, Capitalist Crisis and New Social Subjects 1967–1983* (London: Red Notes).

Negri, A. (1988b) 'Keynes and the Capitalist Theory of the State post-1929', in A. Negri, *Revolution Retrieved* (London: Red Notes).

Negri, A. (1988c) 'Crisis of the Planner-State', in A. Negri, *Revolution Retrieved* (London: Red Notes).

Negri, A. (1988d) 'Crisis of the Crisis State', in A. Negri, *Revolution Retrieved* (London: Red Notes).

Nolan, P. (1989) 'The Productivity Miracle', in F. Green (ed.), *The Restructuring of the UK Economy* (London: Harvester & Wheatsheaf).

O'Connor, J. (1973) *The Fiscal Crisis of the State* (New York: St Martin's Press).

O'Connor, J. (1984) *Accumulation Crisis* (Oxford: Blackwell).

Offe, C. (1984) *Contradictions of the Welfare State*, K. Keane (ed.) (London: Hutchinson).

Panitch, L. (1986) *Working Class Politics in Crisis* (London: Verso).

Pilbeam, K. (1992) *International Finance* (London: Macmillan).

Rowthorn, B. (1992) Government Spending and Taxation in the Thatcher Era, in J. Michie (ed.), *The Economic Legacy, 1979–1992* (London: Academic Press).

Sampson, A. (1983) *The Money Lenders* (London: Hodder and Stoughton).

Schubert, A. (1985) *Die internationale Verschuldung* (Frankfurt: Suhrkamp).

Skidelsky, R. (ed.) (1977) *The End of the Keynesian Era* (London: Macmillan).

Smith, D. (1992) *From Boom to Bust* (London: Penguin).

Stewart, M. (1993) *Keynes in the 1990s: A Return to Economic Sanity* (London: Penguin).

Sutcliffe, B. (1983) *Hard Times* (London: Pluto Press).

Von Mises, L. (1944) *Planned Chaos*, The Foundation for Economic Education (New York: Irvington-on-Hudson).

Von Mises, L. (1949) *Human Action* (New Haven: Yale University Press).

Wachtel, H. (1990) *The Money Mandarins* (London: Pluto Press).

Wolf, W. (1988) 'Casino-Kapitalismus oder die Dialektik von Boom, Crash und Krise', in E. Mandel and W. Wolf, *Börsenkrach & Wirtschaftskrise* (Frankfurt: Internationale Publikationen).

4 Money in the World Crisis: The New Basis of Capitalist Power

Christian Marazzi[1]

One of the major difficulties in analysing the current capitalist crisis and reorganization, whether on the national level or globally, lies in seeing how changes in the international monetary system fit in with changes at the level of the international division of labour and production. To approach this question we must grasp both the nature of the money-form as a *social relationship of power* within capitalism and the historical specificity of the particular organizational forms of that power.

Understood in terms of class power, the money form cannot be grasped simply in terms of 'economic theory' – whether 'Marxist' or not. Rather, we must see how money fits into the antagonistic class relations of capital in order to reappropriate the terrain of revolutionary class struggle. If the crisis of today is an historical crisis of Keynesian development – the crisis of a system of *planned development* based on a certain dynamic equilibrium and internal stratification of class forces (see *Zerowork* 1) – then the breakdown of the international monetary system established at Bretton Woods in 1944 is part and parcel of it. This crisis of the money form is not just the point of arrival of capitalist development; it is both produced by a cycle of class struggle and is the point of departure for a new phase of class confrontation.

It was no accident that the crisis reached the point of no return in the years 1970–1, for that was the moment of maximum tension between all the components of the system; massively generalized wage explosions and price increases following in the wake of the inconvertibility decision, and heavy increases in public and corporate debt to the banking system. The dynamic of this process disclosed the possibility of a classic crisis of overproduction. What was no longer classic, however, were the political relations between the classes, relations which made a repetition of the 1929 crash a *political*

69

impossibility. Not only was it essential to avoid the devaluation of capital that always followed crises of overproduction, but also to avoid a direct political confrontation with the working class, which had established the 'downward rigidity of wages' and undermined the Keynesian use of money.

Marx's understanding of money within capital provides the point of departure for our analysis. He above all understood that 'What appears as a monetary crisis is in fact expressive of anomalies in the process of production and reproduction itself'. We begin with the reconsideration of Marx's analysis of the money form in the *Grundrisse* and *Capital*, for despite the fact that gold has long ceased to be the 'world money commodity' *par excellence*, his notion of money as the ultimate expression of value, and of value as the product of capital's ability to impose work (abstract labour) through the commodity form (exchange value), remains central to grasping capital's attempt to use money against the working class in new ways. The post-war system has shown the possibility of imposing a national currency (the US dollar) as international money, yet the collapse of that system has indicated the limits and weaknesses to which it was prone. The problem, then, is not to try and squeeze contemporary reality into an ossified application of Marx's analysis, but to use that analysis as an entry into an appreciation of the history of money in the last half-century – above all, the challenge launched by the United States in 1971 with the inconvertibility move, the point of departure of capital's counter-attack in the present crisis. On the basis of our current research, we think we can provide some elements for a debate on this question. We argue that from the beginning of the counter-attack, international capital has used money as one of its primary weapons against the working class; indeed, we would argue that money has become the ultimate and most sophisticated instrument for world capitalist restructuring today. On the basis of the analysis which follows, we pose the question of the political elements necessary to bring the debate to the level of working class strategy and organization.

THE CRISIS OF MONEY FORM IN MARX

In Marx's writings, analysis of what he called 'modern crises' is fragmentary. Indeed, analysis of crisis on a world scale, where, as he wrote, production is posed as a totality and where all the contradictions explode, is a chapter Marx never wrote. But from the fragments of such a project which do exist in his works we can follow the direction of his method. It appears that according to Marx what lies at the core of the modern crisis is the contradiction between production and 'loanable capital' – between the factory and the credit system. Marx saw credit as a powerful motor of capitalist development because it places accumulated surplus value – the savings of inactive capitalists – at the disposal of active but 'impecunious' ones. But if credit makes possible the full utilization of the capacities of society, why does it become the 'main lever of overproduction?'

The answer to this problem cannot be presented in static terms, for credit is the means of overcoming the barriers which productive capital encounters from time to time in the course of its activities. Credit is thus the mode by which capitalists *cooperate to overcome the obstacles which lie in their path*, meaning that it is what helps the capitalist *deal with the problems posed for him by worker struggles*. Through credit – that 'powerful instrument of development' – capitalists work together to reassert their command, and as such credit is the pre-eminent means for the *socialization* of capital.

Yet credit does not in itself succeed in overcoming the real contradiction which lies at the root of capitalist development. The fact of being able continuously to overcome through expansion the obstacles posed by workers does not guarantee continued control over labour. The socialization of capitalist development, the 'flight' of the entrepreneur from worker resistance through reorganization, the introduction of new machinery, and the extension of capital to all aspects of the society means that the level of credit always lies at the origin of new levels of class confrontation. It is at this point that we must refer to the theory of money in Marx. Credit, he wrote, is not yet money, because money must be the 'incarnation' and representation of value. Money, if it is to be the universal equivalent of all commodities, must be produced like all other commodities, but at the same time not be a use value. It must, in other words, go out of circulation. Money therefore cannot be understood separately from the commodity and from value. Gold, as money, has to be set apart, to become 'autonomous' from all other commodities. Hence, all other forms of money in circulation – bank notes, national currency, etc. – cannot be perfect representations of 'hard money'. 'Behind the invisible value of commodities', Marx wrote, ' "hard money" lies in wait.' If credit circulates more rapidly than 'real money,' it pushes the cycle of production beyond the limit of its valorization and realization: a point arises at which credit enters into conflict with the factory, because the *realization of value has entered into conflict with production.*

The interruption between production and 'real realization' must be analysed at its point of departure, or else it remains only a *possible* rupture in the circuit rather than an immanent tendency. Commodities, if they are to be sold in circulation, must be 'socially validated,' or else there is the possibility of crisis: speculative turmoil, the devaluation of capital, etc. But we cannot reduce this crisis of the transformation of values into prices to a simple problem of 'transitory disequilibrium,' a problem of realization. We must instead concentrate on the underlying transformations of the organic relationship between capital and labour that occur during the phase of expansion. In this sense crises of overproduction are 'violent manifestations' of the law of value and can never be confronted solely at the level of the market, where the commodity completes its trajectory at the point of sale.

Gold, as 'money of all monies,' symbolizes for Marx the fact that capital cannot escape from the contradiction of the law of value, and thus that every crisis is also a desperate attempt to 'reimpose' the law, which in the expansionary phase capital tries to 'escape.' The way the law is reasserted, the way capital tries to embark on a new cycle of development is through an attack on the obstacles posed by worker resistance and insubordination of all forms. With the development of capital this process is expanded to a global scale, and gold thus becomes the general means of exchange between currencies internationally, the means of payment for regulating international balances: the ultimate determination of the money form. Only on the level of the world market – where money is divested of all local and particular determinations – can the complete 'civilizing activity' of money be understood; and it is therefore at this level that modern crisis between production as a whole and credit must be analyzed. For gold, as money, guarantees the generalization of the law of value over all national currencies. It guarantees that all nations are subjected to the same discipline of capitalist laws in the world market. And it guarantees historically the extension of the world market according to the dictates of capital.

We need to carry the analysis further in order to bring it 'up to date.' First, the increase of *means of payments* – whether nationally or on the international level – has always extended beyond the reserves on which it is supposedly based. During the reign of the gold standard, this disproportionate increase of paper money produced cyclical crises, each of which was marked by the violent reappearance of the law of value. But each of these phases of development crisis was complemented by the progressive enlargement of accumulation on a world scale and the progressive reduction of socially necessary labour time. Credit has acted as a genuine instrument of capitalist socialization. In so far as each phase of development crisis has been accompanied by a drastic rise in the organic composition of capital, each successive phase of the history of capital has involved ever-greater amounts of means of payments in meeting working class demands. In other words, the dynamic development of capital has become ever more detached from the embodiment of the law of value, from its incarnation in gold. Gold has long ceased to function as the sole universal money, as the general means of payment between nations. The important thing here is that it *could not have been otherwise*. Not only has the real, effective appearance of sterling and then the dollar displaced gold as the 'money of all monies,' but international power has increasingly determined the 'value' of all currencies in the last instance. What is even more decisive here is that this transformation of the international monetary system has been the result of the 'long march of necessary labour against surplus value.' It has been the progressive reduction of socially necessary labour time that has precluded gold from functioning as the sole measure of value, precisely because socially necessary labour time has less and less been the basis upon which real wealth rests. (For more on this see the final section of Mario Montano's article in *Zerowork* 1.)

This does not mean that the gold standard has never functioned, but rather that each moment of its imposition has led to its transcendence by the real dynamics of international class relations. In the phase before the First World War, Britain extended its empire beyond the gold standard by investing sterling in its colonies (thus creating an external demand for its commodities), meeting the deficit it had with Europe and the United States by attracting gold through the simple manipulation of the bank rate. The gold standard was in reality always a sterling standard. After 1918 the United States imposed the gold standard on Europe, while divorcing its entire domestic monetary policy from any metallic base. The flow of gold into the United States in the 1920s never increased the money supply on a proportional basis, thus allowing prices to remain low and the volume of trade and direct investments abroad to increase.

Throughout these phases the gold standard was, in other words, a means of imposing a specific imperialist policy, a policy sustained by the key role of first sterling and then the dollar as means of payment, as national currencies given a fundamental role in the *development of the productive forces on a world scale*. It would be wrong to conclude that imperialist development and the extension of the basis for accumulation in this latest period has been something 'fictitious' or based upon pure 'paper money,' just as it would be wrong to conclude that international cyclical crises occurred because of the non-functioning of the 'law of value' embodied in gold. In fact, the increase in the 'monetary consumption' of gold has remained more or less steady from the time when sterling and the dollar began to function as international currencies. Currencies, in other words, have never been completely convertible in any real sense. For if such had been the case, gold reserves would have to have increased in volume to an extent quite disproportionate to annual gold production. In short, gold has always been more or less nominal.

We can now draw some conclusions. First, the international monetary system has more and more grown dependent on the national currencies that have acted as means of payment for world accumulation. Second, both domestic and international credit have been increasingly transformed into credit *ex nihilo*, into artificially created money which is no longer based on accumulated surplus value, but on *no existing value*. The requirement for 'artificial money' to act as a productive force beyond the value embodied in gold reserves is that it must become money as capital, that is, it must become credit which *commands* alien labor: money must become command. But precisely because this form of money as capital makes for both an extension and intensification of the basis of accumulation, gold comes to function increasingly marginally as the measure of value, which in turn comes to depend less and less on socially necessary labour time and increasingly on *imperial command*. In other words, if money becomes increasingly less convertible in terms of gold, it has to become ever more convertible in terms of command of capital over labour power. The problem for capital is that while international credit – the World Bank, the International Monetary Fund (IMF), etc. – has increasingly functioned as the lever of capitalist socialization on a world scale, the command function upon which money now rests is not solid – precisely because of the new era of international working class struggle. What is at the root of the current international monetary crisis is that not only can the international currency – the dollar – no longer be converted to gold, but money as capital itself can no longer be converted into *effective command over labour*.

The establishment of an inconvertible monetary system by Nixon in August 1971 presented challenges to analyses of the monetary crisis. We have said that the crisis, as a crisis of the money form of capital, exploded because international capitalist organization was no longer able to contain the dynamics of the class struggle. Thus, the inconvertibility of the dollar cannot, as is often done, be examined simply in terms of the US refusal to meet its commitments to the other capitalist nations, a refusal to cover with gold all the dollars accumulated in the central banks of Europe and Japan. An examination must begin with a look at the nature of the monetary system of international power constructed after the Second World War.

The system established at Bretton Woods in 1944 represented a US victory in which gold was to play a key political role in determining the composition of the IMF. The United States, which during the 1930s had accumulated two-thirds of the world gold supply, imposed the condition that the IMF would be empowered to allocate to nations in difficulty liquidity (credit) on the basis of given amounts of gold and national currencies already committed to the fund by the member countries. In other words, the amount of credit the IMF would make available would depend on the initial contribution of each member country, an arrangement that would later allow the United States to expand significantly its foreign debt, since the quantity of dollars in international circulation came to exceed, by 1957–8, the quantity established in the statutes of the IMF. The other members were required to maintain a fixed rate of exchange of their currencies against the dollar, so that the central banks of these countries were put in a position of supporting the value of the dollar. This situation produced an automatic inflationary tendency, given the fact that the acquisition of dollars implied an expansion of domestic money supply. It was clear by the mid-1950s that there was a contradiction between the static principle of the international capitalist order originally conceived in the US 'currency principle' and the dynamic development of the new capitalist order that had followed the Second World War. The birth at this time of the Euromarket – a US banking system outside of the US to allow the multinationals to ignore the gold–dollar exchange standard – indicated that the US victory at Bretton Woods had been a Pyrrhic one.

The declaration of dollar inconvertibility in 1971 must be situated in this context. Given that worker struggles could no longer be managed by monetary means as a spur to further investment and productivity, the strategy of 'planned development' – the Keynesian system

– had to be abandoned. The international wave of struggles beginning in the mid-1960s meant the breakdown of the whole system of
international stratification of command over living labour, upon which
the gold–dollar exchange standard was based. Dollar inconvertibility
was imposed on the United States because its control over the international system had reached an impasse. The decision was a means
of escape from the law of value, from the immediate impact of worker
struggles, and from the risk of a dangerous repetition of the classic
type of 1929 crisis, which would have generated an explosive class
confrontation. But at the same time, this means of escape enlarged
the terrain of counter-attack, liberated the range of strategic options
for capital. The United States redefined its leading role by imposing
on the rest of the world a new kind of forced *self-discipline* in which
the ultimate sanction is money as world command, that is, determined and regulated *politically* and hence freed from any commodity
limits. In other words, inconvertibility can only be understood in
political terms; it set the strategic framework for reorganization of
capital by means of the crisis – *a planned crisis against the global
working class through the manipulation of money.*

Given the historical development of capital at the time he was
writing, Marx did not explore the notion of an inconvertible paper
money very far. He saw that theoretically the 'value' of such money
was determined by the value of the commodities circulated and the
labour commanded, but he had few occasions in the periods he examined to study such a situation concretely. Subsequently, the only
serious Marxist effort to do so systematically was that of Rudolf
Hilferding in his work [*Finanzkapital*], (1910/1981), which dealt with
the capitalism of the Austro–Hungarian Empire, which was run
on the basis of inconvertible money. Like Marx, Hilferding saw that
there was no such thing as any real value of money as such; there was
only a quantitatively determined rate of exchange of money, and that
rate was manipulated by 'finance capital.' Hilferding had the merit of
seeing that one aspect of the problem for the recomposition of capital
at that time, and the reason for the way in which money was being
manipulated, was the relation between the banking system and the
capitalization of the rentier class, the mobilization of all 'unproductive income' through credit as capital. This new relation between the
banks and the state – the centralization of credit – he saw to be the
lever whereby such non-productive income could be mobilized for
a relaunching of productive industrial capital. The relevance of this
for the present period should be clear: today, once again, capital is

manipulating money to transfer value from an 'unproductive' role to a 'productive' use in capital investment. But today the unproductive income is not financing a rentier class, but rather the working class, which converts wages to income through its refusal to function as labour power.

But if a rereading of Hilferding reveals this sort of useful similarity, it can also be misleading, because of Hilferding's limitations. For he unfortunately hypostatized the regime of inconvertible money and failed to see the 'finance capitalism' he confronted as an historical phase of capital centred on the emergence of the big banks and joint stock enterprises. The subsequent passage of dominance from the big banks to industrial capital marked the transitory nature of what he studied.

Moreover, even in the period of its usefulness for understanding the mobilization of income for capital, other limitations of Hilferding's analysis led to disastrous political practice. Seeing the big banks as the enemy, his strategy was the social democratic nationalization of the banks, pension funds, insurance funds, etc. 'Socialism' in this perspective becomes the socialization of credit for the development of the productive forces such as capital was 'unable' to achieve. This kind of conclusion was unavoidable, since the problem of money was seen only in terms of dysfunctions *within* capital and between capital and non-productive sectors such as the rentier class. What Hilferding and his successors failed to see, and what we must grasp today, is the process of socialization which was at the root of the finance capital phase. The reorganization he observed, which involved both individual capitals and the banking system, marked a step necessary for the widening of the basis for the extraction of relative surplus value from the working class and the generalization of abstract labour. The working class in Hilferding's approach is seen as external, as an exogenous factor in this reorganization, for he could not see the *historically defined composition of the working class* upon which and against which capital was *forced* to reorganize itself and which had historically contradicted both the previous industrial and monetary systems. What Hilferding and official Marxism of all varieties failed to see was that the gold standard depended on an international class composition that had been superseded. When we examine capital's recourse to inconvertible money in the present crisis, we must see how it is a means of transforming working class conquests into a further socialization and concentration of control.

Yet we must also see that under today's conditions, the capacity for such a transformation is severely limited. The current transition by means of inconvertible money and floating exchange rates is precarious. It appears that money can no longer serve as the lever for further socialization on the basis of the given composition and demands of the working class, and must thus become an instrument for the violent rupture of that composition – a weapon for the dictatorship of capital in its quest to undermine the advanced form of working class power. At this level of confrontation, where money becomes pure unmediated assertion of state power against the working class, the 'transition' is not only more precarious but threatens to become *permanent*: in this lies the uniqueness of the class confrontation today. There is the danger of a direct unmediated class battle with the state, in which money loses its mystical appearance – its so-called independence – and in which the 'revolution from above' opens up a new level of struggle 'from below.' The risk is that short term transitional measures are already taking on the characteristics of a *highly volatile permanent emergency* for the capitalist system as a whole.

THE STATE, MONEY, AND RECESSION

The problem now is to explain why this crisis – a 'transitional solution' – might actually become a state of 'permanent transition.' We must see first what the constraints are which continue to limit the action of the capitalist state in this period of inconvertible money. If the state was able to escape the straitjacket of value embodied in the international monetary system until 1971, why has capitalist reorganisation not yet succeeded in becoming a new process of development?

The state's capacity to act upon the money supply through central banks and hence to promote the reorganisation of manufacture and circulation has, in every capitalist country, been unable to establish the basis for recovery. Both in terms of financing the industrial sector through banking and other financial institutions, and the public sector through the sale of Treasury Bills and other government bonds, it has not been possible to establish global conditions of productivity capable of relaunching the system. This is because the state, from the beginning of the crisis, has found itself confronted with a widening of the terrain of working class struggle, including a convergence of factory struggles and social struggles as a whole. (For more on the beginning of this process in the United States, see Paolo Carpignano's article in

Zerowork 1.) The struggle for wages separated from productivity in the factory became a generalized struggle over the *social wage*, involving both waged and unwaged sectors of the class. This made it no longer possible for the state to manipulate the distribution of consumption, using the spur of consumption to control production. From being 'distributor in the last instance,' the state became *'lender in the last instance.'* The state was forced to run a debt economy not only for industry, but for the public sector, the cities, etc. Given the pressure on the social wage as a whole, the state, acting in the open market through the issuing of money, continued throughout the crisis to pour more and more money into circulation through the purchase of Treasury bonds, commercial guarantees to cover loans to industry, etc. In other words, the increase in money supplies was increasingly 'covered' by the promise of future guarantees of repayment – a practice which continued even when the assets of the banking system no longer corresponded to any real capacity on the part of industry to repay the loans. This is what is at the bottom of the 'financial crisis' of the public sector and the so-called fiscal crisis of the state. The point is that we cannot see this crisis merely in terms of inadequacies of the banking system in relation to industry and the public sector. Given the degree of intervention by the central authorities to support the assets of the major banks in cases where institutional investors have been reluctant to provide direct credit, the state is increasingly *the* source of support for the assets of the whole banking structure, thanks to which the banks are (or were) able to continue to finance the debts of industry and the public sector.

It is, of course, true that this state policy represented nothing new in terms of traditional Keynesian policies throughout the post-war period. But there is a crucial difference – the question of the *time lag* in which social capital has to transform the money issued by the state through 'deficit spending' into capital. The Keynesian model placed the state above the economy as the distributor of income to the whole of society. But the state can only manage global demand if the money created *ex nihilo* by the central authority succeeds in becoming *effective demand*: only, in other words, if the additional demand created by the state succeeds in stimulating a level of overall production above the existing level. Only on this condition can money become an active motor of development. The politics of 'deficit spending' depends on control over the time period in which money becomes money as capital in order to ensure overall balanced 'growth.' As Marx put it: 'Time is everything, man is nothing.'

It is precisely this time period that has become unmanageable in the present crisis. In the Keynesian system this time period is *subjectively* determined; it depends on the subjective choice and cooperation of social agents – capitalists and workers – having a common interest as partners in growth. Such cooperation was not automatic, and had to be constantly readjusted at new points of equilibrium. Now, not only is this process not automatic, it is not functioning at all, both at the level of production and at the level of social reproduction. In production, the leap forward in the organic composition of capital in order to restabilize command over living labour and increase productivity has come up against the real impossibility of using inflation to finance future investments. The cash flow generated during the time of production and circulation of goods has not succeeded in financing on its own the new investments needed, forcing industry increasingly into debt. The resistance of workers to productivity increases and their continuous pressure to push up wages has made it impossible to reduce wage costs relative to new investment projects. As a result, industrial capital has been forced to move further and further along the path of restructuration of more and more investment to reach necessary levels of productivity: this spiral of investment has become an ever-increasing spiral of debt. Second, despite the massive attack on employment, the parallel resistance of the unemployed and wageless has forced the state to continue issuing money to back up the banking system and to finance the growing debt of the cities. It has become impossible for capital to use unemployment to any great extent to depress the general wage level.

Given these parallel pressures in the factory and in the social factory, the time of transformation of money into capital has become the time of the *working class transformation of money into income.* As the time of capital's transforming of money into capital becomes longer and more uncertain, the working class is more and more able to impose its own needs and shorten the time in which money is taken out of circulation. When money is blocked from becoming capital, it can only remain at the level of simple circulation; instead of becoming capital, it becomes 'funny money.' It is in this sense that inflation is no longer 'controllable,' a solution for capital which is no longer a solution, for it has become 'runaway inflation' imposed by working class struggle for income.

Seen in this context, the various attempts to restabilize the international system since dollar inconvertibility have failed in their purpose, in so far as they have not provided the conditions for a new basis of international command. To take only the most striking case of this failure: the attempt through the oil crisis after the Yom Kippur war in 1973 to force a new hegemony of US multinationals by draining dollars from Europe and forcing a drastic deflationary movement on the European states did not produce this result. In fact, the oil crisis was not followed by the necessary deflationary discipline by the diminution of reserves in the oil importing counties; it did not slow down the leapfrogging devaluation of currencies and hence the rate of inflation. Nor did it sufficiently increase the surplus of petrodollars in the oil exporting countries to an extent which could make them into a source for the ever-increasing demand for investment capital by the multinationals. The condition for this deflationary coup to become effective and to provide for the spiralling needs of investment would have been to provoke a head-on class confrontation, which was not a practical possibility. It has been the new socialized terrain of the struggle that has been the limit of any deflationary counter-attack by capital. The oil coup only served to delay the major offensive against the omnipresent working class demands for income.

The same can be said for the introduction of the floating exchange rates, which were resorted to precisely to prevent the 'permissive' expansion of credit through the purchase of dollars within the framework of the old system of fixed rates. This move was not sufficient for limiting money supplies, given that the regulated movement of exchange rates according to the balance of payments – even within the European 'snake' – was counteracted by the continuous increase in money supply by the central banks and flows of speculative capital escaping from the uncertainty of working class struggle, struggle that has forced capital to redefine its strategy, as seen first with Chile, then with New York City, and now throughout the world.

TWO, THREE, MANY NEW YORKS

These elements of the crisis can be concretized if we take the case of the situation in New York in 1975–6, which exemplified the present new line of attack by the capitalist state. The problem of New York was not merely a question of the geographical reorganization of the industrial sector of the United States – the abandonment by industry of urban centres in favour of new poles in other parts of the country. The real problem has been the failure to control the demand for income and services: this is what explains why the federal government turned off the tap of subsidies to the big banks, while blaming the crisis of New York on lack of 'investor confidence.' This use of the argument of 'confidence' as a means of political blackmail had, of course, first appeared in the monetarist policies imposed in South America, especially Chile. The same discipline was then to be imposed in New York as the testing ground in the battle to cut the social wage in the 'metropolis' itself. The important point here is that this strategy was directly imposed by the state in its decision to cut off the flow of liquidity to the banks. To point to speculators and the big banks – finance capital – as the culprit (the mystification which social democracy from Hilferding onwards has always used to cover up the relation between money and the state) is no longer possible. The confrontation was strictly one between the state and the incomes of the working class (especially the unwaged).

The tactics, which are now becoming familiar on a world scale, consisted of increasing the rate of interest on city notes and bonds, creating in this way a climate of loss of confidence and thus provoking a fall in the value of the issues. Basically, the state, as lender in the last instance, refused to lend. But this managed crisis had an extremely significant outcome: it forced the city unions to use their accumulated pension funds to buy the notes and bonds the banking system could no longer cover. The result was a structural change in the financial system in which a new type of attack on the struggle for income by the working class is discernible. On the one hand, the state assumes direct responsibility for paying forms of social wages in order to try to control and regulate the urban unwaged; on the other, it gradually forces the workers in the public sector to cover the borrowing requirements of social expenditures through the investment of their pension funds. This amounts to a transformation of the social wage into a system of reinsurance, forced savings imposed on the working class itself. Thus the political goal of capital becomes clear: the state attempts to divide by this means the various sectors of the class fighting for more income, for more cash. Moreover, this move is covered by the ideology of 'co-responsibility' and co-management in the financing of the public sector – a situation analogous to the co-management, profit-sharing, and other schemes in private industry. It is significant that this attempt to reimpose Say's Law, mobilizing 'deferred wages' for investment and consumption, has been called Pension Fund Socialism.

New York showed the way for the IMF strategy that was already being discussed by the Monetary Negotiations Committee in August

1975. But it was only with the international agreements reached at Kingston (Jamaica) in January 1976 that the full implications of this new strategy were spelled out on a world scale. The agreements included the decisions to sell the gold held by the IMF in a series of auctions on the free market; create a 'trust fund' with the profits from the gold sales to subsidize the poor nations with annual *per capita* income of less than $350; abolish the 'oil facility,' which had been created to cover part of the severe deficits in balance of payments owing to oil price increases; and finally, generalize floating exchange rates to all countries. Not for nothing have these agreements been called 'a new Bretton Woods.'

The implications of these new conditions became clear immediately with the first big devaluation of the Italian lira in January, followed by devaluations of the Spanish peseta, the British pound, the French franc, and later the Australian dollar and the Mexican peso. How can the New York crisis be linked to the international monetary coup that we . . . witnessed in 1976? [See also Chapter 7 in this volume.]

Let us take the first of the IMF decisions – the gold auctions: this establishes two clear conditions of attack. On the one hand, the sharp fall in gold prices from the peak of $200 an ounce in 1974, besides drastically reducing the 'trust fund' for the poor nations devalorized the central reserves of countries like Italy, France, and Portugal – in which gold is a significant component. This means that these countries, when using gold for 'collateral agreements,' receive less money in exchange from lenders. Italy, for example, had contracted for a loan of $200 million from West Germany in 1974 on the basis of a given quantity of its gold reserves. By the summer of 1976 Italy was able to raise only $150 million on the basis of the same quantity of gold as a result of the fall in gold prices decided by the IMF. Similarly, Portugal, wh,ich had contracted a collateral agreement with the Bank of International Settlements (BIS) in 1975, faced severe difficulties in February 1976 when it asked for a new loan from the Bundesbank and the Swiss National Bank. The stumbling block was the 'negative pledge clauses' which regulate the Eurobanks, clauses which prevent a country from seeking a loan more than once by means of gold collateral without doubling the quantity of gold already exchanged for the original loan (in this case the previous loan by the BIS). It was only the political role of the Socialist Mario Soares in the negotiations that allowed the clauses to be waived. Thus we have a clear example of the new *selective political use of gold as a weapon* to impose conditions on a country acceptable to the multinational banks. The demonetarization of gold and the arbitrary, in short political, nature of decisions and conditions attached to international loans which this implies have removed the residual autonomy that national states could previously maintain by means of their gold reserves in the face of foreign deficits – deficits which are, of course, mainly made up of public and social expenditures.

The second effect of the gold auctions is to create a climate of speculative uncertainty between national currencies now that gold prices are no longer a stabilizing factor. As a result, the flight from weak currencies ends up strengthening the strong ones, but above all becomes a tap for the Euromarket and hence the US multinationals and Treasury securities, thus aiding the US public deficit.

Finally, we should not ignore the extremely important effect of these measures on the role of the Soviet Union and the Comecon countries. From 1974 onwards the USSR had a mounting debt to Western countries, especially to West Germany and France for machinery imports and to the United States for grains. This accumulation of debt has been the result of the level of internal class resistance, which prevented the achievement of the goals of the Five-Year Plan. The first phase of detente in the 1960s which allowed the modernization of industry – the 'Third Phase' of Soviet planning – ran up against a hidden inflationary push resulting from working class use of the limited labour mobility that was permitted. The profound effects of the western monetary measures was due to the fact that gold has always been used in the Soviet Union to settle accounts with the 'outside world' – ever since Lenin established the rule. Thus the USSR has become increasingly bound by the conditions of its western creditors, and has thus been pushed into a frenzied quest for higher productivity from its workers – which has resulted in a greatly increased intensity of class confrontation.

If these are the effects of the demonetarization of gold, there are also limits within which gold prices have to be managed. If the price is allowed to fall too far, the struggle of the black workers in South Africa would escalate into an open and overall crisis of political control in all of southern Africa. Upon the maintenance of gold prices depends the future of the mining industry, and hence the control of African labour power. This is the diplomatic constraint (that was represented by Kissinger) within and against which the strategy of the IMF on gold prices has to operate. Indeed, the wave of struggles in South Africa in 1976 was the major 'disequilibrating' element in the entire world monetary strategy adopted at Kingston. The margins of manoeuvre for US polices that this situation imposes are very narrow. If the black struggles cannot be defeated, the choice will be either increasing the price of gold – and hence abandoning the entire deflationary strategy based on demonetarization – or the loss of control over southern Africa. Here we can see how the 'pure' policies of the monetarist coup at the world level – the illusion of pure money which must always be used to exorcise the class struggle – have been met by their 'opposite pole': hence the narrow and treacherous channel between money and politics through which US global strategy has to steer its course today.

Given these effects and limits of gold prices as a means of international control, what is implied by the system, or better, non-system, of floating exchange rates? Here again, in spite of the fact that from a purely monetary point of view there are no limits to the fluctuations of the various currencies, this devaluation–revaluation movement in 1976 has encountered political obstacles, and if carried through according to pure monetarist logic, it could jeopardize the entire strategy of the restructuration of capitalist command – the only long-term way out of the crisis for capital – as well as undermining the basis of the state and the international order.

The operation of floating exchange rates in 1976, with the enormous devaluation crises and the increasing indebtedness of local authorities and the public sector which have resulted, has narrowed in an unprecedented way the margins of manoeuvre – the 'relative autonomy' – of national states, to the extent of dramatically reducing the area of choice within which national politics has to operate. All governments and their oppositions have in this sense been pulled into the narrow area of choice imposed by the logic of international monetary austerity. And the first consequence has been a loss of autonomy of national states and a *shift of state power to the world level – the level at which monetary terrorism operates*. At the same time, however, the downward movement of weak currencies and the upward movement of interest rates has been accompanied by the increasing *regionalization* of monetary control over local authorities, cities, etc. – which in recent years have become more and more dependent on the multinational banks as opposed to state subsidies. In the period from 1974 onwards, in fact, the state (for example in Britain, France, and Italy) has actively promoted this increasing indebtedness of local authorities. In this apparent decentralization of state power (in the form of devolution, regionalization policies, etc.), the conditions are being created for the multiplication of 'New Yorks' on an international scale; what we are witnessing is centralization of a new kind: the *centralization of multinational state power*. The devaluation imposed on countries with large public sector deficits and borrowing requirements – even where cuts have not been drastically and immediately applied – has meant that the local authorities and the public sector as a whole are increasingly caught in a scissors movement between soaring costs and upward interest rates on debts: they thus have to implement their own cuts and become increasingly dependent on the selective decisions of the multinational centres of power. And when, in addition, these mounting debts have to be paid in devalued currency, it is possible for capital to create 'two, three, many New Yorks' at virtually 24-hour notice.

To summarize: the downward spiral of devaluation and the upward movement of interest rates have resulted, first, in the regionalization of power, promoted by the state itself, which ceases to operate as lender in the last instance; and second, in the shifting of *power as lender* to the selective controls exercised by multinational centres of decision making. The political implications of this are enormous. Behind the system of floating exchange rates decided upon at Kingston lies a strategy of austerity by means of forced devaluations that impose self-reduction of spending on local authorities, narrowing the political choice to the point at which the only choice is the *distribution of the cuts*. The room for bargaining over the distribution of income is no longer open and expansive from the class point of view; it is reduced to a restrictive field in which bargaining becomes a purely divisive and disaggregating instrument in the hands of the state. By shifting the selective power to impose the blackmail of crisis to the international level, the entire framework of consensus through the distribution of income – the basis of the Keynesian state – is thrown into crisis. The mediations on which state power has depended – the party system, the distribution of income via local authorities, partnership with the unions for 'planned development,' etc. – are undermined. Their self-justification increasingly relied on the illusion that there is still room for bargaining. The new 'justification' of the state, the rebuilding of its consensus, depends increasingly on the selling of this monetary terrorism by the official organizations of the working class, primarily the parties and the unions. They not only become directly implicated in the running of the crisis, but indeed become *direct agents* in the divisive and terrorist politics aimed at containing and blocking any widening of the class front. It is increasingly up to the official class organizations to create conditions allowing the relative autonomy of the state – by imposing the logic of austerity while fostering the ideology of deferred, future growth. This is the real function of the new social democracy in the crisis; its 'left' component is confined to tilting at windmills. The monetarist blackmail has forced social democracy to become the national government of austerity: whether it is the 'government' or the 'opposition' is unimportant. To cite two obvious examples: the Italian Communist Party, fresh from electoral victories, above all at the regional and local level, now finds itself trapped in a political impasse. From being the party of guaranteed income, it now has to transform itself into the administrator of cuts in local spending. In Britain there has been a similar dramatic change in the physiognomy of the Labour movement: the 'social contract' of 1974 has become the means by which government and the unions impose the deflationary regime, exploiting the monetarist blackmail to the full while externalizing responsibility for the crisis to shadowy and ill-defined 'international financial operations.' The real power and initiative in selectively imposing austerity is hidden behind the smokescreen in which money supposedly obeys its own laws outside and beyond the sphere of political choice — where 'man is nothing.'

The experience of New York is also a paradigm for the likely consequences of this overall strategy of austerity for the so-called developing countries. The loan arranged for New York to cover its immediate liabilities was on the condition of no moratorium. The loan had to be repaid within the time specified. The ending of moratoria also appeared at the United Nations Conference on Trade and Development meeting in Nairobi in the spring of 1976, where the 'developing' countries met to discuss a common policy for confronting their enormous debts abroad and regulating the pricing policy for raw materials. A large part of the debt of these countries has been increasingly held by the commercial and investment banks of the Euromarket. It is estimated that just over half of these are financed by official agencies – the World Bank, the OECD, OPEC, the socialist countries, etc. – while almost half are from the private banking sector. The total amount of credit required by the poorer countries has been calculated at $40 billion for 1976, while about 50% of the profits of the major US banks now come from loans to these same countries – a situation which makes it unlikely that moratoria will be widely permitted. To do so would lead to an open-ended system of 'international welfare'. The refusal of moratoria on the part of the 'advanced countries indicates the strategy of privatization of aid on a world scale by means of conditional, fixed-term credits provided by the multinational banking system, with the result being the proliferation of the 'debt economy' on a global level. As in the cases of New York and the western European countries, the poor countries – the debtors *par excellence* – can only repay their debts by devaluation, which in turn lowers the purchase price of their raw materials – while their imports from the western countries have to be paid for in dollars.

A NEW LEVEL OF CLASS CONFRONTATION

If this monetary strategy arising from the restructuration of the financial system represents the general line of deflationary attack on the working class internationally, to what extent can it provide the *solution* for capital? How far can it succeed where previous deflationary attempts have failed? Rather than providing a solution – that is, a way out of the 'open-ended transition' that capital has been faced with – the application of the monetarist policy contains its own inherent and unavoidable contradiction. Monetarism and policies deriving from it presuppose a relation of class forces completely subordinated to money as capital. But such a relation cannot be assumed in the present situation. The prerequisite for this strategy to provide the solution, and not merely a response, to the already existing level of international class attack is an ability to exorcise the class struggle, not only in theory but in reality. Yet this strategy is premised upon the already existing open-ended crisis, but contains in itself no inherent capacity to solve the political confrontation which its application implies. On the one hand, it subordinates politics, the arena of subjective decisions and class forces, to the dictates of money: when Milton Friedman says, in an interview during a visit to Chile in March 1975, 'Last year New York and Chile, this year Britain,' he assumes that the political conditions are already everywhere favourable to monetary attack, that the battle is already won. On the other hand, these conditions are clearly not given: politics cannot be eliminated by a voluntaristic solution to the problem of power. Earlier deflationary attempts failed to solve the political problems of the resistance of the working class -- a spectre which cannot be exorcised. Equally, monetarist strategy can only establish the basis for the relaunching of the capitalist system by eliminating this contradiction, or else the crisis remains open-ended and the contradiction is merely pushed up to a higher level of class confrontation.

It is against this threat that the state must measure its use of terrorist measures to isolate potential vanguard sectors in order to avoid a generalized class confrontation: the only political 'solution' in sight for capital is a long, drawn-out process of (hopefully) eroding working class power, of 'holding the fort' – in short, a war of position. Hence capital once again faces the political 'limits' that ultimately represent the 'limits' or contradiction of the money form itself. To return to Marx: 'From the fact that capital posits every such limit as a barrier and hence gets *ideally* beyond it, it does not by any means follow that it has *really* overcome it.' In subjecting the state to international monetary dictates, there is a grave risk for capital that these 'limits' may not only create a vicious circle in which the contradiction within monetary policy is constantly reproduced, but that they may escalate the crisis of money into the crisis of the state itself.

In October 1976 representatives of the member countries of the IMF met in Manila to re-examine the world situation in the wake of a new wave of devaluations. What soon became clear was that the general strategy would not change – not until wages, income, and social discipline had been brought back under capitalist control. The terrorism imposed by money will continue, checked only when the political price is too high. The attack on employment will continue, as will the dependence of industrial development, local government, and the public sector on the selective political controls exercised more and more by the multinational banks. In short, each crisis leads on the next, and the monetary transition threatens to become more and more a permanent state of international emergency. This undermines the entire system of mediations on which the state has relied in the past: from the state as distributor, to the state as lender, to the state as distributor of cuts – what comes next?

What is clear is that the longer this period of transition lasts – the more permanent the monetary attack becomes – the more it can develop into the terrain of a subjective reorganization of the working class. While the overall dimensions of this new cycle of struggles are not yet clear, its characteristics have begun to emerge in confrontations ranging from the uprisings of black youth in Soweto and London, to the food price riots in Poland and Egypt, to the pitched battles between students and police in Italy and Britain. What seems to tie these struggles together is that in a crisis situation in which capital is forced to abandon the Keynesian form of money as mediator of class relations in order to maintain its power, the working class – whose very struggles generated that crisis – is pushing forward with demands that aim at the elimination of work altogether and appropriation of social wealth as a whole.

This is not a dream of a future society; rather it is the practical requirement posed by the present situation of class confrontation. And it is not the planning of a party central committee, but the expression of the new needs and new demands of the various sectors of the working class. For, given the new forms of capital's attempt to reimpose command through centralized multinational state power and regionalized implementation of austerity, these very struggles over money, work, and all the conditions of life are immediately *struggles against the state.* To speak of attacking the coercive power of the state can no longer mean the *coup d'etat,* the storming of the Winter Palace. It means an attack on the 'social contracts' and incomes policies in Western Europe, an attack on the fiscal crisis in the United States, an attack on 'socialist discipline' in the Eastern bloc – in short, generalized resistance to capital's plans everywhere for the erosion of working class power.

The overriding question before us now is one of determining the forms of organization which can carry out these attacks. This is not a matter of establishing a party that attempts to manage the struggle from above and 'lead the working class to socialism'. Rather it is a matter of analyzing the successes and failures of the modes of working class organization in the previous cycle of struggle, primarily the organizations of the unwaged in the struggles against the state over the social wage. Only then can we begin to grasp the mechanisms of the *circulation of struggles,* both across geographical areas and among different sectors of the class, and thus organize ourselves in ways that accelerate that circulation. And it will be only then that we may see what it truly means for the working class not just to *have* power, but to be *in* power; and what it means for us not just to *fight against* capital, but to *destroy* capital in all its forms.

Note

The article was first published in English in *Zerowork: Political Materials*, 2 (1977).

1.   This article is the result of discussion and collaboration among a group of comrades linked to *Zerowork* in London. John Merrington and Mike Sonenscher have made major contributions to the final result.

References

Hilferding, R. (1910/1981) *Finance Capital* (London: Routledge & Kegan Paul).

Marx, K. (1973) *Grundrisse* (Harmondsworth: Penguin).

Marx, K. (1966) *Capital vol. III* (London: Lawrence & Wishart).

Marx, K. (1970) *Capital vol. I* (London: Lawrence & Wishart).

5 Capital, Crisis and the International State System

Peter Burnham

INTRODUCTION

The closing months of 1993 saw the conclusion of two agreements heralded by liberals as setting the world economy on a new and sound footing. The United States' ratification of the North American Free Trade Agreement (NAFTA) in November was capped in December 1993 when the Director-General of the General Agreement on Tariffs and Trade (GATT) brought down the gavel on the Uruguay Round, which had been formally launched in September 1986. Amid the popping of champagne corks the *Financial Times* declared that the agreements would provide, 'powerful underpinning for the world economy, fresh impetus to competition, and fresh hope for those developing and former communist countries that have been opening up to international commerce'.[1] By the opening months of 1994 this liberal triumphalism looked somewhat premature in the face of the Zapatista revolt in Chiapas (see Chapter 7; and Cleaver, 1994) and tension in Europe occasioned by persistent economic stagnation and disputes over the enlargement of the European Union.

Whilst it is commonplace to point out that the re-regulated financial and trade markets of contemporary capitalism have considerably enhanced the power of internationally mobile capital, the implications of this shift for national states are less clear. The 'social costs' arising from the 'structural adjustment' of economies in the wake of trade liberalisation are likely to heighten class conflict within states in addition to exacerbating fiscal crisis and adding to the mountain of international debt. The aim of this chapter is to provide a Marxian framework for understanding how the crisis of contemporary capitalism is experienced as a crisis of the national form of the state. In so doing the chapter contributes to overcoming a weakness in Marxist state theory which has typically stopped short at theorising inter-state relations.

In 1969 Ralph Miliband relaunched the state debate amongst western radicals by highlighting the paradox that whilst a 'theory of the state' underpins all political analysis, the state itself as an object of political study had long been neglected.[2] Although Miliband's char-acterisation of the capitalist nature of the state has long been super-seded, his focus on the capitalist state (in the singular) rather than on the multiplicity of states which comprise the international state sys-tem has remained the norm in Marxist accounts. With the notable exceptions of von Braunmühl (1978) and Barker (1978/1991), this deficiency has passed almost unnoticed, with the result that one might easily get the impression from a survey of Marxist literature that capitalism has but one state. The guiding theme of this chapter is that a materialist analysis of the inter-state system is a prerequisite for understanding current developments in the global political economy.

The first part of this chapter shows the importance of Marx's dia-lectical method in theorising the relationship between class and state. For Marx the state is perceived as the concentrated and organised force of class divided societies controlling and subduing the popular masses – the organised force of their suppression (Marx, [1871] 1986, pp. 486–7). However unlike Weber who reifies the notion of domina-tion and thereby sees 'the political' as a distinctive form of action always and everywhere distinguishable from 'economic action' in terms of ends and means, Marx understands the 'moment of coercion' and the 'moment of appropriation' as elements of a totality, differences within a unity – the case with any organic entity (Marx, [1857] 1986, pp. 36–7). From a dialectical viewpoint therefore the state is not au-tonomous, or simply *related to*, 'the economy'. Rather it is an integral aspect of the set of social relations whose overall form is determined by the manner in which the extraction of the surplus from the imme-diate producer is secured.[3] This conceptualisation provides a basis for analysing the historical specificity of the particular state forms (ancient, feudal, capitalist) which arise out of the social organisation of production in class societies.

From the vantage point of 'form analysis'[4] the capitalist state is understood as the historically specific condensation of the 'political' in capitalism. The *particularisation* of the state (that is, its institu-tional separation from the immediate production process) is an im-portant defining feature of its capitalist form. However it is only by locating the class character of the capitalist state in the context of the historical separation of state and civil society, achieved with the gradual disintegration of feudal social relations, that we can fully understand the specificity of the capitalist state form.

The third section of the chapter supplies a systematic account of the national states which comprise the international system. Only at this point (on the basis of a prior analysis of state forms) is it appropriate to introduce discussion of particular national states and their distinctive historical development. The weakness of much state theory becomes evident at this level. It is important to break free from studies which see the world system as an aggregation of compartmentalised units.[5] The flaw in such studies has been well identified by von Braunmühl (1978, p. 162), who cogently argues that the international system is not the sum of many states, but on the contrary the international system *consists* of many states. Furthermore as Barker (1978/1991, p. 207) recognises, the dual determination of the state (*vis-à-vis* 'its citizens' and the international system) is a permanent feature informing all aspects of state policy and activity. Therefore, the appropriate focus for conducting theoretically guided empirical analysis of national states, is the world market – a single system in which state power is allocated between territorial entities. In this section I will map out one of the most important yet undertheorised tensions of late capitalism, that between the present national political constitution of the state and the global character of accumulation.

On this basis, the final part of the chapter will show how the overaccumulation crises of post-war capitalism are manifest in terms of the national state–global economy relationship. From the post-war settlement, through the reconstitution and decline of Bretton Woods, to the multilateral trade talks and the process of financial re-regulation, national states have struggled in the post-1945 period to mediate the consequences of this national–global tension. Rather than focus on realist debates couched in terms of the loss of state sovereignty I will conclude that Marxist analysis must begin to understand 'international relations' as the national processing of global class relations.[6] Struggle between labour and capital at all points in the circuit of accumulation produces crisis situations which are exacerbated by global competition (see Chapter 4 in this volume). Such crisis is manifest at the level of the state as a national crisis experienced in terms of balance of payments difficulties, fiscal crisis, low levels of productivity, political overload, etc. The contradictory basis of capitalist social relations ensures that crisis is endemic, producing constant change throughout the global system. National states, seen as the political form of capitalist social relations, are not simply affected by 'economic trends' or 'globalisation', rather they are part of this crisis of the social whole. In response to the latest and deepest crisis of post-war global capitalism we have not yet witnessed the extinction of the national state but the concerted and paradoxical attempt to retain the national form of the political, through schemes aimed at the regionalisation of the world market. Nevertheless the experience of the European Union points, in many ways, to the reformulation of the basis of national state relations towards an inchoate system of regional political co-ordination. In this way the recasting of class relations which has occurred since the demise of the Keynesian 'mode of domination' in western Europe in the mid-1970s, has now reached a new level of intensity and instability with the refashioning of the global political framework which maintains the 'real freemasonry' of the capitalist class *vis à vis* the working class as a whole. In short we are witnessing the restructuring of relations of conflict and collaboration between national states. The moves to regionalism evident across the globe (European Union, NAFTA, APEC) represent an attenuation of the tension between national states and the global economy as the crisis of the class relation is simultaneously expressed as a crisis of the international state system.

MARX, METHODOLOGY, AND 'POLITICAL DOMINATION'

It is common for 'Marxist' approaches to the state to be character-ised as adopting one of two positions. Either, it is alleged that the state is capitalist because the economically dominant class is also politically dominant, or the state is interpreted as a *deus ex machina* divined from the structural logic of capital. Whilst the first position is simply radical-sounding pluralism, the second is an equally unten-able Marxified Parsonian structural functionalism.[7] The deficiencies of these approaches cannot be corrected simply by seeing the argu-ments as complementary.[8] Both are flawed since they implicitly sanction a base–superstructure model of capitalism, denigrate the concept of struggle to that of an exogenous variable, and are pre-dominantly ahistorical. But more importantly these viewpoints are deficient because they mirror the errors committed by orthodox political science, which takes the estranged forms of appearance of capitalist social relations and fails to trace what Marx refers to as their 'inner connections'.[9] To appreciate the importance of this critique in relation to the state debate it is necessary to show how the notion of 'inner connection' is central to dialectical methodologies.[10]

The error of positivistic orthodoxy, Marx outlines in the *Grundrisse*, is that it simply brings outward appearances into an external relationship with one another, 'the crudity and lack of comprehension lies precisely in that organically coherent factors are brought into a haphazard relation with one another, i.e. into a purely speculative connection' (Marx, [1857] 1986, p. 26). Unlike non-dialectical research which begins with an isolated unit and attempts to reconstruct the whole by establishing external connections, dialectical research starts with the whole and then searches for the substantive abstraction which constitutes social phenomena as interconnected, complex forms different from, but united in, each other (Bonefeld, 1993, p. 21; Ollman, 1993, pp. 12–17). Notions of externality and structure are replaced by the dialectical categories of process and contradictory internal relationship.[11] Whilst non-dialectical methodologies segment the social world and analyse the contingent relations of external phenomena, Marx focuses on how social relations take different *forms*, creating a differentiated, contradictory unity. Rather than understanding form in terms of species (the form of something more basic which lies behind the appearance), this view sees form as a mode of existence – something exists only in and through the forms it takes (see Bonefeld *et al.*, 1992, p. xv). Hence diverse phenomena such as the state and the economy do not exist as externally related entities but as moments of the class relation from which they are constituted (Bonefeld, 1992, p. 100). As Clarke (1978, p. 42) clarifies, it is the concept of class relations as being analytically prior to the political, economic and ideological forms taken by those relations (even though class relations have no existence independently of those forms) that makes it possible for a Marxist analysis to conceptualise the complexity of the relations between the economic and the political, and their interconnections as complementary forms of the fundamental class relation, without abandoning the theory for a pragmatic pluralism.

This approach clarifies Marx's advance over the classical political economists who mistook the bourgeois form of social production for eternal, natural relations of production thereby failing to see the specificity of the value form and consequently of the commodity form, the money form and the capital form. In the work of the classical writers production is presented as governed by eternal natural laws independent of history, 'and then bourgeois relations are quietly substituted as irrefutable natural laws of society *in abstracto*. This is the more or less conscious purpose of the whole procedure' (Marx [1857] 1986, p. 25). The importance of this emphasis on 'form analysis' is not only that it sensitises us to the fluidity of social relations but more fundamentally it breaks with the old essence–appearance distinction and implores us to decode forms in and of themselves. The inability of orthodox political science to develop 'form analysis' is responsible for much of the confusion in discussions of the state.[12] Similarly, no longer can we remain fixed in Leninist fashion to notions of the enduring nature of the nation-state. Instead our focus is on the changing nature of state form as the mode of existence of class relations.

Applying the dialectical method to the study of the state involves firstly specifying, on a very general level, the relationship between labour and political domination. Marx is emphatic that the most significant distinguishing feature of each social formation is not so much how the bulk of the labour of production is done, but how the dominant propertied classes controlling the conditions of production ensure the extraction of the surplus which makes their dominance possible (de Ste Croix, 1981, p. 52). Marx's clearest exposition of this point is in *Capital*, Vol. 3 ([1894] 1981, p. 927), where he writes:

The specific economic form in which unpaid surplus labour is pumped out of the direct producers determines the relationship of domination and servitude, as this grows directly out of production itself and reacts back on it in turn as a determinant. On this is based the entire configuration of the economic community arising from the actual relations of production, and hence also its specific political form. It is in each case the direct relationship of the owners of the conditions of production to the immediate producers . . . in which we find the innermost secret, the hidden basis of the entire social edifice, and hence also the political form of the relationship of sovereignty and dependence, in short the specific form of state in each case.

The 'state' understood as 'politically organised subjection',[13] charged with the enforcement of rule, empowered to exercise force to safeguard the relations which constitute the social order, is to be understood as the 'moment of coercion' without which no class divided society can exist. Throughout history the form of this enforcement has changed radically. However, all hitherto existing societies (above primitive levels) have presupposed establishing means of political domination (means which have gone far beyond Weber's stress on the *claim* to the legitimate use of physical force[14]).

Whilst this general analysis of the internal relationship between the organisation of labour and political domination tells us nothing about actual historical societies, it is nevertheless the bedrock which enables us to understand the development of the capitalist form of the state. This is the second step which is required before we consider in detail the specificity of the modern national states (the British and French states, for example) which comprise the international system. This task Marx achieves in his seminal, 'Contribution to the Critique of Hegel's Philosophy of Law' ([1843] 1975).

THE CLASS CHARACTER OF THE CAPITALIST FORM OF THE STATE

Marx's account of the rise of the modern political state is set against the social struggles which accompanied the overthrow of feudal relations of property and production. Whilst drawing attention to the exercise of monarchical power (based on property) within feudal relations, Marx argues that 'the abstraction of the state *as such* belongs only to modern times. The abstraction of the political state is a modern product' ([1843] 1975, p. 32). This argument needs close attention.

For Marx, the character of old civil (feudal) society was directly political. The elements of civil life – property, the family, the mode of labour – were raised to the elements of political life in the form of seigniory, estates and corporations. In this sense, an individual's position within an estate determined his/her political relation, that is, his/her separation and exclusion from other components of society. As he later clarified in *Capital*, Vol. I, ([1867] 1976, p. 170), 'here, instead of the independent man, we find everyone dependent – serfs and lords, vassals and suzerains, laymen and clerics. Personal dependence characterises the social relations of material production as much as it does the other spheres of life based on that production'. In these circumstances different subdivisions of trade and industry are the property of different corporations; court dignities and jurisdiction are the property of particular estates; and the various provinces the property of individual princes. Hence, in the Middle Ages we find serfs, feudal estates, merchant and trade guilds, and corporations of scholars, with each sphere (property, trade, society, man) directly political – 'every private sphere has a political character or is a political sphere; that is, politics is a characteristic of the private spheres too' ([1843] 1975, p. 32). Marx characterises the Middle Ages as the 'democracy of unfreedom', since in a context where trade and landed property are not free and have not yet become independent, the political constitution also did not yet exist. This discussion of the identity of civil and political society in feudalism has important ramifications for theorising the emergence of the capitalist state form. Marx saw the identity of the civil and political *estates* as the expression of the identity of civil and political *society*. Within each individual principality, the princedom (the sovereignty), was a particular estate – 'their estate was their state' ([1843] 1975, p. 72) – which had certain privileges but which was correspondingly restricted by the privileges of the other estates. Their activity as a legislative power was simply a complement to their sovereign and governing (executive) power, directed largely to civil affairs. As Marx summarises, 'they did not become *political* estates because they participated in legislation; on the contrary, they participated in legislation because they were *political* estates' ([1843] 1975, p. 73). To this can be added the significant rider that the relation of estates to the Empire was merely a treaty relationship of various states with nationality, 'their legislative activity, their voting of taxes for the Empire, was only a particular expression of their general political significance and effectiveness' ([1843] 1975, p. 72).

The emergence of the capitalist state form was neither an automatic response to the development of world trade, nor simply a matter of the transfer of power from one class to another. The historic change in the form of the state occurred gradually as political revolutions overthrew sovereign power (which constituted the political state as a matter of general concern), and fundamental social struggles, which were both prompted by and were expressions of, changing social relations of production, 'necessarily smashed all estates, corporations, guilds, and privileges, since they were all manifestations of the separation of the people from the community' ([1843] 1975, p. 166). These struggles simultaneously abolished the direct political character of civil society whilst creating the modern state. Gradually relations within civil society were transformed from the 'motley feudal ties' characterised by 'the most heavenly ecstacies of religious fervour . . . and chivalrous enthusiasm' (Marx and Engels, [1848] 1976, p. 487), to the crass materialism of modern private property relations subject to the rule of money and law, and the egotistical struggle of each against all. Marx is emphatic, 'the establishment of the political state and the dissolution of civil society into independent individuals – whose relations with one another depend on law, just as the relations of men in the system of estates and guilds depended on privilege – is accomplished by one and the same act' ([1843] 1975, p. 167).

Social struggle therefore is at the heart of Marx's account of the rise of the modern state. The unity of the feudal state rested on the political unity of estates comprising the principality. The social struggles which dissolved the personal and corporate foundations of this power effected the separation of state from civil society – which paradoxically underscores the dependence of the contemporary state on the reproduction of capitalist social relations. As Clarke (1988, pp. 127–8) makes clear, the formal separation of the capitalist state from civil society sets limits to its powers. The state merely gives form to the social relations whose substance is determined in civil society, so that the state 'has to confine itself to a formal and negative activity, for where civil life and its labour begin, there the power of the administration ends' (Marx, [1844a] 1975, p. 198). The formal and regulatory activity *par excellence* of the state is to uphold the basis of the new social relations which comprise the framework of civil society.

For Marx, the state is 'based on the contradiction between public and private life, on the contradiction between general interests and private interests' ([1845–6] 1975, p. 46). By positively upholding the rule of law and money, the state maintains the formal discipline of the market, and thereby mediates the contradiction between the expression of general and particular interests. This discipline must necessarily be *imposed* in an 'independent form' which is divorced from private interests: 'Just because individuals seek only their particular interest, which for them does not coincide with their common interest, the latter is asserted as an interest "alien" to them, and "independent" of them . . . in the form of the state' ([1845–6] 1975, pp. 46–7).

From the foregoing discussion it is clear that the class character of the capitalist state is not determined by the dominance of capitalists or the 'primacy of the economy'. Rather it is determined by the historical form of the separation of state from civil society. It is in this sense that we should see the perspicacity of Holloway and Picciotto's (1977/1991, p. 112) statement that a materialist theory of the state begins not by asking in what way the 'economic base' determines the 'political superstructure', but by asking what it is about the social relations of production under capitalism that leads to the creation of *apparently separate economic and political forms*. Within feudal social relations although the Holy Roman Emperor and the Pope stood at the apex, the structure was not a continuous hierarchy but rather sovereignty was fragmented and acts of force were not centrally orchestrated or rooted in a general system of right (Kay and Mott, 1982, pp. 80–4). In the feudal *corvée* force was directly applied to the serf as producer compelling him to produce rent for the lord. This force was particular, applied to each serf separately, in contrast to the compulsion to work in capitalism which operates through an impersonal labour market. Relations therefore were not mediated through a central authority, but were made directly at all points. Feudal relations of production were immediately relations of power. By contrast capitalist relations take place through the apparent exchange of equivalents. Labour and capital meet in the 'exclusive realm of Freedom, Equality, Property and Bentham' (Marx, [1867] 1976, p. 280), brought together by a contract whose very nature expels all immediate political content. As Kay and Mott (1982, p. 83) make clear, a crucial presupposition of modern contract is that both parties are deprived of the right to act violently in defence of their own interests, with the consequence that, 'in a society of equivalents relating to each other through contract, politics is abstracted out of the relations of production, and order becomes the task of a specialised body – the state'. In this way, the state as the particularised embodiment of rule, and the replacement of privilege by equivalence, are part of the same process, since 'citizens' only face each other through the medium of the state which is 'equidistant' from them.

Our second level of abstraction has therefore located the specificity of the modern state in the historical form of the separation of state from civil society achieved gradually with the dissolution of feudal social relations. The enforced separation of state and civil society is, of course, an institutionalised illusion.[15] The institutional existence of the state as a 'political' sphere presupposes the 'depoliticising' of civil society. The act of 'depoliticising' is itself political and this is the reality which the institutional state obscures, a reality founded on the basis of private property. An important conclusion of deriving the capitalist state form in the foregoing manner is that it reveals the notion of the 'autonomy' of the state to be pure sophistry. The power of the state in its liberal capitalist form is embodied in the rule of law and money (which are at the same time its own presupposition[16]). This is the most appropriate form to serve the expansion of capitalist social relations since the social power of the bourgeoisie is embodied in the abstract form of money. The political monopolies and privileges of feudalism are replaced by the 'divine power of money', whilst man as a 'juridical person' is not freed from property or the egoism of business but receives freedom to own property and to engage in business.[17] The institutional separation of the public state represents the historically specific form of political domination – the political moment – characteristic of capitalist social relations. Marx's dialectical approach reveals this separation to be illusory and opens up space to theorise the state–civil society nexus in terms of *differentiated forms of capitalist power*.

NATIONAL STATES IN THE INTERNATIONAL SYSTEM

One of the major difficulties which has been encountered in developing a Marxist theory of the interstate system has turned on reconciling a view of the state primarily defined relative to a domestic class structure, with the fact that the state is a component of a state system.[18] As Picciotto (1991, p. 217) has pointed out, this tendency has been greater in Marxist than non-Marxist writing, since the Marxist emphasis on the class nature of the state has made it necessary to discuss the state in relation to society, and it has become convenient to assume a correlation between the society and the classes within it and the state within that society.

This difficulty however is again a product of conflating levels of analysis. The capitalist state form is not derived from a 'domestic' analysis, to which 'external' determinants are then appended *a posteriori*. As I have indicated above, the form of state specific to capitalism is derived from Marx's analysis of the fundamental change in social relations wrought with the demise of feudalism. This level of analysis (as with most of *Capital*) is neither 'purely historical' nor 'purely abstract', but instead utilises the dialectical approach to approximate the concrete.

When turning to analyse the contemporary international system it is fundamental to switch our focus and level of abstraction from 'the state' (capitalist state form) to particular national states (the Swedish or Mexican state).[19] In so doing we are confronted with the following paradox. Whilst from its earliest stages accumulation has proceeded on a global level, capitalist states have developed on the basis of the principle of territoriality of jurisdiction. The fragmentation of the 'political' into national states, which from their very inception comprise an international system, has developed in an uneven fashion along-side the internationalisation of capital. As Picciotto (1991, p. 217) clarifies, the transition from the personal sovereign to an abstract sovereignty of public authorities over a defined territory was a key element in the development of the capitalist international system, since it provided a multifarious framework which permitted and facilitated the global circulation of commodities and capital. However the neo-realist image of independent and equal sovereign national states is a fetishised form of appearance, since the global system does not comprise an aggregation of compartmentalised units, but is rather a single system in which state power is allocated between territorial entities. This is significant since exclusive jurisdiction is impossible to define, so in practice there is a network of overlapping and interlocking jurisdictions.

Whilst therefore the class character of the capitalist form of the state is globally defined, the political stability of individual states has up until the present been largely achieved on a national basis – although alliance and treaty have occasionally broadened the man-agement of stability. The question of why the 'political' fragmented into national states (which is to be answered through detailed historical analysis of the overhang from absolutism) is less important than the implications which this fragmentation has for national states today. One of the most important features therefore of the global capitalist system – a feature which itself is a historical product of the class struggles which overturned feudal social relations – is the *national political constitution of states and the global character of accumulation*. Although exploitation conditions are standardised nationally, sovereign states via the exchange rate mechanism are interlocked internationally into a hierarchy of price systems. In the same way that jurisdictions transcend national legal systems, world money tran-scends national currencies. National states therefore founded on the rule of money and law (as the source of their revenue and claim to legitimacy) are at the same time confined within limits imposed by the accumulation of capital on a world scale – the most obvious and important manifestation of which is their subordination to world money (see Marazzi's, 'Money in the World Crisis', Chapter 4 in this volume).

National states (understood as the historically shaped political form of bourgeois class relations) in addition to upholding the authority of the market, through forms of regulation of law and money, respond in policy terms to the crises which result from the contradictory basis of their social form. 'Politics' is not therefore to be read off from 'economics'. Rather, the political and the economic are both to be seen as forms of social relations, whose differentiation enables the everyday conduct of government and yet whose contradictory unity circumscribes the volition of states. Governments thereby respond to (and take pre-emptive action in relation to) the power of labour at home and are forced to deal with the consequences of labour–capital struggles on a global level. The contradictory basis of capitalist accumulation[20] is expressed in class terms as capital's ability to impose work (abstract labour), in ever-greater degrees of intensity, through the commodity form (exchange value). The fallout from these endemic class struggles confront national states in terms of declining national productivity and financial crises. Moreover, the anarchic condition of international politics, itself a consequence of the fragmentation of the 'political', necessitates that national states attend to security issues, with the probable consequence of having to mediate the effects of the power–security and defence dilemmas (Buzan, 1991). Whilst the national state cannot ultimately resolve these contradictions (since it is itself an expression of the crisis on the political level), it may be able to mobilise resources and refashion international political and economic relations, to gain a more favourable temporary position in the interstate system characterised by uneven development.[21] National states provide both the domestic political underpinning for the mobility of capital and offer rudimentary institutional schemes aimed at securing international property rights as a basis for the continued expansion of capital. In this way, national states are best theorised as differentiated forms of global capitalist relations. The contradictory basis of class relations however ensures that far from accommodation and even development being the norm, interstate relations are instead characterised by conflict and collaboration, as national states struggle to mediate the consequences of the national–global tension. Whilst each national state strives to regulate the terms of class conflict within its jurisdiction, the overall interests of national states are not directly opposed, and relations of antagonism and collaboration are thereby reproduced at the interstate level.

The national–global tension confronts individual national states with the following dilemma. The world economy is driven by the creed, 'Accumulate, accumulate! This is Moses and the prophets' (Marx, [1867] 1976, p. 724). In response to the vulgar economists who claimed that capitalist overproduction was impossible, Marx ([1884] 1978, p. 156) clearly outlines that the volume of the mass of commodities brought into being by capitalist production is determined by the scale of this production and its needs for constant expansion, and not by a predestined ambit of supply and demand, of needs to be satisfied. The continued extension of the market has thus accompanied increases in both the production and realisation of surplus value which has depended not only on the globalisation of trade but also of production, capital export, the purchase of labour power and the globalisation of capital ownership.

National states ultimately derive both their revenue and their power from capital. This is true in the abstract sense inasmuch as the power of the national state is expressed in the rule of law and money which are the fetishised forms of the power of capital, and in the concrete sense that revenue derives from the capital outlaid and the working class subsequently employed within the bounds of its jurisdiction. To increase the chances of attracting and retaining capital within their boundaries (see Holloway's 'Global Capital and the National State', Chapter 6 in this volume) national states pursue a plethora of policies (economic and social policy, cooption and enforcement, etc.) as well as offering inducements and incentives for investment. However the 'success' of these 'national' policies depends upon re-establishing conditions for the expanded accumulation of capital on a world scale. The dilemma facing national states is that whilst participation in multilateral trade rounds and financial summits is necessary to enhance the accumulation of capital on the global level, such participation is also a potential source of disadvantage which can seriously undermine a particular national state's economic strategy. The history of the post-war international system is the history of the playing out of this contradiction. An important feature of the tension is its spatial dimension, which guarantees uneven development and shifts the manifestation of capital's global crisis to particular national states and regions. The crisis of the capital relation is thus at the same time a crisis of the international state system. Crisis, the endemic feature of the capital relation, is therefore less the result of a blanket exhaustion of a particular 'regime of accumulation', and more the consequence of the social form of capitalist production itself (Clarke, 1991b), leading to overaccumulation, the effects of which are worked out differentially across the globe. The final section of the chapter will illustrate these remarks through a brief review of the restructuring of the interstate system in the post-war period.

CONCLUSION: MANAGING POST-WAR CRISIS

The disorganisation of the working classes in 1945 enabled politics once again to be channelled through the form of the national state. As in the aftermath of the First World War, the European working class forewent the opportunity for unity and struggle over the form of the state, opting instead to alienate their social power and seek political representation *through* the national state.

The most immediate task facing the war-torn societies of western Europe in 1945 was physical reconstruction. The achievement of reconstruction aims and the expansion of economic growth depended however on the more subtle diplomatic reconstruction of international trade and payments systems which would facilitate international exchange and secure the regular import of essential commodities and raw materials.[22] The primary barrier to rapid accumulation in 1945 was the uneven development of world capitalism which had produced a serious disequilibrium in production and trade between the eastern and western hemispheres, as experienced in the 'dollar gap'. The economic strategy of European national states therefore turned on finding a solution to recurrent balance of payments crises which were a manifestation of this uneven development, itself a consequence of the contradictory basis of the class relation. For these national states the need to maximise accumulation was translated into the need to accumulate world currency. Britain (acting largely on behalf of European states) and the United States thereby engaged in a series of protracted negotiations to restore global circuits of accumulation. In conditions of such fundamental structural imbalance the United States' multilateral objectives (immediate full currency convertibility, non-discrimination in trade and reduction of tariffs) were successfully resisted by Britain and, contrary to popular perception, the Bretton Woods system was effectively shelved until 1959 (see Chapter 4 in this volume). The key episodes of intergovernmental negotiation which characterised the restoration of post-war capitalism clearly illustrate the contradictory relations of conflict and collaboration which exist between national states. Constructing an efficient mechanism for international exchange was a prerequisite for all nations in 1945. However the struggles in determining the pattern of European trade and payments agreements illustrate the degree of conflict which existed both within Europe and between European states and the United States, as each national state sought a competitive advantage in relation to the dollar gap.

Towards the latter stages of the reconstruction phase, rising wages and the growth of consumer credit maintained steady, but far from uniform, economic development in western Europe. By the late 1950s however the controls and exchange restrictions which European national states had used to husband world currency after the war, appeared as a fundamental barrier to further growth. With controls now perceived to be redundant, liberalisation of trade and payments led to the intensification of competitive pressure in world markets culminating, by the late 1960s, in the overaccumulation of capital and overproduction of commodities. As Clarke (1988, p. 125) cogently argues, the fundamental error of Keynesianism is the belief that overaccumulation and underconsumption are two sides of the same coin, so that the expansion of the market will resolve a crisis of accumulation. However once we locate the source of crisis in the social form of capitalist production itself (in the uneven development of the forces of production within branches of production), it is clear that neither the growth of the market nor the expansion of credit can 'resolve' capitalist crisis. Whilst credit temporarily frees capital from the limits of monetary constraint, it simultaneously relieves the pressure on backward capitals to restructure, thereby creating the potential for even more devastating crisis in the future.

By the 1970s it was clear that many European national states had failed to develop economic policies capable of delivering sustained growth. In Britain for example, liberalisation of trade and sterling convertibility ended the relatively inefficient 'domestic' production of goods destined for safe Commonwealth markets. Despite the attempt of the British state to devalue the cost of labour power through a restructuring of the organisations of labour, it was nevertheless unable to effect a radical reconstitution of the institutional structures which affect 'competitiveness'. By contrast, freed from the necessity of maintaining a high ratio of military expenditure to GNP and with no effective legal limit to the length of the working day, the Japanese state, through the utilisation of innovative production methods (and backed by American capital during the period of the Korean War), achieved a dramatic reconstitution (Morioka, 1989). As the penetration by advanced capitals operating out of Japan and Germany into formerly protected markets gathered pace, the fragility of the Bretton

Woods gold–dollar exchange standard became evident. As early as 1950 the United States had begun to record balance of payments deficits. Between 1950 and 1964 the governments' foreign accounts showed an accumulated deficit of $35 billion, the result of military assistance and direct defence expenditure abroad (excluding the direct budgetary cost of the Korean War, Burnham, 1991). Reeling from both the social struggles and the expenditure generated by the Vietnam offensive, the United States brought the international financial system to the brink of crisis in the early 1970s, unable to devalue with the liquidity problem stimulating intense speculation against the dollar. Although Germany and Japan prized the effects of the overvalued dollar on their own exports, the stabilisation of the world financial system demanded the introduction of a system of floating exchange rates (amended in 1978 to enable further diversity in IMF members' exchange rate arrangements).

The crisis of 'Bretton Woods' is predominantly interpreted in technical terms as one of 'liquidity'; 'adjustment'; 'seigniorage'; and/ or as an illustration of 'Gresham's Law' (Pilbeam, 1992). These explanations accurately convey the surface manifestation of crisis, yet conceal its source. To locate the root we need to focus on production, and in particular how the national–global tension shifted the overaccumulation crisis to American shores as a more intensive imposition of work and associated capitalist strategies revolutionised the labour process in the Pacific Basin. Evidence for this can be gleaned from US balance of payments figures which show that in April 1971 the US trade balance went into deficit for the first time this century (US Dept of Commerce, 1975). Whilst Japan's crude steel production was only 5.5% of that of the United States in 1950, by 1980 it had exceeded the US level, with Japan even outstripping the United States in passenger car production by 1988. Similarly whilst the period 1981–7 saw Reagan unsuccessfully attempting to lift the American economy by borrowing over $531 billion, Japan became the biggest creditor nation in the world with its net overseas asset balance, which stood at $11.5 billion in 1980, increasing to $291.7 billion by 1988 (Rothschild, 1988; Shinohara, 1991).

The success of capital located in and operating out of the Japanese state illustrates that although national states experience crisis most sharply in fiscal and financial form, the source of crisis is to be located in the production process reflecting uneven development. In the same way that domestic credit temporarily shores up inefficient capitals, international borrowing is an option for national states struggling to generate the institutional structures which could enable capital to increase its scale of production, enhancing the attractiveness territories for further investment. The tragic lesson of the debt crisis in Latin America is that this option risks a further overaccumulation crisis with even deeper attendant consequences.[23]

The cause of contemporary crisis is often attributed to the whirlwind process of the internationalisation of capital (particularly financial capital) affecting the sovereignty of national states.[24] Globalisation is not however the cause but is rather the result of crisis. The successful reproduction of accumulation within national state boundaries is premised on the reproduction of accumulation on a global scale. Whilst the integration of global circuits of accumulation is always contingent, resting on the continued subordination of the working class and the containment of militancy, it sets the context for the relations between national states vying to minimise the consequences of global overaccumulation. For national states capable of reconstituting the institutional structures which enhance 'competitiveness', the internationalisation of capital presents an opportunity for temporarily lifting the barrier to economic growth and penetrating world markets. The appearance of crisis is then not the result of the process of internationalisation itself, but rather is the consequence of capital attempting to overcome its inherent contradiction, thereby producing overaccumulation on a global scale. Global crisis is then experienced by capitalist states in a national form. This contradiction although it is mediated by national states through multilateral rounds, financial summits and limited forms of regionalism cannot be resolved within the framework of capitalist social relations since it is an expression of the social form of those relations.

The liberalisation of trade and finance which has occurred since the late 1950s has revealed with each new bout of global crisis that the national form of the state is increasingly unable to function as an integrated unit supplying the political stability which is the prerequisite for global class relations. Even the most powerful national states (Germany, the United States and Japan) are now turning to seek regional solutions to national balance of payments problems and the regulation of trade and finance. The 'hollowing out' of the national form of the state is not (*pace* Jessop, 1992) a response to 'post-Fordism' but is rather a recognition that the revolutionising of relations and the uninterrupted disturbance of all social conditions which Marx had already associated with capitalist society in 1848 extends also to the restructuring of the interstate system. The signs in western Europe are that the European Union could – however falteringly – transform political relations between western states. If present trends continue, then it is possible that the creation of a European currency and central bank and the increased transfer of political authority to Brussels could ultimately result in the establishment of a complex system of regional political coordination throughout Europe. This restructuring (unless it extends to fully fledged political regionalism) would not free the present states of western Europe from the monetary and fiscal problems which now appear so intractable. However, regionalisation of the world market and regional political coordination will set the context for a more intense phase of global class struggle.

The prospect of a *simple* transfer of authority from the national to the regional is most unlikely. Rather it seems that a more complex pattern will emerge whereby some national state capacities are transferred to pan-regional or international bodies, others devolved to local levels within the national state, and yet others are usurped by emerging horizontal networks (local and regional) which by-pass central states and connect localities and regions in several nations (Jessop, 1992; Rosewarne, 1993). The management of monetary relations looks set to follow a similar line as evidenced in the changing role of the IMF (there has not been a single western borrower from the IMF since 1979, reflecting the enhanced role of the European Monetary Committee–European Commission).

If the national form of the state is now undergoing transformation and we are witnessing a regional coordination of political relations, this will simply reproduce on a larger scale the pattern of conflict and collaboration which currently characterises the inter-state system.[25] However it may also foster closer cooperation between 'national' labour movements and further increase the concentration and centralisation of capital moving closer to the situation depicted in the *Communist Manifesto* where national differences diminish owing to 'the development of the bourgeoisie, to freedom of commerce, to the world-market, to uniformity in the mode of production and in the conditions of life corresponding thereto' (Marx and Engels, [1848] 1976). In the present context of the revival of political nationalism (as well as neo-fascism) the moves already made towards the regional coordination of political relations look fragile, and Marx's prognosis overly optimistic. Nevertheless this restructuring creates opportunities for socialist strategy which can no longer be hidebound by the 'internationalism versus socialism in one country' dilemma.

The struggle of national states in the global economy is not to be perceived as a struggle between 'social democratic Sweden' and 'monetarist Britain', but as one of warring political brothers (necessarily united *vis à vis* the working class) competing to avoid the deleterious consequences of an overaccumulation crisis erupting on their shores courtesy of uneven development. The theoretical lesson of this chapter is that national states are a differentiated form of capitalist power – a complementary and contradictory form of class relations. The crisis of the national form of the state is producing a restructuring of interstate relations. The indeterminate outcome of a shift to complex political and economic forms of regional coordination (and more pertinently the outcome of a crisis of this regionalisation) throws open real opportunities for global socialist strategies and finally lays to rest all talk of a national road to liberation.

Notes

1. *Financial Times* (16 December 1993), p. 18.
2. Miliband (1969, pp. 3–4). The nature of the state had of course been widely discussed in socialist and anarchist circles at the turn of the century. See DeLeon (1896); Kropotkin (1897); Paul (1916); Lenin (1917); Hunter (1918). However, serious analysis largely perished from the early 1930s onwards under the twin influence of Stalinist state monopoly capital theory and western social democratic pluralist viewpoints.
3. See Marx's famous section in *Capital* Vol. III, Chapter xlvii; and for a clear exposition de Ste Croix (1981, p. 52).
4. For a discussion of form analysis see the Introduction to Bonefeld *et al.* (1992).
5. The most eloquent defence of this position remains Bukharin ([1917] 1972). Bukharin, of course, fully recognised that 'national economies' no longer exist. However he presents an aggregate account of the world economy, with states simply the 'state capitalist trusts' of nationally based groups of bourgeoisie. The simple identification of state and capital in this fashion is both historically inaccurate and theoretically bankrupt. The whole point of state theory is to explain why and how state and capital are related. Bukharin begins from an assertion which itself must be the object of critical appraisal.
6. For a more extensive analysis of this point see Burnham (1993).
7. The first account is pluralist because it locates the capitalist nature of the state in terms of interest articulation rather than the social relations of production. The second is functionalist because it assumes that 'capital' has *a priori* needs which are met by the state. 'Relative autonomy' conceptions of the state are equally unsatisfactory since

they tend towards tautology. Carnoy (1984), provides a good summary of Marxist debates, as does Jessop (1990). Seminal critiques are Clarke (1977/1991) and Holloway and Picciotto (1977/1991).

8. This is the surprising solution offered by Miliband (1991, p. 521).
9. Marx ([1894] 1981, p. 956). A good example of the 'inconsistencies, half-truths and unresolved contradictions' of orthodox political science is found in the work of the guru of realist international political economy, Robert Gilpin. In discussing the contemporary political economy Gilpin (1987, p. 10 n. 1) writes:

> the historical relationship of state to market is a matter of intense scholarly controversy . . . but one whose resolution is not really relevant to the argument of this book. State and market whatever their respective origins, have independent existences, have logics of their own, and interact with one another.

10. For useful accounts of Marx's dialectical method, see Rosdolsky (1977); Murray (1988); Bonefeld (1993).
11. For an account, see Bonefeld *et al.* (1992, p. xv).
12. A good example of such confusion is found in the debate between Wallerstein (1984) and Skocpol (1979) on the relation of 'the state' to the development of capitalism. Neither has grasped that the *form* of the state can be understood only on the basis of the historically specific social relations of which it is a part. In posing the question of whether 'states' postdate or antedate capitalism, these writers are already guilty of conflating levels of analysis, thereby guaranteeing erroneous conclusions.
13. This is the useful term coined by Philip Abrams (1977) in preference to the 'state' – which Abrams argues lends itself too easily to reification.
14. Weber (1918, p. 78). Also see Corrigan and Sayer (1985).
15. This is emphasised by Murray (1988, p. 32), and demonstrated by Holloway and Picciotto (1977/1991).
16. A point well made by Clarke (1988, p. 127).
17. Marx ([1844b] 1975, p. 325) and ([1844c] 1975, p. 167).
18. See the debate between Chris Harman, Alex Callinicos and Nigel Harris, summarised in Callinicos (1992).
19. A point well made by John Holloway's 'Global Capital and the National State', Chapter 6 in this volume.
20. Clarke (1991b) offers a useful view of the primary contradiction being the tendency to develop the productive forces without limit, whilst confining the development of those forces within the limits of profitability.
21. See Hall (1986) for a useful analysis of the institutional structures which affect 'competitiveness', namely, the organisation of labour; the organisation of capital; the organisation of the state; the position of the state within the international economy; and the organisation of its political system.
22. For details see Burnham (1990).
23. Consequences, which as Cleaver (1989) highlights, are heaped on the working class and which themselves are products of global class struggle.

24. See for instance the special issue of *Capital and Class*, 43 (1991), continuing the debate begun between Robin Murray and Bill Warren; see Radice (1975).
25. It should be clear that I am not offering a version of Kautsky's ultra-imperialism thesis. Regional coordination is not to be equated with the 'peaceful alliances' of internationally united finance capital which resolve the contradictions of imperialism. On the contrary, moves toward the complex political and economic regionalisation of the global system intensify contradiction and uneven development.

References

Abrams, P. (1977) 'Notes on the difficulty of studying the State', *Journal of Historical Sociology*, 1.

Barker, C. (1978/1991) 'A Note on the Theory of Capitalist States', *Capital and Class* 4, and in S. Clarke (ed.), *The State Debate* (London: Macmillan).

Bonefeld, W. (1992) 'Social Constitution and the Form of the Capitalist State', in W. Bonefeld, R. Gunn and K. Psychopedis (eds), *Open Marxism Vol. I: History and Dialectics* (London: Pluto Press).

Bonefeld, W. (1993) *The Recomposition of the British State During the 1980s* (Aldershot: Dartmouth).

Bonefeld, W., and Gunn, R. and Psychopedis, K. (eds) (1992) *Open Marxism, Vol. I: History and Dialectics* (London: Pluto Press).

Bukharin, N. [1917] (1972) *Imperialism and World Economy* (London: Merlin).

Burnham, P. (1990) *The Political Economy of Postwar Reconstruction* (London: Macmillan).

Burnham, P. (1991) 'Imperialism and post-revisionism: reassessing the role of the United States in the global political economy 1900–1960', *CSE Conference Papers* (July).

Burnham, P. (1993) 'Marxism, Neorealism and International Relations', *Common Sense*, 14.

Buzan, B. (1991) *People, States and Fear* (London: Harvester).

Callinicos, A. (1992) 'Capitalism and the state system: A reply to Nigel Harris', *International Socialism*, 54.

Carnoy, M. (1984) *The State and Political Theory* (Princeton: Princeton University Press).

Clarke, S. (1977/1991) 'Marxism, Sociology and Poulantzas' Theory of the State', *Capital and Class*, 2, and in S. Clarke (ed.), *The State Debate* (London: Macmillan).

Clarke, S. (1978) 'Capital, Fractions of Capital and the State', *Capital and Class*, 5.

Clarke, S. (1988) *Keynesianism, Monetarism and the Crisis of the State* (Aldershot: Edward Elgar).

Clarke, S. (1991) 'Overaccumulation, Class Struggle and the Regulation Approach', in W. Bonefeld and J. Holloway (eds), *Post-Fordism and Social Form* (London: Macmillan).

Clarke, S. (ed.) (1991) *The State Debate* (London: Macmillan).

Cleaver, H. (1989) 'Close the IMF, abolish debt and end development: a class analysis of the international debt crisis', *Capital and Class*, 39.

Cleaver, H. (1994), 'The Chiapas Uprising and the Future of Class Struggle', *Common Sense*, 15.

Corrigan, P. and Sayer, D. (1985) *The Great Arch* (Oxford: Blackwell).

DeLeon, D. (1896) *Reform and Revolution* (Glasgow: Socialist Labour Press).

de Ste Croix, G.E.M. (1981) *The Class Struggle in the Ancient Greek World* (London: Duckworth).

Gilpin, R. (1987) *The Political Economy of International Relations* (Princeton: Princeton University Press).

Hall, P. (1986) *Governing the Economy* (Oxford: Blackwell).

Holloway, J. and Picciotto, S. (1977/1991) 'Capital, Crisis and the State', *Capital and Class* 2, and in S. Clarke (ed.), *The State Debate* (London: Macmillan).

Hunter, R. (1918) *Bolshevism and the Labour Movement* (London: Routledge).

Jessop, B. (1990) *State Theory* (London: Polity Press).

Jessop, B. (1992) 'Towards the Schumpeterian Workfare State', *Lancaster Regionalism Group Working Paper*.

Kay, G. and Mott, J. (1982) *Political Order and the Law of Labour* (London: Macmillan).

Kropotkin, P. (1897) *The State: Its Historic Role* (London: Freedom Press).

Lenin, V.I. (1917) *The State and Revolution* (Moscow: Progress Publishers).

Marx, K. [1843] (1975) 'Contribution to the Critique of Hegel's Philosophy of Law', in K. Marx and F. Engels, *Collected Works* (MECW), Vol. III (London: Lawrence & Wishart).

Marx, K. [1844a] (1975) 'Critical Marginal Notes on the article by a Prussian', in K. Marx and F. Engels, *Collected Works* (MECW), Vol. III (London: Lawrence & Wishart).

Marx, K. [1844b] (1975) 'Economic and Philosophical Manuscripts', in K. Marx and F. Engels, *Collected Works* (MECW), Vol. III (London: Lawrence & Wishart).

Marx, K. [1884c] (1975) 'On the Jewish Question', in K. Marx and F. Engels, *Collected Works* (MECW), Vol. III (London: Lawrence & Wishart).

Marx, K. [1845–6] (1975) *The German Ideology* (MECW), Vol. V (London: Lawrence & Wishart).

Marx, K. [1857] (1986) *The Grundrisse* (MECW), Vol. XXVIII (London: Lawrence & Wishart).

Marx, K. [1867] (1976) *Capital*, Vol. I (London: Pelican).

Marx, K. [1871] (1986) *The Civil War in France* (MECW), Vol. XXII (London: Lawrence & Wishart).

Marx, K. [1884] (1978) *Capital*, Vol. II (London: Pelican).

Marx, K. [1894] (1981) *Capital*, Vol. III (London: Pelican).

Marx, K. and Engels, F. [1848] (1976) *The Communist Manifesto* (MECW), Vol. VI (London: Lawrence & Wishart).

Miliband, R. (1969) *The State in Capitalist Society* (London: Weidenfeld & Nicolson).

Miliband, R. (1991) 'The State', in T. Bottomore *et al.* (eds), *A Dictionary of Marxist Thought* (Oxford: Blackwell).

Morioka, K. (1989) 'Japan', in T. Bottomore and R. Brym (eds), *The Capitalist Class: An International Study* (London: Harvester).

Murray, P. (1988) *Marx's Theory of Scientific Knowledge* (London: Humanities Press).

Ollman, B. (1993) *Dialectical Investigations* (London: Routledge).

Paul, W. (1916) *The State. Its Origin and Function* (Glasgow: Socialist Labour Press).

Picciotto, S. (1991) 'The Internationalisation of Capital and the International State System', in S. Clarke (ed.), *The State Debate* (London: Macmillan).

Pilbeam, K. (1992) *International Finance* (London: Macmillan).

Radice, H. (ed.) (1975) *International Firms and Modern Imperialism* (London: Penguin).

Rosdolsky, R. (1977) *The Making of Marx's Capital*, Vol. I (London: Pluto Press).

Rosewarne, S. (1993) 'The Transnationalisation of the State', paper presented to the CSE Annual Meeting.

Rothschild, E. (1988) 'The Real Reagan Economy', *New York Review of Books* (30 June).

Shinohara, M. (1991) 'Japan as a World Economic Power', *The Annals* (January).

Skocpol, T. (1979) States and Social Revolutions. (Cambridge: Cambridge University Press).

US Department of Commerce (1975) *Survey of Current Business.*

von Braunmühl, C. (1978) 'On the Analysis of the Bourgeois Nation State Within the World Market Context', in J. Holloway and S. Picciotto (eds), *State and Capital* (London: Edward Arnold).

Wallerstein, I. (1984) *The Politics of the World-Economy* (Cambridge: Cambridge University Press).

Weber, M. (1918) 'Politics as a Vocation', in Hans Gerth and C.W. Mills (eds), *From Max Weber* (London: Routledge).

6 Global Capital and the National State

John Holloway[1]

The dilemmas of 'left' politics at the moment have much to do with the shattering of the myth of socialism in one country, whether in its 'communist' or social-democratic form. It has been made clear by the collapse of the Soviet Union and the regimes of Eastern Europe, by the increasing integration of China into the world market, by the changing orientation of so many 'socialist' regimes in different parts of the world, by the right-wing policies of social democratic parties in Europe, that the only possible way to think of socialism today is as a global project.

Just what this means or how it is to be achieved may not be clear, but it is clear that rigid conceptions of the state are a major obstacle to be overcome by such a project. As always, any attempt to conceptualise socialism must come to grips with the significance of the state and its relation to capital, but it is now clearer than ever that this relation can be understood only in a global context.

The immediate stimulus for writing this chapter was the experience of teaching a course on 'The Crisis of the Welfare State' in the Latin American Faculty of Social Sciences (FLACSO, Mexico). To talk about the crisis of 'the welfare state' or the reform of 'the state' in an international setting immediately raises the question of 'which state? where?' To someone who has lived most of his life in Europe, there is an additional problem: of what relevance are ideas developed in Europe about 'the state' to people whose main point of reference is the Paraguayan, Bolivian or Argentinian state? The answer can only lie through some concept of the fragmentation of a united world.

THE STATE

The very concept of the 'crisis of the welfare state' (or the 'reform of the state', another expression used widely to discuss current changes

116

in the different states) points to the fact that we are identifying something common in the development of different states, and therefore proclaiming that an analysis oriented to one particular state is insufficient. The states appear to be quite distinct, separate entities, and yet we speak of the reform of 'the state' or the crisis of 'the state' as though there were just one state, assuming some sort of unity between that which appears to be separate. How can we understand the relation between the development of different states as a unity of the separate, the unity-in-separation/separation-in-unity of the state and the multiplicity of different states?

In the tradition of political science, the state is taken as a basic, and largely unquestioned, category. The state's existence is taken for granted before any discussion begins. In the tradition of Political Theory (at least as taught in British universities), categories such as authority, obligation and rights are discussed, but the state, as a category, is simply assumed. In the study of contemporary politics, the determinants of state action, the relations between states, the changing forms of government, and so on, are analysed, but all on the basis of an assumed starting point, the 'state'.

The overwhelming majority of work in the discipline takes one particular state as its almost exclusive framework, analysing political developments as though they could be understood in purely national terms. This is particularly true of work in the United States and Europe: for example, it has been common, on both left and right, to analyse 'Thatcherism' or 'Reaganism' as purely national phenomena, rather than as part of a global shift in the relation between the state and the market. Such analyses not only beg the obvious question of how then the global trend is to be understood, but they also focus political opposition on the national state, suggesting by the very terms of the analysis that all would be well if only Thatcher, Major or whoever were not in office. In Latin America people have been far more conscious of the world context within which current changes are taking place, but there is still a sense in which the unquestioned category of 'the state' restricts and defines discussion.

If the state is taken as the starting point for analysis, then the world (in so far as it appears at all) appears as the sum of nation-states. Trends or developments which go beyond the borders of one state are discussed either in terms of inter-state relations (as in the tradition of the 'subdiscipline' of 'international relations') or in terms of analogy (as in the 'subdiscipline' of 'comparative politics'). Both approaches start not from a concept of the unity of the different states but from an assumption of their separation: common trends can be understood only as part of the inter-state network of power relations exercised either directly or through institutions such as the International Monetary Fund; or else in terms of the similarities between states in ideas, political institutions or social structures. An important example of the latter, comparative approach is the currently influential regulation theory, which establishes nationally-defined concepts of Fordism and post-Fordism and then proceeds by analogy to discuss their applicability to different phenomena.

Inter-state pressures, pressures from international organisations, and institutional and theoretical fashions can certainly be seen as playing an important role in shaping the development of the state, yet they are insufficient to explain the depth and the global dimensions of the changes currently taking place. To explain the changes in terms of pressure from the IMF, for example, simply throws the question to a different level: what lies behind the policy orientation and influence of the IMF? Similarly, to explain the changes in terms of the influence of neo-liberal thought simply raises the question of why neo-liberal thought should have gained such influence in different countries at this particular time. Comparative analyses which focus on the occurrence of similar socioeconomic changes in the different countries, as in the regulationist analysis of Fordism, take us deeper, but the analogies, although suggestive, tend to be sketchy and superficial (Clarke, 1988/1991): the unity on which the analogies are inevitably based remains untheorised. To reach a satisfactory understanding of the changes taking place at the moment we need to go beyond the category of 'the state', or rather we need to go beyond the assumption of the separateness of the different states to find a way of discussing their unity.

Here, dependency theory offers itself as an attractive alternative, in so far as it emphasises the unitary character of the world, insisting on the importance of understanding the actions of particular states in the context of the bipolar relationship between centre and periphery, the periphery being subject to exploitation by the centre. Here there is a concept of the unity of the separate states, in so far as all are elements of a bipolar world. However, in so far as the 'centre' and the 'periphery' are understood as the 'central states' and the 'peripheral states' (or groups of states as in 'Latin America', cf. Marini, 1973), the analysis remains very state oriented. In this sense it is closely related to the tradition of international relations: although the emphasis is on the primacy of the world system over particular states, the world system is understood basically as an international state system, with the central states as the dominant actors, and with the only possible path out of dependence lying through the action of peripheral states.[2] As in the mainstream tradition, the state defines a distinction between internal and external, the difference being that in dependency theory, the emphasis (in relation to the dependent states) is very much on the external, rather than the internal determinants of state action. Developments such as the state reforms being carried out in the peripheral states can, in this perspective, be understood only in terms of the external constraints arising from the centre–periphery relationship, but there is no concept which allows us to understand the dynamic of that relationship.

THE STATE AS A FORM OF SOCIAL RELATIONS

Each state proclaims its own separateness from other states, its own national sovereignty. In order to understand that which allows us to speak of the crisis or reform of 'the state' as though there were only one state, we need to soften that separateness, to dissolve the state as a category.

To dissolve the state as a category means to understand the state not as a thing in itself, but as a social form, a form of social relations. Just as in physics we have come to accept that, despite appearances, there are no absolute separations, that energy can be transformed into mass and mass into energy, so in society too there are no absolute separations, no hard categories. To think scientifically is to dissolve the categories of thought, to understand all social phenomena as precisely that, as forms of social relations. Social relations, relations between people, are fluid, unpredictable, unstable, often passionate, but they rigidify into certain forms, forms which appear to acquire their own autonomy, their own dynamic, forms which are crucial for the stability of society. The different academic disciplines take these forms (the state, money, the family) as given and so contribute to their apparent solidity, and hence to the stability of capitalist society. To think scientifically is to criticise the disciplines, to dissolve these forms, to understand them as forms; to act freely is to destroy these forms.

The state, then, is a rigidified (or 'fetishised', to use Marx's term) form of social relations. It is a relation between people which does not appear to be a relation between people, a social relation which exists in the form of something external to social relations. This is the starting point for understanding the unity between states: all are rigidified, apparently autonomous forms of social relations.

But why do social relations rigidify in this way and how does that help us to understand the development of the state? This was the question posed by the so-called state derivation debate, a slightly peculiar but very important discussion which spread from West Germany to other countries during the 1970s.[3] The debate was peculiar in being conducted in extremely abstract language, and often without making explicit the political and theoretical implications of the argument. The obscurity of the language used and the fact that the participants often did not develop (or were not aware of) the implications of the debate left the discussion open to being misunderstood, and the approach has often been dismissed as an 'economic' theory of the state, or as a 'capital–logic' approach which seeks to understand political development as a functional expression of the logic of capital – thus leaving no space for class struggle. While these criticisms can fairly be made of some of the contributions, the significance of the debate as a whole was precisely the opposite: it provided a basis for breaking away from the economic determinism and the functionalism which has marred so many of the discussions of the relation between the state and capitalist society, and for discussing the state as a moment of the totality of the social relations of capitalist society.

The focus of the debate on the state as a particular *form* of social relations is the crucial break with the economic determinism implied for example by the base–superstructure model (and its structuralist variants). In the base–superstructure model, the economic base determines (in the last instance, of course) what the state *does*, the functions of the state. The focus on the functions of the state takes the existence of the state for granted: there is no room in the base–superstructure model to ask about the form of the state, to ask why, in the first place, social relations should rigidify into the apparently autonomous form of the state. To ask about the form of the state is to raise the question of its historical specificity: the existence of the state as a thing separated from society is peculiar to capitalism, as is the existence of the 'economic' as something distinct from overtly coercive class relations (Gerstenberger, 1990). The question then is not: how does the economic determine the political superstructure? Rather, it is: what is peculiar about the social relations of capitalism that gives rise to the rigidification (or particularisation) of social relations in the form of the state?[4] The corollary of this is the question: what is it that gives rise to the constitution of the economic and the political as distinct moments of the same social relations? The answer is surely that there is something distinctive about the social antagonism on which capitalism (like any class society) is based. Under capitalism, social antagonism (the relation between classes) is based on a form of exploitation which takes place not openly but through the 'free' sale and purchase of labour power as a commodity on the market. This form of class relation presupposes a separation between the immediate process of exploitation, which is based on the 'freedom' of labour, and the process of maintaining order in an exploitative society, which implies the use of coercion (cf. Hirsch, 1974/1978).

Seeing the state as a form of social relations obviously means that the development of the state can only be understood as a moment of the development of the totality of social relations: it is a part of the antagonistic and crisis-ridden development of capitalist society. As a form of capitalist social relations, its existence depends on the reproduction of those relations: it is therefore not just a state in capitalist society, but a capitalist state, since its own continued existence is tied to the promotion of the reproduction of capitalist social relations as a whole. The fact that it exists as a particular or rigidified form of social relations means, however, that the relation between the state and the reproduction of capital is a complex one: it cannot be assumed, in functionalist fashion, either that everything that the state does will necessarily be in the best interests of capital, nor that the state can achieve what is necessary to secure the reproduction of capitalist society.

To speak of the state as a rigidified form of social relations is to speak both of its separation from, and its unity with, society. The separation or rigidification (or fetishisation) is a process constantly repeated.[5] The existence of the state implies a constant process of separating off certain aspects of social relations and defining them as 'political', and hence as separate from the 'economic'. The antagonism on which society is based is thus fragmented: struggles are channelled into political and economic forms, neither of which leaves room for raising questions about the organisation of society as a whole. The riots in Los Angeles and other cities last year are an obvious recent example, where the stability of the existing society depended very much, not just on the use of brute force, but on the society's ability to channel social discontent into the established procedures of the political system, to impose certain definitions on an often ill-defined rejection of the existing order. This process of imposing definitions on social struggles is at the same time a process of self-definition by the state: as a rigidified form of social relations, the state is at the same time a process of rigidifying social relations, and it is through this process that the state is constantly reconstituted as an instance separate from society. The very existence of the state is a constant process of struggle. Revolution, by implication, involves the development of anti-state organisation, of social relations which defy rigidification (Holloway, 1980/1991, 1992).

NATIONAL STATES AS FORMS OF THE GLOBAL TOTALITY OF SOCIAL RELATIONS

'The state' is thus doubly dissolved: it is not a structure but a form of social relations; it is not a totally fetishised form of social relations but a process of forming (fetishising) social relations (and hence a constant process of self-constitution). But the discussion is still at the level of 'the state': nothing has yet been said of the fact that 'the state' is not one state but a multiplicity of states. As otherwise sympathetic critics of the 'state derivation' approach have pointed out (Barker, 1978/1991; von Braunmühl, 1974, 1978), the debate 'treats the state as if it existed only in the singular. Capitalism, however, is a world system of states, and the form that the capitalist state takes is the nation-state form' (Barker, 1978/1991, p. 204).

At one level, this criticism is misdirected, because the state derivation debate was concerned not with the understanding of a particular state, but rather with the understanding of 'statehood' or, better, 'the political'. The derivation of 'the political' from the nature of capitalist social relations abstracted from the fact that 'the state' exists only in the form of a multiplicity of states. In the context of analysing the general relation between state and society, it was, as Picciotto points out, 'convenient to assume a correlation between the society and the classes within it and the state within that society'.[6] Yet, convenient or not, this point was never made clear in the debate, and the result was a serious confusion between 'the state' in the sense of 'the political' (henceforward referred to simply as 'the political') and 'the state' in the sense of the Mexican, Argentinian or German state (henceforward referred to as 'the national state').[7] This led to an impoverishment of the concept of 'the political', and it also contributed to some of the difficulties in carrying the debate further once the general theoretical argument had been made.[8]

What are the implications of opening up this distinction between the political and the national state? The political, it was seen, is a moment of the totality of capitalist social relations. The 'totality of capitalist social relations' is a global (world-wide) totality. Capital, by its nature, knows no spatial bounds. The 'freedom' of the worker which distinguishes capitalism from earlier forms of class exploitation is at the same time the freedom (in a much more real sense) of the exploiter. When serfs freed themselves from feudal bondage, they became free to wander wherever they would in search of a means of survival: no longer tied to a particular place of exploitation, they could go and be exploited wherever they chose, providing they could find an exploiter willing to accept them. By the same token, the lord was no longer tied to exploiting the serfs he had inherited, but could convert his wealth into money and use the money as capital to benefit from the exploitation of workers in any part of the world. The freeing of the worker from a particular exploiter, the freeing of the exploiter from a particular group of workers, implied the establishment of social relations in which geographical location was absolutely contingent, in which capital could, and did, flow all over the world. The destruction of personal bondage was also the destruction of geographical constraint. The lord-turned-capitalist may or may not know where his money is being used for the exploitation of labour: that is in any case irrelevant, since all capital shares in the exploitation of all labour through the equalisation of the rate of profit through competition. Relations of exploitation exist in space, since people exist in space, but the space is undefined and constantly changing. The absolute contingency of space is epitomised in the existence of capital as money. Whenever money capital moves (i.e. constantly), the spatial pattern of the relations between capital and labour changes.

The global nature of capitalist social relations is thus not the result of the recent 'internationalisation' or 'globalisation' of capital,[9] both concepts which imply a moving out from a historically and logically prior national society. Rather, it is inherent in the nature of the capitalist relation of exploitation as a relation, mediated through money, between free worker and free capitalist, a relation freed from spatial constraint. The aspatial, global nature of capitalist social relations has been a central feature of capitalist development since its bloody birth in conquest and piracy.

The political, then, as a moment of the relation between capital and labour, is a moment of a global relation. However, it is expressed not in the existence of a global state but in the existence of a multiplicity of apparently autonomous, territorially distinct national states.[10] Historically, the liberation of the relations of exploitation from spatial constraint was accompanied by the development of a new territoriality in the form of the national states. The particularisation of the state, the abstraction of coercion from the immediate process of exploitation, was expressed in a contrasting movement: as the relation of exploitation was liberated from spatial bonds, the coercion which provided the necessary support for capitalist exploitation acquired a new territorial definition. An important activity of the emerging national states was the territorial definition of coercion, the limiting of the mobility of the newly 'free' workers through measures such as the series of laws to define and control vagabondage.

The political, then, is fractured into territorially defined units: this fracturing is fundamental to an understanding of the political, a crucial element that is lost if it is assumed that society and state are coterminous. The world is not an aggregation of national states, national capitalisms or national societies: rather the fractured existence of the political as national states decomposes the world into so many apparently autonomous units.

The distinction between the political and the national state thus gives a new dimension to the concept of the state as a process of fetishising or rigidifying social relations. The decomposition of global society into national states is not something that is accomplished once national boundaries are set. On the contrary, all national states are engaged in a constantly repeated process of decomposing global social relations: through assertions of national sovereignty, through exhortations to 'the nation', through flag ceremonies, through the playing of national anthems, through administrative discrimination against 'foreigners', through war. In short, the very existence of the state is racist. The more feeble the social basis of this national decomposition of society – as in Latin America, for example – the more obvious its forms of expression. This decomposition of global social relations is a crucial element in the fragmentation of opposition to capitalist domination, in the decomposition of labour as a class.[11]

The national state, then, is crucially a form of fracturing global society. Seen in this light, there is a basic territorial non-coincidence between the state and the society to which it relates. The 'convenient' assumption, mentioned by Picciotto, of a correlation of state and society is quite simply wrong, crucially wrong. If capitalist social relations are inherently global, then each national state is a moment of global society, a territorial fragmentation of a society which extends throughout the world. No national state, 'rich' or 'poor' can be understood in abstraction from its existence as a moment of the global capital relation. The distinction so often made between 'dependent' and 'non-dependent' states falls. All national states are defined, historically and repeatedly, through their relation to the totality of capitalist social relations. The distinction made by Evers, for example, in his development of the state derivation debate in relation to the capitalist 'periphery', between the 'central' states in which there is a 'social identity between the economic and the political sphere' and the 'peripheral' states, in which there is no such identity (Evers, 1979, pp. 77–9), is quite invalid. In spite of the national orientation of most theorists in the 'richer' countries, the existence of the national state as a moment of the global capital relation is no less crucial for an understanding of Thatcherism in Britain, say, than it is for an understanding of the rise of neo-liberalism in any so-called 'peripheral' country (as Bonefeld, 1993, convincingly shows).[12]

This is not to say that the relation between global capital and all national states is the same. On the contrary, although all national states are constituted as moments of a global relation, they are distinct and non-identical moments of that relation. The fracturing of the political into national states means that every state has a specific territorial definition and hence a specific relation to people within its territory, some (usually but not always – South Africa, Kuwait – the majority) of whom it defines as 'citizens', the rest as 'foreigners'. This territorial definition means that each state has a different relation to the global relations of capitalism.

The contrast between the spatial liberation of the process of exploitation (mediated through the flow of capital as money), on the one hand, and the spatial definition of coercion (expressed in the existence of national states), on the other, is expressed as a contrast between the mobility of capital and the immobility of the state. The territorial definition of the state means that each state is immobile in a way that contrasts strongly with the mobility of capital. The national state can change its boundaries only with difficulty, whereas capital can move from one side of the world to the other within seconds. Where national states are solid, capital is essentially liquid, flowing to wherever in the world the biggest profits are to be made. Clearly there are obstacles to this flow, limits to this mobility. Crucially, the reproduction of capital depends on its (transitory) immobilisation in the form of productive capital, involving its embodiment in machinery, labour power, land, buildings, commodities. Other obstacles also impede the free flow of capital, such as state regulations or the existence of monopoly situations but, in its most general and abstract form, money, capital is global, liquid and fast-flowing. Money knows no personal or national sentiments.

The relation of the national state to capital is a relation of a nationally fixed state to a globally mobile capital. It is in these terms that both the relation between the national state and the world and the relation between national states must be conceptualised. This is important because it has been common, particularly on the left, to discuss the relation between the state and capital as though capital were immobile, as though it were attached to particular activities, places or persons. This gives rise to analyses of political development in terms of conflict between capital fractions (textile capital versus chemical capital, say, or banking capital versus industrial capital) as though capital were in some way tied down to a particular activity[13] or, more to the point in the present discussion, to the discussion of the state in terms of some sort of fusion, unity or interlocking between the state and 'national capital', as though capital were tied down in some way to some particular part of the world. The link between the state and capital is shown in terms of family links, personal connections, the existence of military industrial complexes, and these links are theorised as showing the capitalist nature of the state (as in Miliband, 1969), or in terms of a 'fusion' of state and monopolies (as in state monopoly capitalist theories), or as the formation of competitive state-capitals (as in state capitalist theories such as Barker, 1978/1991[14]), or in classic theories of imperialism. All of these approaches treat capital as though it could be understood in terms of its personal, institutional or local attachment, instead of seeing these attachments as transitory moments, staging posts in the incessant flow of capital. Certainly personal, institutional and political links exist between groups of capitalists and national states, but 'groups of capitalists' are not the same as capital and often national states are obliged to break their links with their capitalist friends and act against them in the interests of securing the reproduction of capital as a whole (cf. Hirsch, 1974/1978). The relative immobility of the national state and the extremely high mobility of capital makes it impossible to establish such a simple relation between a national state and any particular part of world capital (Murray, 1971; Picciotto, 1985/1991).

The competition between states and the changing positions of national states in relation to global capital can therefore not be adequately discussed in terms of competition between 'national capitals'. The discussion must start not from the immobility of capital but from its mobility. In so far as the existence of any national state depends not just on the reproduction of world capitalism, but on the reproduction of capitalism within its boundaries, it must seek to attract and, once attracted, to immobilise capital[15] within its territory.[16] The competitive struggle between national states is not a struggle between national capitals, but a struggle between states to attract and/ or retain a share of world capital (and hence a share of global surplus value). In order to achieve this end, the national state must try to ensure favourable conditions for the reproduction of capital within its boundaries (through the provision of infrastructure, the maintenance of law and order, the education and regulation of labour power, etc.) and also give international support (through trade policy, monetary policy, military intervention, etc.) to the capital operating within its boundaries, largely irrespective of the citizenship of the legal owners of that capital.

In this competitive struggle positions of hegemony and subordination are established, but a hegemonic position does not free states from the global competition to attract and retain capital. Relative positions of hegemony and subordination are based ultimately on the existence of more or less favourable conditions for capital accumulation in the different state territories: hence the long-term decline of Britain as a hegemonic power and the present instability of the international position of the United States. Conditions for capital accumulation depend in turn on the conditions for the exploitation of labour by capital, but there is no direct territorial relation here. Capital may accumulate in the territory of one national state as the result of the exploitation of labour in the territory of another state – as in the case of colonial or neo-colonial situations, but also in cases where states, through tax advantages or other incentives, make themselves into attractive locations for capital accumulation (the Cayman Islands and Liechtenstein are obvious examples).

National states thus compete to attract to (or retain within) their territory a share of global surplus value produced. The antagonism between them is not an expression of exploitation of the 'peripheral' states by the 'central' states (as dependency theorists suggest) but rather expresses the (extremely unequal) competition between them to attract to their territories (or retain within their territories) a share of global surplus value. For that reason, all states have an interest in the global exploitation of labour. It is true, as dependency theorists argue, that national states can be understood only by reference to their existence in a bipolar world characterised by exploitation, but the exploitation is not the exploitation of rich countries by poor countries but of global labour by global capital, and the bipolarity is not a centre–periphery bipolarity but a bipolarity of class, a bipolarity in which all states, by virtue of their very existence as states dependent on the reproduction of capital, are located at the capitalist pole.[17]

The relation between national states is thus not adequately understood as an external relation, even though it presents itself as such. If the national state is a moment of the global capital relation, then neither the global capital relation ('international capital') nor other states can properly be understood as being external to it. In trying to understand the development of any national state, it is thus not a question of choosing between the 'external' determinants of state development (favoured by dependency theory in the case of 'peripheral' states) and the 'internal' determinants (preferred by regulation theory, Hirsch, 1992). Nor can state development be understood as being the result of a combination of endogenous and exogenous motor forces, the solution pursued by Dabat (1992). The distinction between inside–outside, internal–external, endogenous–exogenous reproduces the apparent autonomy of national states, and so reinforces the murderous rigidification of social relations which national boundaries represent, but is not adequate as an explanation of state development. All national states manipulate the internal–external distinction as a crucial element of practical politics. All states which have dealings with the IMF, for example, present the results of such dealings as being externally imposed, whereas in reality they are part of the seamless integration of 'national' and global political conflict. This is equally true of the terms 'imposed' by the IMF on Britain in 1976 (an important victory for the Right in Britain) and the terms recently 'imposed' by the IMF on Venezuela, which form an important element of the Venezuelan state's strategy to restructure society in such a way as to create more favourable conditions for capital accumulation. Global capital is no more 'external' to Cochabamba, Zacatlán or even Tannochbrae than it is to New York, Tokyo or London, although the forms and consequences of its presence differ enormously.

Understanding the development of the state cannot be a question of examining internal and external determinants, but of trying to see what it means to say that the national state is a moment of the global capital relation. Most obviously, it means that the development of any particular national state can be understood only in the context of the development of capitalist social relations, of which it is an integral part. The 'global development of capitalist social relations' is not a logical process nor something 'out there', but a historical process of conflict, a conflict which, although fragmented, is global. The structure of that conflict (ultimately the form of capital's dependence on labour, the relation of surplus value production) gives to capitalist social relations a characteristic instability which is expressed in capitalism's tendency to crisis. It follows that the development of national states, their relation to each other and their existence as moments of global capital can be understood only in the context of the crisis-ridden development of capitalist class struggle (cf. Holloway, 1992).[18] However, the relation between any particular national state and global development is a complex one. Although the fact that all national states are moments of the same global relation is expressed in the occurrence of common patterns of development, as illustrated by the 'reform of the state' in so many countries in recent years, the differential relation of national states to global capital means that the forms taken by the struggles around the development of global capital, and hence the development of the national states, can differ enormously, and often what appears at first to be a common development (the neo-liberal reform of the state, for example) conceals a large number of different (and competing) strategies to achieve a redefined relation to a global capital in the process of restructuring.[19]

THE REFORM OF THE STATE AND THE NATIONAL POLITICS OF GLOBAL OVERACCUMULATION

Capitalism is a restless mode of domination. If the dissolution of feudalism liberated exploiters from their ties to particular workers, and from a relation of exploitation which no longer functioned, it also condemned them (or rather their wealth) to an endless search for a new, stable relation of exploitation. The history of capital is the history of a constant flight forward, a constant flight from the inadequacy of existing relations of exploitation, from the inadequacy of its own domination of the power of labour on which it depends. This flight exists all the time, but acquires a particular intensity in times of crisis, crisis being the manifestation of the inadequacy (for capital) of existing relations of exploitation.

The restlessness of capital is epitomised in its existence as money. In its existence as money, capital is free, free to flow globally in pursuit of obtaining maximum benefit from the exploitation of labour, in pursuit of profit. Capital, of course, does not exist only as money: it flows constantly through its different functional forms, existing now as money, now as productive capital embodied in means of production and labour power, now as commodities. Each form has different implications in terms of spatial mobility. Capital in the form of money can travel from London to Tokyo in seconds. Capital in the form of productive capital embodied in machinery, buildings, workers, etc. is much less mobile geographically. Capital in the form of commodities is clearly somewhere in between the other two forms in terms of mobility.

In the shifting forms of capital, production plays a decisive role, since it is production which is the sole source of surplus value and hence of the reproduction and expansion of capital. Capital, however, is blind to such theoretical considerations: in its endless restlessness, it will flow into whatever form appears to offer the biggest profits, the best possibilities for expansion. Thus, if the inadequacy of existing relations of production express themselves in a fall in the profitability of production and the saturation of commodity markets (what 'Marxist economists' – a contradiction in terms – refer to as 'economic crisis'), then capital will flow into the money form. The result will be a radical change in the mobility of capital.

Changes in the mobility of capital are crucially important for the development of the national state. While capital flows globally, the national state is fixed. Capital flows globally, but at any given moment it has some spatial location, be it in the account of some financial institution or tied up in the bricks and mortar of some factory. The different states compete to attract and immobilise the flow of capital. The relation of particular national states to global capital is mediated through this competitive process of attraction-and-immobilisation.

The relation can perhaps be imagined in terms of a series of reservoirs seeking competitively to attract and retain the maximum amount of water from a powerful and largely uncontrollable river. As the metaphor suggests, national states do not control the overall pressure, speed and volume of the flow of water. This can be understood only in terms of that which produces the movement of the water in the first place. The national states, the reservoirs of the metaphor, can only respond to changes in the magnitude and power of the river.

The major changes in the organisation and conceptualisation of the state which have taken place over the last fifteen years or so throughout the world are a response to a radical change in the flow of the river of capital. This radical change is the expression of crisis, the intensified flight of capital from the inadequacy of its own basis, from the insufficiency of its own subordination of the power of labour.

The destruction caused by the Second World War and the pre-war depression, combined with the experience of fascism in a number of countries, created favourable conditions for capitalist exploitation globally. The twenty-five years or so after the war was generally a period of high and steady growth based on the profitability of capitalist production. The resulting relative stability of capital created the basis for the development of a certain type of relation between national state and global capital, giving credibility to a world composed of 'national economies'. The relative stability also created an environment in which it was possible for the international agreements established after the war to regulate the economic relations between national states: particularly important in this respect was the Bretton Woods agreement which, by creating a system of fixed exchange rates, regulated to some extent the movement of money between national states and hence insulated national states to some degree from the global movement of capital (cf. Bonefeld, 1993). This relative insulation, founded on the relative stability of productive capital and bolstered by international regulation and by international policies to control the movement of capital, provided the basis for the state-oriented politics of this period, be it the politics of the Keynesian welfare state or the politics of import substitution. The same relative stability also made possible the creation of reasonably stable alliances between the national states and groups of capitalists – the sort of alliances fixed conceptually in the theories discussed above (military–industrial complex, state monopoly capitalism, etc.); and also between the state and bureaucratised labour movements, as found in many varieties of corporatist political development.[20] Many of the theoretical conceptions concerning the state that are still common – particularly the abstraction of 'the state' from the world, discussed above – arose from the experience of this period, which was also a period of rapid expansion for 'political science' and the social sciences in general.

The relative insulation of the national state came to an end with the end of the long period of post-war boom. From the mid-1960s there were clear signs of growing instability. The conditions which had made production profitable throughout the post-war period were weakening: the costs associated with the exploitation of workers (often referred to as the organic composition of capital) were rising, the labour discipline (and general social discipline) established by the experience of war was weakening, the state bureaucracies associated with the post-war pattern of development were proving costly for capital. Investment in production came to be a less secure means of expanding capital. The inadequacy of the existing relations of exploitation as a basis for the expansion of capital was manifested in falling profits.

In these circumstances the inherent restlessness of capital asserted itself. Capital, in order to survive, needed to free itself from the existing relations of exploitation, to spit out some of the workers currently being exploited, to restructure its relations with others, to go in search of new people to exploit. Capital takes flight from the inadequacy of its own basis: this flight is expressed in the conversion of capital into money and the movement of that money in search of profitable means of expansion.

This process can be described in terms of the over-accumulation of capital. In the years of the boom there had been a rapid accumulation of capital: more capital had accumulated than could now find a secure and profitable outlet in productive investment. When that happens, then, in much the same way as bees swarm when there is no longer enough honey in the hive to support an expanded population, capital swarms – part of it gets up and flies in search of a new home.[21] Capital assumes the liquid form of money and flows throughout the world in search of profit. Instead of embodying itself in the bricks and mortar, machinery and workers of productive investment, it flows in search of speculative, often very short-term means of expansion. Many of the factories which have now become unprofitable are closed down, the buildings and machinery sold, the workers laid off: the capital released remains as money, which may be transformed into productive investment elsewhere, but is more likely to remain in the form of money as long as conditions for productive investment remain relatively unfavourable. The difficulties of production express themselves in an increase both in the supply of money, as previously productive capital converts itself into money and offers itself for loan, and in the demand for money, as the capital which remains in production tries to overcome difficulties through borrowing, and states try to reconcile growing social tensions through increasing their debt.

The crisis of production relations is expressed in the liquefaction of capital. There is a sharp change in the relation between productive capital and capital held in the form of money:[22] money, instead of appearing to be subordinate to production, now appears as an end in itself. Inevitably, the shift in the form of capital means a change in the relation between the territorially fixed national states and the global movement of capital. This is not an 'internationalisation' or 'globalisation' of the economy, as it is often called, but a change in the form of the global existence of capital. The flow of capital, previously relatively stable, turns into a fast-moving torrent and this torrent[23] sweeps away the institutions and assumptions of the post-war world. One of the first pillars of the post-war world to collapse was the Bretton Woods system of fixed exchange rates based on a fixed parity of the dollar with gold. The rapid growth in the 1960s in the quantity of dollars held as money outside the United States (and outside the regulatory powers of any national state), the so-called Eurodollars, led to an undermining of the position of the dollar and the abandonment in 1971 of the Bretton Woods system, which was eventually replaced by a system of floating exchange rates. This was just the first step. The rapid growth and the increasing integration of world money markets throughout the 1970s and 1980s, together with the increased speed of movement of money facilitated by the application of new technology, has had drastic consequences for the organisation of national states.[24] National states seek to attract and retain capital within their territories: what this means changes radically with the new liquidity of capital. Competition between states to attract their share of capital increases sharply, obliging all national states to find new ways of making themselves attractive to capital. The fact that a higher share of capital is invested on a short-term basis means that states are under constant pressure to maintain conditions which will hold capital within their territory.[25] States, as states, must bend to the restlessness of capital. The old ideologies go: the new rule of money finds expression in the new ideologies of neo-liberalism, supply-side theory, monetarism, all of which say in one way or another: money rules. The old alliances go. The established links between groups of capitalists and the state come to be seen as a hindrance once it is seen that capital in its money form attaches to no group of people and no particular activity. The patterns of corporatist domination through trade unions also come under strain:

what is needed to attract global money is a new organisation of work, a new 'flexibility' and new discipline that is incompatible with the old trade union structures, a new way of 'learning to bow' (cf. Peláez and Holloway, 1990/1991). Money, in its desperation to find a way of expanding itself, forces open areas previously closed to private capitalist investment: everywhere areas of activity previously controlled by national states are privatised, opened up to the torrent of money in search of a profitable home.[26] Even the most solid bastion of them all, the Soviet Union, is opened up and torn apart by money.

And then there is debt. The transformation of capital into its money form means that much of that money is offered for loan, that it is converted into credit and debt. The last years of the post-war boom were sustained by a rapid expansion of debt. In the late 1970s, after the crisis of profitability had made itself felt in the richer countries and monetary austerity had been proclaimed, the flood of money moved south, particularly to Latin America, offering itself to governments looking for a way of containing social tensions, and converting itself into debt. After it became clear, on the Mexican government's declaration of difficulties in 1982, that Latin America was not a safe location for loans, the money flowed north again, breaking the short-lived attempts at tight monetary control in the United States and giving rise to a massive expansion of consumer debt and of military-led government debt. With debt comes a new politics of debt, both internationally and within national states (cf. Cleaver, 1989; Holloway, 1990). The growth of debt means the growth of discrimination, discrimination between those deemed worthy of credit and those who are not, a new division that has made itself horribly obvious both between national states and in society throughout the world.

The shift in the relation between national state and global capital means a significant change in the forms of global capitalist domination. There is, as Marazzi puts it, 'a shift in state power to the world level – the level at which monetary terrorism operates' (see Marazzi's 'Money in the World Crisis', Chapter 4 in this volume). Political decisions taken at the level of the national state are now more directly integrated into the global movement of capital.[27] The obviousness of this shift brings its problems, however: the subjection of the national state to the global movement of capital makes more difficult the national decomposition of society, and gives rise to tensions evidenced in very different ways by the recent difficulties of the Venezuelan government, the fall of Thatcher in Britain or the speech of President Salinas in Mexico distinguishing his patriotic 'social liberalism' from the neo-liberalism which knows no national sentiment.

In all this, capital appears all-powerful. Money is the brashest, most arrogant form of capital. Its successes throughout the world have been many and obvious. And yet the dominance of money is the manifestation of capital's weakness. Bees in swarm too are the brashest, most arrogant form of bee, yet they are in swarm precisely because there is not enough honey to go around. Money dominates because production has ceased to be so attractive for capital, but ultimately it is production and only production which provides the honey: production is the sole source of capital's self-expansion. The violent restlessness of capital is the clearest indication of the inadequacy (for capital) of the existing relations of exploitation, of capital's incapacity to subordinate the power of labour on which it depends. Despite appearances, the restless movement of capital is the clearest indication of the power of the insubordination of labour. It is not the breaking of old patterns by money, not the 'reform of the state', which holds the key to the recovery of capitalist health, but the reorganisation of exploitation, the restructured subjection of the power of labour to capital; and despite all the changes in the organisation of production, and despite all the aggressive politics of capital over the last ten or fifteen years, it is not clear that capital has yet succeeded in achieving this end.

Notes

1. This chapter, first published in English in *Capital & Class*, 52 (Spring 1994), is a modified version of an article originally published in Spanish in *Perfiles Latinoamericanos*, 1, FLACSO (Facultad Latinoamericana de Ciencias Sociales), Mexico City (December 1992). The theme of the issue is the Reform of the State in Latin America. Many people have provided helpful comments on the chapter: my particular thanks to Colin Barker, Werner Bonefeld, Peter Burnham and Eloina Peláez.
2. See Dabat (1992) for a similar critique of dependency theory.
3. On the state derivation debate and its spread, see, for example: Holloway and Picciotto (1978); Clarke (1991) (*Great Britain*); Vincent (1975) (*France*); Perez Sainz (1981) (*Spain*); *Críticas de la Economía Política* (1979, 1980); Sánchez Susarrey (1986) (*Mexico*); Archila (1980); Rojas and Moncayo (1980) (*Colombia*); Fausto (1987) (*Brazil*).
4. The state derivation debate revived the question that Pashukanis had posed in 1923:

why does the dominance of a class not continue to be that which it is – that is to say, the subordination in fact of one part of the population to another part? Why does it take on the form of official state domination? Or, which is the same thing, why is not the mechanism of state constraint created as the private mechanism of the dominant class? Why is it disassociated from the dominant class – taking the form of an impersonal mechanism of public authority isolated from society? (Pashukanis, 1923/1951, p. 185).

This question eventually cost Pashukanis his life, since its implication, namely that the state is a specifically capitalist form of social relations, was incompatible with Stalin's attempt to build a statist 'socialism in one country'.

5.   It cannot be assumed, as Jessop does (1991), and as Hirsch seems to assume, at least in his later work, that the particularisation of the state is a process completed at the origins of capitalism. Such an approach inevitably leads to functionalism. For a critique of Jessop, see Holloway (1991).

6.   'There has been a tendency for Marxist analysis of the capitalist state to focus on the state, the individual state. This is perhaps a greater tendency in Marxist than in non-Marxist writing, since the Marxist emphasis on the class nature of the society makes it necessary to discuss the relation to the structure of society, and it becomes convenient to assume a correlation between the society and the classes within it and the state within that society' (Picciotto, 1985/1991, p. 217).

7.   In that sense, Barker (1978/1991, p. 208) is quite right when he criticises an article by Picciotto and myself (Holloway and Picciotto, 1977/ 1991), saying 'their whole article is concerned with an abstraction called "the state" whose connection with the actual states of the capitalist system is not adequately developed'.

8.   For a related discussion of this issue, see Burnham (1992).

9.   The editorial introduction to *Capital & Class*, 43 (1991) maintains that 'fundamental issues of analysis and theory are raised by the globalisation of capitalism', and goes on to ask: 'must we now adopt a more "globalist" framework of analysis, or does the nation-state still provide a satisfactory framework within which we can understand capitalist development and change, and struggle for socialist objectives?' The 'fundamental issue' is surely that there is no globalisation of capitalism, and that the nation-state never provided a satisfactory framework for understanding and struggle. Important is rather that the change in the form of global nature of capitalism makes more obvious the failings of the previous analyses oriented towards the national state. As Barker puts it in a comment on an earlier draft of this chapter, 'What marks the present is that we are emerging out of a period in which the predominant theories and practices of the world's left took national arguments for granted, whether in theories of purely national reformism or in arguments for 'socialism in one country', or again in arguments for 'national-developmental-socialism'.

10.   A similar point is made by Burnham (1992, p. 12).

11. The recomposition of labour as a class, it follows, thus involves the fundamental rejection of all forms of nationalism, of all forms of discrimination against 'foreigners', however defined. In so far as the very existence of the state is racist, an anti-racist politics must be anti-state.
12. In the case of Britain, a dramatic example of this point is provided by 'Black Wednesday', 16 September 1992, and all the political consequences that have flowed from it.
13. For a seminal critique of fractionalism, see Clarke (1978).
14. Although Barker's critique of the limitations of the state derivation debate is basically correct, the conclusion he draws about the need to analyse the national states in terms of competing state-capital blocks is thus quite wrong.
15. Protectionism is just as much an expression of the global existence of capital as free trade policies designed to attract capital.
16. The extent to which particular states can break from these constraints in revolutionary situations would require a separate discussion, which is not attempted here.
17. For a discussion of the relations of conflict and collaboration between national states, see Burnham (1992).
18. It is surprising that Picciotto, in his discussion of the internationalisation of the state (1991), does not relate international state development either to the concept of capital or to a concept of crisis. This leads him to separate social and class relations, the economic and the social, and class and popular struggles.
19. In all this there must be no functionalism. One of the problems associated with the analysis of the 'capitalist state' as though there were only one state was that it led very easily to the functionalist assumption that because the state was a capitalist state it therefore performed the functions required of it by capital. As pointed out in the account of the state derivation debate, this is already an unjustifiable conclusion at the level of 'the state', but the weakness of the functionalist argument becomes much clearer when it is borne in mind that capital is global and 'the state' is a multiplicity of national states: it cannot be assumed from the fact that the reproduction of global capital would be promoted by some political action that some state or states will achieve what is required (Picciotto, 1985/1991). It cannot be assumed that capital will always solve its crises.
20. Many of these interconnections have been analysed in the regulationist discussion of Fordism, but since regulation theory takes the national state and not global capital as its frame of reference (cf. Clarke, 1988/ 1991; Hirsch, 1992), it has not succeeded in relating these issues to the mobility of capital. The orientation of regulation theory to the national state is a reflection of the fact that the national state in the post-war period probably played a more central role in the global containment of labour than at any other time; but because the national state is taken as given in regulation theory, this remains quite untheorised.
21. Metaphors mix without shame in this section. But bees and rivers are enough.
22. For a much more detailed account of the processes described in these

paragraphs, see Bonefeld (1993), to which the present chapter owes a considerable debt. See also Bonefeld (1992).

23.   On the scale of the change in the transnational flow of capital, see Crook (1992, pp. 6–9). Among the figures which he gives to indicate the scale of the growth of the international movement of money: 'during the past decade the stock of international bank lending (i.e. cross-border lending plus domestic lending denominated in foreign currency) has risen from 4% of the OECD's GDP to 44%'; 'turnover in foreign exchange, including derivatives, is now put at roughly $900 billion each day . . . Currency trading has grown by more than a third since April 1989, when a central bank survey estimated net daily turnover at $650 billion – and that was double the previous survey's estimate for 1986'.

24.   The World Bank makes the point succinctly, pointing out 'that in a global marketplace there is a sharply-reduced tolerance for poor policies': Fidler (1993, p. v).

25.   The nature or the pressure in the case of Mexico, for example, can be inferred from the fact that the inflow of capital to Mexico in 1992 represented over 8.4% of GDP; of this between one-third and one-half is short-term funding, ' "hot money" – money attempting to capture profit from interest differentials or foreign exchange market inefficiencies, and which is likely to be withdrawn as soon as the perceived risk associated with the investment increases': Fidler (1993, pp. ii, iii).

26.   This 'torrent of money' can be seen as the assertion of the tendency of the equalisation of the rate of profit. On recent trends, see Marx (1971, pp. 195–6).

27.   One implication of this development is that, paradoxically, it becomes easier to reconcile the democratic political form with the interests of capital. It is this, Cavarozzi *et al.* (1992) suggest, which is the key to understanding why the growth of democracy in Latin America in recent years has gone hand in hand with a growth of poverty and social inequality.

References

Archila, M. (coord) (1980) *Del Estado Instrumento a la Forma-Estado* (Bogotá: CINEP).

Barker, C. (1978/1991) 'A Note on the Theory of Capitalist States', *Capital & Class*, 4; reprinted in S. Clarke (ed.), *The State Debate* (London: Macmillan).

Bonefeld, W. (1992) 'Money and Liberty: The Constitutive Power of Labour and Capitalist Reproduction', paper presented to the Seminar on Global Money and the National State (Mexico City: FLASCO) (July).

Bonefeld, W. (1993) *The Recomposition of the British State During the 1980s* (Aldershot: Dartmouth).

Bonefeld, W., Gunn, R. and Psychopedis, K. (eds) (1992) *Open Marxism, Vol 1: History and Dialectics; Vol. II: Theory and Practice* (London: Pluto Press).

Bonefeld W. and Holloway, J. (eds) (1991) *Post-Fordism and Social Form. A Marxist Debate on the Post-Fordist State* (London: Macmillan).

Burnham, P. (1992), 'The International State System and Global Crisis', paper presented to the Seminar on Global Money and the National State (Mexico City: FLASCO) (July).

Cavarozzi, M. *et al.* (1992) 'Rethinking Development Theories in Latin America: Democratic Governance, the International Economic System and Domestic Social Structures', unpublished paper, Flacso, Mexico City.

Clarke, S. (1978) 'Capital, Fractions of Capital and the State: neo-Marxist analyses of the South African State', *Capital & Class*, 5.

Clarke, S. (1988/1991) 'Overaccumulation, Class Struggle and the Regulation Approach', *Capital & Class*, 36; reprinted in W. Bonefeld and J. Holloway (eds), *Post-Fordism and Social Form. A Marxist Debate on the Post-Fordist State* (London: Macmillan) (1991).

Clarke, S. (1988) *Keynesianism. Monetarism and the Crisis of the State* (London: Edward Elgar).

Clarke, S. (ed.) (1991) *The State Debate* (London: Macmillan).

Cleaver, H. (1989) 'Close the IMF, abolish debt and end development: a class analysis of the international debt crisis', *Capital & Class*, 39.

Críticas de la Economía Política (1979), 12/13, *Estado y Capital*, Mexico City.

Críticas de la Economía Política (1980), 16/17, *Historia y Teoria del Estado*, Mexico City.

Crook, C. (1992) 'World Economy', *The Economist*, Survey (19 September), pp. 5–48.

Dabat, A. (1992) *Capitalismo Mundial y Capitalismos Nacionales* (Mexico City: Fondo de Cultura Economica).

Evers, T. (1979) *El Estado en la Periferia Capitalista* (Mexico City: Siglo Veintiuno).

Fausto, R. (1987) *Marx: Lógica e Política* (Rio de Janeiro: Editora Brasilense).

Fidler, S. (1993) 'The Return of Capital to Latin America', *Financial Times* Survey on Latin American Finance (29 March), pp. ii–v.

Gerstenberger, H. (1990) *Die subjektlose Gewalt: Theorie der Entstehung bürgerlicher Staatsgewalt* (Münster: Verlag Westfälisches Dampfboot).

Hirsch, J. (1974/1978) 'The State Apparatus and Social Reproduction: Elements of a Theory of the Bourgeois State', in J. Holloway and S. Picciotto (eds), (originally published in German in 1974).

Hirsch, J. (1992) 'Interpretations of Capital, State and World Market in terms of Regulation Theory', paper presented to the Seminar on Global Money and the National State (Mexico City: FLACSO) (July).

Holloway, J. (1980/1991) 'The State and Everyday Struggle', in S. Clarke (ed.) *The State Debate* (London: Macmillan) (originally published in Spanish in 1980).

Holloway, J. (1990) 'The Politics of Debt', *Common Sense*, 9.

Holloway, J. (1991) 'Capital is Class Struggle (And Bears are not Cuddly)', in W. Bonefeld and J. Holloway (eds), *Post-Fordism and Social Form. A Marxist Debate on the Post-Fordist State* (London: Macmillan).

Holloway, J. (1992): 'Crisis, Fetishism, Class Decomposition', in W. Bonefeld, R. Gunn and K. Psychopedis (eds), *Open Marxism, Vol I: History and Dialectics; Vol II: Theory and Practice* (London: Pluto Press).

Holloway, J. and Picciotto, S. (1977/1991) 'Capital, Crisis and the State', in S. Clarke (ed.) *The State Debate* (London: Macmillan).

Holloway, J. and Picciotto, S. (eds) (1978) *State and Capital: A Marxist Debate* (London: Edward Arnold).

Jessop, B. (1991) 'Polar Bears and Class Struggle: Much Less than a Self-Criticism', in W. Bonefeld and J. Holloway (eds), *Post-Fordism and Social Form. A Marxist Debate on the Post-Fordist State* (London: Macmillan).

Marini, R.M. (1973) *Dialectica de la Dependencia* (Mexico City: Ediciones Era).

Marx, K. (1971) *Capital*, Vol. III (Moscow: Progress Publishers).

Miliband, R. (1969) *The State in Capitalist Society* (London: Quartet Books).

Murray, R. (1971) 'The Internationalisation of Capital and the Nation State', *New Left Review*, 67.

Pashukanis, E. (1923/1951) 'The General Theory of Law and Marxism', in J.N. Hazard (ed.), trans. I. Babb, *Soviet Legal Philosophy* (Cambridge, Mass.: Harvard University Press) (new translation: *Law and Marxism: A General Theory*, ed. Ch. Arthur (London: Pluto Press).

Peláez, E. and Holloway, J. (1990/1991) 'Learning to Bow: Post-Fordism and Technological Determinism', *Science as Culture*, 8; reprinted in W. Bonefeld and J. Holloway (eds), *Post-Fordism and Social Form. A Marxist Debate on the Post-Fordist State* (London: Macmillan).

Perez Sainz, J.P. (1981) *Mercancía. Capital y Estado*, doctoral thesis, Universidad Libre de Bruselas.

Picciotto, S. (1985/1991) 'The Internationalisation of Capital and the International State System', CSE Conference Papers; reprinted in S. Clarke (ed.), *The State Debate* (London: Macmillan).

Picciotto, S. (1991) 'The Internationalisation of the State', *Capital & Class*, 43.

Rojas, F., and Moncayo, V. (eds) (1980) *Crisis Permanente del Estado Capitalista*, Bogotá.

Sánchez Susarrey, J. (1986) *La Forma Estado. La Forma Mercancía*, Universidad de Guadalajara.

Vincent, J.M. (1975) *L'Etat Contemporain et le Marxisme* (Paris: Maspéro).

Von Braunmühl, C. (1974) 'Kapitalakkumulation im Weltmarktzusamenhang. Zum methodischen Ansatz einer Analyse des bürgerlichen Staates', *Gesellschaft*, 1, Frankfurt-am-Main.

Von Braunmühl, C. (1978) 'On the Analysis of the Bourgeois Nation State within the World Market Context', in J. Holloway and S. Picciotto (eds), *State and Capital: A Marxist Debate* (London: Edward Arnold).

7 The Subversion of Money-as-Command in the Current Crisis

Harry Cleaver

Over a period of two decades money has emerged as a central axis of class conflict in much of the world. Beginning in the early 1970s with the shift from fixed to flexible exchange rates, developing through the rise of monetarism and 'tight money' policies to the 'debt crisis' of the 1980s, money has been used by capital against the insurgent power of the working classes. During this period, it has become impossible to continue to treat money technically as 'standard of price', 'means of circulation', 'means of payment' or 'store of value'. It has become a weapon of command in new and unusually brutal ways. Yet, at the same time, as we will see, in comparison to the earlier Keynesian use of money, monetarist money has proven to be, at best, a blunt and crude instrument. It has been useful for hammering down real wages and standards of living, for creating massive unemployment and widespread suffering. But its ability to transform itself into truly productive capital has been limited. It has been, so far, unable to organise a new cycle of accumulation. This inability, we will see, has been due to two processes of subversion: one from within capital, where money has been used for the redistribution rather than generation of surplus value and one from the working class, where money has been subverted into non-capitalist uses in ways which undermine the foundations of accumulation.

In what follows, I shall sketch four arguments: first, that in Marxist theory money under capitalism is the embodiment of class power, second, that in the era of the Keynesian state money played a fundamental role in the capitalist management of class relations at both the national and international levels, third that the cycle of working class struggle that brought that era to an end involved, in part, an undermining of the Keynesian uses of money, and fourth, that in the recent period of capitalist counterattack the new ways of using money as a weapon have failed to achieve their most important ends.

THE MARXIST THEORY OF MONEY-AS-COMMAND

Marx's point of departure in his analysis of money was the roles it plays in capitalist society; his point of arrival was an understanding of the various roles of money in the dynamics of class struggle. The subordination of money-as-mediator of exchange (C-M-C) to money-as-end (M-C-M') is a crucial differentia of the capitalist economy and society. But what does 'money-as-end' mean? To stop with the mere quantitative augmentation of money (profit) is to fall prey to fetishism. Marx shows us rather that the essential social role played by money in capitalism is the command of people's lives as labour. The 'capitalists' are not just the rich who consume luxuriously – the pre-capitalist landed gentry did that. They are not just merchants who buy and sell for profit – those have been around since the Sumerians. They are a new breed who use their money to put people to work where the production of use values is merely the necessary means to the end of organizing society around endless work. Yes, that work produces more value and surplus value (profit in money terms) but that surplus money (*qua* capital) is merely the means to put people, often more people, to work once again. Capital, Marx often insisted, is a social relation – an antagonistic relation of the imposition of work and the resistance to it. Thus historically the capitalists rose against the leisure and consumption of both the landed aristocracy and the working classes raising instead the banner of frugality, investment and work.

This is the secret of primitive accumulation: the creation of a new class structure in which one class (the capitalists) uses money to put others to work (the 'working' class). The story is one of the expropriation of the majority from tools and land and of their concentration in the hands of a new master class which uses them to subordinate the lives of that majority to work. As Marx and others since have shown, this was no easy subordination because of the stiff and unending resistance of most people to being forced into this new position of working for others under difficult conditions of exploitation. That widespread resistance took on a diversity of forms, as diverse as the circumstances of the imposition of work. Overcoming that resistance required capitalist control over two interlinked institutions: *money* and *the state*.

The centrality of money in the new class relations was precisely the centrality of command. The creation of the working class was first and foremost, the imposition of the mediation of (capitalist-controlled)

money between people and the means of subsistence. The expropriation of land and tools made it impossible for people to live independently. But the imposition of the money wage and of money prices
was necessary to force people to work for capital. This imposition
required, above all, new powers of a new capitalist state: the control
over the creation and regulation of money and the police power to
inflict money as a universal measure and mediator on society. Thus
the 'bloody legislation' against the expropriated – implemented by
whip, the branding iron and the gallows – was above all the imposition of monetary relations: making money the only means to
subsistence and access to money dependent on the sale of one's life as
labour power. All of the multiple and widespread attempts at independence – from the retaking of land (e.g. the Diggers) through the
direct appropriation of wealth (e.g. begging, 'theft') to outright rebellion (e.g. the rising of the Scottish Highlands in 1745) – had to be
suppressed viciously and thoroughly in order to impose the new
monetary rules of the capitalist game.[1] The rule of capital was a rule
of money and it required, as Peter Linebaugh has recently shown, a
new 'thanatocracy' to impose it.[2] 'If money,' as Marx wrote, came
'into the world with a congenital blood-stain on one cheek, capital
[the capitalist use of money] comes dripping from head to toe, from
every pore, with blood and dirt'.[3]

At the same time, the imposition of money – like all the other
mechanisms of domination – involved a constant risk: namely that
the working class might make use of it for its own purposes. By this
I do not mean simply the expenditure of money for the means of
subsistence, that purpose, *per se*, is fully consistent with the needs of
capital as long as it merely involves the *reproduction of labour power*.
However, we need to recognize that there is only a limited auto-
maticity in this role of money. The working class must spend its wage
to reproduce itself and as long as capital is able to continue to impose work, consumption will inevitably reproduce labour power, at
least to some degree. At the same time, workers have also proven
quite capable of using money for purposes antithetical to such reproduction. Obvious cases are those where money has been used by
workers to finance their struggles against capital, from strike funds
and weapons to the periodical avoidance of work made possible by
sufficiently high money income.[4] Beyond such negative subversion of
money is the use of money by workers to finance their own creative
forms of self-activity in which they pursue ways of being alternative
to capital – from innovations in traditional cultural activities to the

development of new forms of communist social patterns.[5] In both cases, of course, there is a dynamic dimension that has to be taken into account in evaluating the degree to which money has really been subverted, in as much as the harnessing of class struggle itself provides the motor of capitalist development. Nevertheless, the ability of capital to limit and reinternalize forms of working class struggle is never given *a priori* and, as we know, it has often failed to do so, resorting instead to the straightforward repression of working class self-activity. The point is that from the beginning right through to the present, the imposition of money as universal mediator carried with it such potential for working class subversion as I have described.

Beyond the original imposition of money and its role as the vehicle of capitalist command, lay the maintenance and adaptation of these relations in the course of accumulation. Despite the supposedly subtle role of 'market' pressures in controlling the working class – as opposed to the naked relations of force supposedly dominant in earlier societies – working class resistance has been such that capital has never been able to dispense with the powers of the state, both direct and indirect. Always, need has been found for police controls over working class behaviour: from the suppression of sabotage, strikes and 'riots' of industrial waged workers through the policing of the unruly, unwaged lumpenproletariat in the industrial cities to the military quelling of insurgent peasants and plantation workers in the colonies. Again and again, repeated threats to the role of money has required state action: from the direct regulation of the mediator itself to the management of the flow of money.

Thus, the role of the state has had to be maintained and even expanded in the creation and management of money, from the minting of metallic coin to the printing of paper to the regulation of banking reserves and the management of fiscal affairs (taxation and expenditures). The development of such state policies and the philosophical and political economic debates about them have constituted a long history of trying to find the best means to realize the role of money as an essential moment of capitalist class relations. Within the framework of capitalism there have been two great obstacles to such realization: first, among the capitalists themselves, a money fetishism which has obscured more fundamental social relationships, and second, originating in the antagonism of the working class, the power to separate money from capitalist command and utilize it for autonomous purposes.

In the classical political economy of the eighteenth century, the struggle against the first of these obstacles, money fetishism, took the form of an attack on the various strands of mercantilist thought and policy which saw money, in its gold and silver forms, as the essential form of wealth – to be sought primarily through trade. Despite the survival of a certain fetishism in the form of variations on Hume and Locke's quantity theory, the classical economists broke the back of money fetishism by re-identifying the source of wealth as labour, especially industrial labour producing commodities for the market. Their labour theory of value thus gave expression to the most basic characteristic of capitalism (the centrality of the subordination of life to work) and articulated labour value as the measure of all wealth. In a progression through Steuart and Smith to Ricardo, they would thus be able to situate money as an endogenous element in these social relationships rather than as a power in its own right. It remained for Marx to elaborate a theory of those relationships which brought out their exploitative character of class domination and struggle. These intellectual efforts against the 'monetary system', not only served to support a wide variety of policies conducive to industrial investment and development (e.g. the abolition of the Corn Laws) but they also served to ground new policies for the state with respect to the direct management of money, especially with respect to the growth and regulation of bank money: notes and credit. Ricardo's work on money, for example, would be used to justify Sir Robert Peel's Bank Acts of 1844 and 1845 and the efficacy of the not so invisible hand of the gold standard.[6]

The struggles in the seventeenth and eighteenth centuries against the second major obstacle to the capitalist use of money – the working class – apart from the kinds of measures taken to impose increasingly universal monetary relations which I have already mentioned, included the imposition of a unique monetary standard and its defence against debasement. While the creation of such a standard could be handled physically by the state through coinage and later through the printing of paper money, its social employment and maintenance was a more difficult matter. First, because early on 'money' circulated in a wide variety of forms – both official and private – and had to be displaced and replaced by the unique state-sanctioned standard. This was even true after the advent of paper money when, in places like eighteenth century Scotland local authorities could issue notes in response to whatever pressures they were subjected to, from the need for wage money to the avoidance of highway robbery.[7] Second, because ever-present forms of resistance represented by clipping, counterfeiting, and smuggling had to be repressed. One such period of conflict between the state and the widespread and largely invisible 'debasers' of the currency was the 1790s when John Locke mobilized both his monetary theory and the persecutory powers of the Mint to defend the currency. He utilized a combination of hanging and recoinage to restore the power of money and defend the power of the state.[8]

A second employment of both money and economic theory to overcome working class resistance concerned the unemployed and their relation to the waged. Whether money was spent (on poor rates and the work house) or money was withheld (the abolition of the poor laws, the limitation of wages) the object was the same: the maintenance of sufficient economic coercion to force workers into the labour market and into work on the job. Through such infamous arguments as those of Malthus, political economists called for the limitation of wages to mere subsistence and for the goad of poverty and suffering to guarantee work. Money had to be ceded to workers for them to reproduce themselves, but too much money would lead only to self-indulgence, less work and, in the end, more workers whose competition for jobs would force wages back down to subsistence. Almost explicit in this argument is the fear of the working class subversion of the power of money to their own ends.[9]

Marx's own work on money took two forms: a thorough critique of earlier writers and policy makers and an ongoing study of the class dynamics of money in the nineteenth century. Thus he moved from the reading and critique of Hume, Locke, Steuart, Smith and Ricardo to contemporary conflicts around issues of money and finance. Not only did he provide a theoretical analysis of the general roles of money-as-command within capitalism but he also closely examined a number of specific monetary phenomena.

One of his first (and most interesting in the light of the current debt crisis) analyses revealed how the Revolutionary French government in 1848 had wielded its debt against the Parisian working class. He showed how its honouring of the pre-revolutionary state debt to the French bankers became a vehicle for pitting peasants against workers by raising taxes on the former while blaming the latter – a strategy which enabled it to crush the workers within months.[10]

Marx also recognized and examined some of the same kinds of obstacles to the successful use of money in accumulation, as preoccupied the apologists of capital. For example, he studied closely the development of capitalist finance – the rise of the banking system and of the stock exchange – and the problems faced by the state in its efforts to regulate it. Although his view of the role of banks and public debt in primitive accumulation, i.e. their role in centralizing the money necessary for capitalist investment through interest bearing loans to the state repaid out of taxes, seemed unproblematical, Marx's studies of the experience of the Crédit Mobilier showed that this was by no means the case.[11] On the contrary, in that case of the first French 'investment' bank as well as his work on the stock exchange, Marx showed how the temporal and spatial separation of monetary transactions from real investment in building factories and putting people to work, led to a new kind of fetishism: speculation on fictitious capital with the sole aim of monetary enrichment. While the Crédit Mobilier claimed to be playing the role of financial intermediary, centralizing money to be made available for others' large scale investments (e.g. railroads), its creators and managers were actually playing speculative financial games to raise the value of their shares and enrich themselves. The same kind of fetishistic pursuit of money for the sake of money was rampant in all nineteenth century financial markets and Marx's analysis of the dynamics associated with such speculation showed how it contributed to the destabilization and crisis of capitalism more generally.

Parallel to this work on the sphere of 'private' finance was Marx's study of official state monetary and financial policies. Besides his relatively limited study of flows of money involved in public debt, taxation and state expenditures, we should note his more extensive work on the abortive attempts by the English state to intervene constructively in the monetary cycle associated with the Gold Standard. As mentioned above, Ricardo's work on money undergird Peel's Bank Acts which were aimed at imposing the discipline of the species flow mechanism on English domestic finance. The Bank Acts were aimed at tying the amount of currency to the amount of bullion and to make the former fluctuate with the latter. Marx pointed out the theoretical flaws at the heart of this doctrine (e.g. that the amount of money in circulation is a function of the value of commodities and not of bank reserves) and the practical impossibility that proved itself during each crisis when the Bank Acts had to be suspended to meet urgent demands for money and avoid the bankruptcy of the Bank of England. Moreover, Marx's work on the history and theory of crisis more generally, led him to argue that such financial booms and busts were excrudescences on the more fundamental industrial basis whose instability was rooted primarily in class conflicts rather than monetary exchanges. Marx thus showed the limits to the power of the English state to regulate directly a financial system which only seemed to have detached itself from its class basis.

With regard to the obstacles created by the working class to the capitalist use of money, Marx not only provided a theory of the working class as an autonomous and increasingly revolutionary subject, but also the elements of a theory of the wage as an expression not of exploitation but of working class power. In his own political work, this thrust was implicit in his endorsement of wage struggles against Weston.[12] Workers had to fight for higher wages and resist wage decreases, he argued, to develop their ultimate power to overthrow the system. Moreover, there was in his formulation of the circuit of the working class acquisition and expenditure of money (LP-M-C) a view that, from the point of view of the workers (as opposed to that of capital) the purpose of money was life through consumption (as opposed to the reproduction of life as labour power).[13] However, it was also clear in his work that he saw real short term limits to wage struggles (e.g. in the ability of capital to respond to reductions in profits by a strike on investments).[14] Indeed, his other well known argument with fellow leftists over the politics of money also emphasized the limits to ability of the working class to use money in its own interest. That second debate was with Proudhon and his followers over the idea of a People's Bank. They thought that if the working class could take over and control increasing amounts of money it could undercut capitalist power while building its own alternative social order. Marx blasted this scheme as illusory arguing that no manipulation of money could do away with the social relations of capitalism (e.g. the imposition of class domination through work) and that they had to be overthrown directly.[15] Beyond these moments of argumentation, however, there was much in his theory yet to be developed and it would take a generation of struggle to reveal and develop those elements which could articulate other aspects of the working class use of money against capital.[16]

For the moment, I want to employ these elements of Marx's analysis of the class character of money in an analysis of a later period, the one immediately preceding the current crisis, a period many of us call the Keynesian era and others call that of Fordism.

MONEY IN THE KEYNESIAN ERA

If Marx's theoretical critique and careful historical examination could leave no doubt about the crudity of the Bank of England's attempts to manage the amount of money in circulation, and through it the rhythm of development, that critique can provide only a starting point to grasp the much more sophisticated efforts of the Keynesian state, first in its American incarnation and then in its world-wide embodiments. For although the Keynesian state arose on the ashes of the Great Crash of 1929 – brought on in part by precisely those speculative monetary fevers which Marx had identified in the 1850s and in part by other sources of crisis which he had also located in the class dynamics of capitalist development – it had much more power-ful tools for the management of monetary flows. While we can easily imagine Marx's satisfaction at the spectacles of the Crash, of the counter-productive monetary policies which followed it and at the explosions of working class struggles which ensued, it is certain that he would have had to seriously evaluate the new kinds of monetary manipulation which Keynes suggested and which came to be practiced in the wake of his *General Theory of Employment, Interest and Money*.

What Marx's analysis of money has shown is that at the heart of all the roles played by money, both actual and possible, are the power relations of class in any given period. In the period at hand, that of the Great Depression following the Crash, those power relations were shifting in epochal ways. On the material foundations reorganized a decade earlier by Frederick Taylor and Henry Ford (the develop-ment of mass production) and the IWW (with its broad organization of unskilled workers) arose a wholly new structure of working class power: that of the factory mass workers to impose collective bargaining and a new kind of unionism at the industrial level coupled with the social power to impose full employment, rising wages, social security, unemployment compensation and other pillars of a new 'welfare' state. The mandate was for a truly 'new deal' and it was one to which only state institutions at the federal level had the power to respond. At the heart of Keynes' theory, and subsequently of capitalist state policy, was an understanding of the need to respond positively and creatively to that mandate.[17] The vehicle of response was money.

Despite the usual division of Keynesian policy into 'monetary' and 'fiscal' realms, we must not overlook how both involve a highly so-phisticated manipulation of the class content of monetary flows. In both cases the basic Keynesian response to the stagnation of the Great Depression was the same: permit and stimulate an expansion of the flow of money in such ways as to stimulate not only expendi-ture but also investment, employment and output.

On the monetary side, Keynesian policy could build on the insti-tutional structures established in reaction to the kinds of destabilizing speculation that Marx had analyzed. In response to recurrent waves of financial speculation, bank panics and collapse (and to populist demands for banking regulation) in the nineteenth century, the Federal Reserve System had been created in 1913 to stabilize banking practices through the regulation of reserves and more flexible issue of bank notes. In response to the speculative stock market boom which began in the mid-1920s and crashed in 1929 (financed in large part by bank credit) and resultant failures of thousands of banks, and to the powerlessness of the Federal Reserve to counteract the collapse, new financial legislation was passed to further dampen speculation and prevent financial instability. The Federal Reserve System was given the power to raise and lower reserve requirements (and thus control the amount of bank credit). The stock market was regulated by the Fed and a new Securities and Exchange Commission. The Federal Deposit Insurance Corporation was created to insure demand deposits – long since the largest component of the money supply – and implement rigorous new policies of bank examination. Commercial banks were barred from the securities markets. These measures, together with a variety of new federal lending facilities such as the Federal Housing Administration, expanded the availability of money to the banking system and lowered interest rates in ways that increased the availability of money for real rather than speculative investment. Before long the rise in working class income would lead to a further adaptation of capitalist finance: the emergence of widespread consumer credit, from lines of retail and bank credit to omnipresent credit card usage.

So important were these new powers and constraints on the fetishistic pursuit of monetary profit without regard to real investment, that the kind of speculative financial instabilities of the sort that had characterized the whole of the nineteenth and the first decades of the twentieth century virtually disappeared. The period of the Keynesian state was one that saw 'monetary' policy (i.e. those activities of the Fed aimed at regulating banks and financial flows) preoccupied not with avoiding speculation or panics but rather with encouraging the financing of accumulation through low interest rates, the achievement of full employment and the management of the price level. Its success was partially manifested in high corporate profits which made possible a new era of self-financed investment with historically low recourse to outside financial capital.[18]

On the fiscal side, Keynesian policy was employed, in the aggregate, to encourage accumulation through the expansion of federal government expenditures, the limitation of taxation and deficit financing when necessary.[19] In more detailed terms, the Keynesian budget was structured to support consumption (from social security and welfare through the National Labor Relations Board to progressive income taxation) while also expanding expenditures which supported investment and raised productivity (from well established funding of R&D in agriculture through the direct support for new Cold War industries and the development of whole new technologies to investment in 'human capital').

Keynesian control over money required 'fine tuning' in a class sense: at the heart of the expansion of aggregate demand was the working class struggle to raise wages and benefits. Keynes had accepted that henceforth wages would ratchet upwards and policy makers from Roosevelt onward had supported changes that would virtually institutionalize this dynamic. But those increases had to be kept in line with the growth of productive capacity. Linking the growth of wages to the growth of productivity would harness the wage struggle to the development of the capitalist system as a whole – an institutionalization of relative surplus value. At the margin, monetary and fiscal policy in the aggregate could increase the flow of money to generate a little inflation to keep real wages in line with productivity growth, or reduce the flow to raise unemployment and slow the growth of nominal wages to the same purpose.

At the micro level, this meant formal 'productivity deals' in union collectively bargained contracts[20] and at the molecular level it meant that rising wages (increased money flows to workers) must be turned into kinds of consumption that led to more work. Thus, higher wages and consumer credit had to be channelled into the reproduction of life as labour power, more money bought automobiles to drive to work, more education as job training, and mass media with its purveyance of norms and values consistent with the dynamics of accumulation.[21] Similarly, money for the unemployed was not aimed at supporting autonomous lives of leisure or struggle but was tied to job search and the functioning of the labour market. Welfare and education money were not merely 'entitlements' but came to be conceptualized as investments in the creation of 'human capital' and higher levels of productivity.[22] In these ways, the Keynesian state control over money flows sought to permeate and direct virtually every sphere of society through the relative sizes of the flows and the conditions and constraints laid down on them. This complex system of manipulation has not always been visible because of the division of labour

– macroeconomists deal only with aggregate flows, public finance economists deal with fiscal balances, and specialists, of many different stripes, manage the particular monetary aspects of the elaborate social factory.[23]

The victory of the allies in the Second World War, the overthrow of colonialism and the pre-eminence of the United States imposed a new Pax Americana on the western world. This meant that the Keynesian solution to class contradictions in the United States became the norm in the western world, to be replicated or adapted in country after country. At the negotiations of Bretton Woods the American state was able to impose (against Keynes' own preference for an international currency and bank) fixed exchange rates, the hegemony of the dollar and the International Monetary Fund (IMF) as the key elements of a new international monetary order. That order depended on the ability of the Keynesian nation state to so manipulate internal money flows as to be able to achieve any required adjustments in international accounts. For example, an excess of imports over exports could be financed temporarily from reserves of foreign monies or by borrowings from the IMF but eventually the state would have to impose contraction and deflation – i.e. hammer down the growth of local working class wages – in order to cut imports and boost exports. The international regulation of the system of nation states thus depended on the internal power to regulate the balance of class power in money terms. Any fundamental collapse in that internal ability would, in turn, threaten the system as a whole.

Over time, the dominance of the American economy coupled with the rapid growth of trade and investment that accompanied the reconstruction of Europe and Japan (together with the much slower growth of the supply of monetary gold) meant not only the emergence of an effective dollar standard in the western world economy but before long a vast Eurodollar market as well. This evolution of international liquidity confirmed in the case of fiat money as well as in that of a metallic standard, and on a global scale, one of Marx's most dearly-held contentions: namely that the amount of money in circulation is determined primarily by the expansion of commodity trade and financial transactions.[24] Handled in part by the growing numbers of multinational industrial corporations, and in part by increasingly multinational private commercial banks, this dollar liquidity (that had been pumped into the world through American imports and foreign investments) became generally available to finance most monetary exchanges of the global system. In relation to this rapid expansion of private international money, the role of the IMF shrank although it continued to play a key backup role for countries unable to resolve their adjustment problems quickly enough to avoid crises.

THE CRISIS OF KEYNESIAN MONETARY CONTROL

The eventual failure of the Keynesian use of money, which had begun so powerfully in the 1930s and 1940s and been so successful on a global scale during the 1950s and early 1960s, was rooted in processes of political class recomposition by which workers, both waged and unwaged, launched new forms of struggle with which neither the existing monetary nor other state strategies were able to cope. By 'political recomposition' I mean changes in the distribution of class power among workers, and thus between workers as a whole and capital.[25] With respect to the United States, still dominant in the late 1960s, the most fundamental of these processes of recomposition had begun with a new wave of struggles by the unwaged which grew from dispersed origins in the late 1950s to uncontrollable mass movements capable of setting waged workers into motion by the middle of the 1960s. One of the important starting points was the Civil Rights Movement in the United States which mutated into the Black Power Movement, continued with the welfare rights movements and the urban insurgencies that exploded in several American cities, and spurred the development of minority student movements on campuses across the nation. Another set of starting points were the peasant struggles of Southeast Asia which soon circulated to American campuses, spurring a white student movement already in motion in response to human capital strategies which had turned universities into factories. The result was the anti-war movement that spread throughout society and helped give birth to both the environmental and women's movements.

Many of these struggles of the unwaged circulated in turn into the factories and offices of the American economy, both directly through the activities of militants and indirectly as a result of material changes they brought about. For example, black youths with experiences of struggles in the streets brought their militancy into factories already burgeoning with black workers who had come North in the 1940s and formed groups like the League of Revolutionary Black Workers which spearheaded rank and file struggles against the domination of union bureaucrats.[26] At the same time, the welfare rights struggles and urban insurgencies had provoked a vast expansion of 'human capital' investments which raised the floor of money income underlying the whole wage hierarchy and strengthened the battles of factory workers for higher wages and better benefits.[27]

What is important to see in the context of this discussion of the crisis of the Keynesian strategic use of money, is how these various struggles ruptured so many of the particular monetary moments of what had been a carefully crafted social organism held together with monetary sinews. In the case of the unwaged, the development of the various movements subverted the growing amounts of money invested to improve 'human capital' into resources for struggle. The 'Great Society' welfare monies being spent to pacify the cities and improve the production of labour power financed expanded struggles. Vast sums of money dispensed to education for the same purpose, were diverted into fighting the subordination of the universities to business and to financing the development of a whole anti-capitalist and anti-state counter-culture. The unyielding resistance of Southeast Asian peasants, soon supported by the American anti-war movement, forced capital to divert hundreds of billions of dollars from investment into police work on both sides of the Pacific.[28]

On the job, a new cycle of rank and file struggle for higher wages and better benefits, buttressed as we have just seen by the rising floor of unwaged income and streetwise militancy, undermined both the control of union bureaucrats and the all-important Keynesian 'productivity deals' it had been their duty to manage. Not only was this true in the private sector, but as the wave of struggle grew, it influenced public sector workers who launched their own new battles for self-organization and better compensation.[29] Moreover, the proliferation of access to consumer credit decreased the strength of the tie between consumption and work.[30] The manifestations were accelerating wage growth (and consumption which grew even faster thanks to credit) and declining productivity growth. Gains in wages were in turn ploughed back into new struggles and participation in the emerging counter-culture. The results were declining profits, accelerating inflation, growing corporate debt and 'fiscal crisis'.[31] While corporate price rises and the accommodating monetary policies of the Fed which made them possible, were largely able to limit the increase in real wages, this was no marginal Keynesian fine tuning but rather a wage–price spiral increasingly out of control. Whether the economists' analyses spoke of 'demand-pull' or 'cost-push' inflation, the meaning was the same: the Keynesian state had lost the ability to wield money in ways compatible with stable accumulation. At the heart of the growing economic and monetary crises was a loss of capitalist power – and as I have just explained, not only in the formal economy but in the larger social factory. Everywhere money which had heretofore acted as a tool of capital was serving instead to finance working class self-activity.

These ruptures in the Keynesian use of money at the domestic level had equally profound ramifications at the international level. The international monetary system, as we have seen, depended for its functioning on the Keynesian nation state being able to handle most problems of adjustment internally. The system had only limited capability for supranational remedies. National monetary crises not only had their manifestations at the international level but were rapidly destroying the ability of the institutions of the Bretton Woods system to solve those emerging problems.

One such problem, increasingly a direct spin-off of internal and external American crises, was that of a rapidly expanding international dollar liquidity. Whereas the earlier post Second World War period had been one of 'dollar scarcity' when dependable American money had been sought after to finance the regeneration of Europe and Japan, accelerating inflation at home coupled with American expenditures abroad associated with the Vietnam War (which contributed to a growing American balance of payments deficit), led foreign policy makers (whose banking systems it will be remembered were holding and using the growing quantity of 'Eurodollars') to speak of a 'dollar glut' and to blame the American state for exporting inflation and to complain about having their own monetary policies subordinated to the neutralization of American inflationary influence.

At the same time, the growth of the Eurodollar market, unregulated by any national or supranational institution, had recreated on a global scale some of the old dangers of financial speculation and instability that had been largely constrained locally. The existence of vast quantities of unregulated deposit money in commercial banks made possible a very high volitility in the Eurodollar market. Multinational corporations, as well as the banks themselves, could and did with growing ease shift funds from country to country, or from currency to currency in hedges or speculative betting on future changes in national policies or business conditions (which might well be the result of anticipated future changes in local balances of class power). So for example, if any given nation-state was having particular difficulty in imposing a 'cooling off' on its economy (i.e. rising unemployment and slower wage growth) due to working class resistance, massive movements of funds out of that country or out of its currency could provoke crisis or devaluation. In this way, such international movements of money were undermining the Keynesian framework created at Bretton Woods that left adjustment in the hands of local authorities. Changes in fixed rate parities became less frequent and more dramatic and the declining ability of national monetary authorities to cope with their own internal class problems led to increasingly widespread and deep dissatisfaction among them. The result was growing antagonism between nation-states as many European countries, led by French President De Gaulle, began to demand not only that America stop pumping dollars into the world economy but that the international monetary system be fundamentally changed.[32]

All of these crises, rooted as we have seen in a recomposition of class power, came to a head in 1971. The failure of a Keynesian-engineered recession in 1970 in the United States to slow the growth of wages, coupled with the emergence of an American trade deficit and a run on the dollar in the spring of 1971 forced the Nixon adminstration to make fundamental changes. The action taken was the ending of the convertablity of the dollar into gold (and thus of the Bretton Woods system of fixed exchange rates), state intervention into domestic wage bargaining and price setting (a wage–price freeze) and a 15% import tax surcharge which, along with the forthcoming devaluation of the dollar, undercut real wages in the United States and shifted costs of adjustment to America's trading partners. In the background lay further, less immediately visible, but no less important changes in state management of money flows – including the beginning of American withdrawal from Vietnam and of the federal government from the war on poverty and the welfare state.

COUNTER-ATTACK: NEW APPROACHES TO THE CAPITALIST USE OF MONEY

Grasped in terms of the class conflict over money, the present period really dates from either the late 1960s or from 1971, depending upon whether you want to put emphasis on the working class subversion of money or the capitalist counter-attack against the crisis it caused. For the purposes of this chapter I have chosen the latter approach and in this final section I deal with the period of the last twenty years, during which time the policy makers of the capitalist state – in both its national and supranational forms – have repeatedly sought, and have been repeatedly frustrated in their attempts, to regain control over money and to create an effective role for it in managing the accumulation of capital.

The central, and so far the most successful, element of this capitalist effort has been the attempt to withdraw money from the control of workers, both directly and indirectly. During the first decade of the period under consideration the withdrawal of money took the form of direct attacks on income subsidies and the indirect inflationary undercutting of the real wage. In the second decade, while attempts to lower income subsidies persisted and intensified, the use of inflation was abandoned in favor of massive unemployment and attacks on nominal wages. In both periods, state policies (both monetary and fiscal) played an active role at all levels: local, national and international.

The other, and so far only partially successful, element of this capitalist effort has been the attempt to redirect money flows into a renewed imposition of work under conditions profitable enough to fuel a new cycle of accumulation. The mechanisms of this redirection have been both financial and otherwise, both national and international. They have been managed by banks, corporations, government agencies and international institutions. Let us examine some examples of both of these efforts and what has become of them.

First of all, in the 1970s, capitalist policy makers sought to turn two of their monetary problems into solutions to their underlying problem of eroded class power. One of these problems was accelerating inflation; the other was the breakdown of fixed exchange rates. The conversion of these two problems into solutions were pursued simultaneously during much of the decade. In both cases the international dimension was essential.

Efforts, which had begun in the late 1960s, to work out and formally agree upon a new international monetary system were abandoned under the pressure of crisis and disagreement. Between 1971 and 1973, the unilateral abrogation of Bretton Woods by the US government was followed up by a halting and antagonistically negotiated transition to an ad hoc regime of flexible exchange rates – a solution that would eventually be legalized at the IMF meetings of 1976 at Jamaica.[33] Essentially, faced with a crisis of Keynesian control at the level of national class relations, the major western governments opted for a monetary mechanism of international adjustment which would, in principle, occur automatically without their having to intervene overtly with domestic policy measures subject to working class attack. International difficulties, such as the American trade deficit whose emergence in early 1971 had helped precipitate the crisis of the old regime, would be solved by changes in exchange rates which would automatically float to the level required to bring about adjustment, e.g. a depreciation of the value of the dollar *vis-à-vis* other currencies would make imports more expensive and exports less so and thus tend to correct the imbalance. At the same time, those same national governments accorded a greatly expanded power to the supranational IMF to exercise 'surveillance' over exchange rate practices as well as increased resources which buttressed the role of the IMF in managing adjustment financing. In these ways, national governments sought to insulate themselves from domestic class conflicts over economic policy by shifting to international adjustment mechanisms virtually invisible to the average worker.

The increased resources for the IMF were also required to help manage the other monetary strategy of this period: the financing of a rapid acceleration in inflation that would go beyond limiting the growth of real wages to undercut them and transfer value from workers to capital. The vehicles for this acceleration were provided by changes in American domestic policies and by the acceptance of certain policy changes by other nation states. The former involved the quite conscious effort on the part of the Nixon administration to raise dramatically agricultural prices by cutting back on production and expanding export demand (mostly through the infamous Russian grain deal of 1972). The ostensible purpose of these efforts were to increase the value of American exports to help cope with the new trade deficit. The result was also to dramatically raise food prices – which would undercut real wages – both at home and abroad.[34] The acceptance of outside policy changes came with the passive American reaction to the OPEC-engineered dramatic rise in oil prices in 1974. Despite public protestations to the contrary, the American government sanctioned the price increases and international capital sought to utilize them to achieve a gigantic transfer of value from oil consumers to business as OPEC surpluses were deposited in the commercial banking system. Oil, like food, was a basic good whose price increase tended to undercut the real wage as it was passed along through the economy into the prices of all consumption goods produced with its help – either directly as an input (gasoline, fertilizer, plastics) or indirectly (as an energy input in virtually all production).[35]

Thus, while national governments demonized the 'Arabs', blamed them for this inflationary assault on western wages and used oil inflation as an excuse to impose recession via tight money, international capital quietly went to the bank to borrow OPEC petrodollars for new capital investment.[36]

Unfortunately for capital neither of these manipulations of money flows worked out as planned. Instead of bringing about international adjustment in ways that preserved national governments from popular reproach, not only did flexible exchange rates in the presence of the enormous quantity of highly liquid Euromonies turn out to be highly volatile and destabilizing to the 'international investment climate', but national states were repeatedly forced by popular pressure to intervene in foreign exchange markets, buying and selling their currency to insulate their working classes from the effects that would have resulted from free floats. Such repeated interventions resulted in the system being called one of 'dirty floats' and proved that there was no easy monetary escape from confrontation with their domestic class problems. Dissatisfaction also lead the monetary authorities of several European countries to move back towards fixed exchange rates, through the 'snake' and the European Monetary System (EMS) in 1979 to recent negotiations for the creation of a single European currency. As Robert Triffin explained to US policy makers, the European return to at least locally fixed exchange rates was an attempt to create a situation where local attacks on the working class (e.g. imposition of austerity) could be justified by the moral obligation to adhere to international commitments.[37]

In the case of food and oil driven inflation, the working classes of the oil-consuming world proved to be more powerful than anticipated and were able, despite recession and higher unemployment in 1974–5, to drive up money wages enough to prevent a fall in their real value. The result was an acceleration of inflation which did nothing to restore profits or business stability and burgeoning trade deficits as sustained demand kept oil imports high and recession limited exports. The need to finance those trade deficits, in turn, meant that vast quantities of the petrodollars that had been expected to be available for investment had to be recycled to balance of payments support – partly with the help of a new IMF Oil Facility. In short, neither strategy was able to bring about a dramatic reduction of the money wage toward the restoration of an equality with productivity or of an earlier Keynesian era share of profits.

More successful in this period of the 1970s were the efforts of the state to cut the flow of money to the unwaged and to public workers through either piecemeal attacks on particular programmes or more general austerity through the mechanism of 'fiscal crisis'. While some attacks failed, such as those on Food Stamps which began under Nixon and were renewed under Ford and Carter, others were more successful.[38] In retrospect, the 1974–5 fiscal crisis of New York City proved to be the forerunner of a much more generalized state strategy of using budgetary (as well as international) imbalances and public debt as levers to attack all forms of working class income. The 'crisis' in the New York City budget derived from three phenomena: first, working class struggles which diverted city expenditures into social programmes and higher public employee wages and benefits that had to be financed in part by increasing taxes, second, an eroding tax base as businesses and high income white collar workers fled the growing power of other workers in the city, and third, a growing recourse by the city to borrowing in order to finance its deficits. The development of these trends from the mid-1960s to the mid-1970s prepared the way for a bank and state monetary counterattack against the New York City working class. It came with the refusal of the banks to roll over the city's debt except on condition of the imposition of austerity, i.e. cuts in city worker wages and reductions in public services. At the same time, oversight of the management of city government was granted to a series of specially created oversight and control boards, further undercutting the ability of local workers to resist (see also Chapter 4 in this volume).[39]

The application by capital of the methods used in New York spread quickly to other parts of the world, e.g. Egypt and Poland in 1976 where other 'fiscal crises' and the pressure of financial bodies (the IMF) were used to attack wages and standards of living, and was eventually generalized through the international debt crisis beginning in 1982. Because I have dealt with the debt crisis elsewhere,[40] here I only want to point out that as in New York City it often involved both the working class subversion of borrowed money and the use of monetary terrorism by the state (both national and supranational) to end that subversion by reducing both the flow of money to workers and its real value. Not only have all IMF 'adjustment programmes' which have been imposed as a condition of the roll over of debt called for the reduction of public expenditures that put money in the hands of workers (food subsidies, public employee wages, investment in higher education) but they have also imposed local currency devaluations, privatizations, drastic cutbacks in consumption imports, recession and high unemployment – all of which effectively undercut workers' ability to obtain and use money.

Historically, however, the generalization of the strategy of monetary austerity, originated not with particular private creditor institutions as it did in New York, but rather with the highest levels of capitalist policy making: the IMF and the executive branch of the United States government. Throughout the late 1970s, the IMF called repeatedly for the subordination of macroeconomic policy to a concerted attack on inflation – its euphemistic way of calling for an attack on the working class whose power it quite correctly perceived to be at the base of rising prices. Whereas the European ruling class had sought these ends through a return to locally fixed exchange rates, Jimmy Carter and the Federal Reserve responded to this call when they adopted a militant anti-working class monetarism at the end of the 1978.[41]

'Monetarism' is understood here as both economic theory and economic policy. Throughout the Keynesian period, when money was being wielded with finesse to manage class conflicts within growth, the economic theory of 'monetarism' existed only at the margins of theoretical and policy discussions, mainly within the walls of the University of Chicago where it was being crafted by Milton Friedman and his colleagues. As long as inflation was a minor phenomenon, indeed could be seen as useful in 'greasing the gears of the economy' and in moderating real wages, the monetarist desire to limit the role of the Fed to the management of a slow and steady growth of the money supply received little attention from those responsible for 'fine tuning' the class relations of accumulation. When, however, the productivity deal was ruptured and inflation began to grow in the late 1960s and accelerated in the mid-1970s with the incease of basic good prices and wages, the failures of Keynesian policies (and thus theories) opened space for a rapid increase in the influence of monetarist theories and policies. If Keynesianism had become hegemonic because of its ability to cope with the deflation of the Great Depression, monetarism replaced it by offering an analysis (too rapid growth of the supply of money) and a cure for inflation.[42]

The cure, of course, was monetary restriction and a shift in Fed policy from the accomodation of wage increases and the attempt to encourage investment by keeping interest rates low to the limitation of the growth of the money supply to make accelerating inflation impossible. This shift occurred in 1979 when Carter appointed Paul Volcker as head of the Fed. He immediately imposed a dramatic reduction of the money supply which drove interest rates to record highs and plunged the country and the world into depression. The economic theory of monetarism – which includes a modern variant of the quantity theory – was almost as full of money fetishism as the mercantilist thought fought by the classical political economists. But while this provided surviving Keynesians with endless material for critique by insisting that theory should explicitly grasp the real economic relations of which money is only a part, monetarist policy had a much more obvious class content: not only did depression and high unemployment attack working class wages directly by throwing millions out of work and indirectly through the dramatic growth of the reserve army, but part of the limitation of credit was aimed directly at reducing the availability of consumer credit, and thus retying consumption more directly to work.[43] Marx's old warnings about the ability of capital to limit wage increases through crisis and unemployment were suddenly relevant in a way they had not been since the 1930s.

This class content was made even more visible by the budgetary strategies of the 'fiscal crisis' discussed above. The monetary attack on the wage was complemented by supply-side budgetary measures to shift value–money from the working class to capital. Although this process began under Carter, it accelerated and received a much clearer articulation under the Reagan adminstration in the 1980s. 'Supply-side' economics, along with monetarism, became the new state economic doctrine, definitively displacing Keynesianism. Deregulation to cut business costs, tax cuts in favour of business, and a shift in the composition of government expenditures from those benefiting workers to those benefiting capital were, along with tight money, the explicit policies of the new regime.[44]

Although, once again, as in the 1970s there were successes in cutting social programmes, especially in the first year of the first Reagan adminstration, there were also failures. The defensive countermobilization of a wide variety of targeted groups, from those defending food stamps for the poor to those defending social security for the middle class, succeeded in preventing much of what had been slated for elimination under Reagan's supply-side programme.[45] Given the successful resistance to such cuts, the Reagan programme of reduced taxes but not-adequately-reduced expenditures produced a skyrocketing budget deficit which could be funded only by massive foreign borrowing from Europe and Japan. The result was that when business discontent over the depression and over federal crowding-out in money markets combined with the threat of Mexico to default in the debt crisis, Volcker was forced to ease up on monetary policy and lower interest rates in the Fall of 1982. When he did so, his explicit emphasis was on stimulating consumption, not investment. The long slow recovery that followed had something of a Keynesian flavor to it, much to the distaste of monetarists and supply-siders. The fact that the pattern of unemployment, income tax cuts and financial deregulation had had the effect of shifting money income from waged workers to salaried workers and managers – financing the yuppy generation – meant that this 'consumption-led' recovery was based on a new class composition, but it was not the investment-led growth envisaged by the supply-side policy makers.

This history of class conflict over money at the level of the state was taking place in the midst of a much wider set of conflicts in the private sphere between workers and individual employers. Although initially in the background of Reagan policy, the administration's hardline attack on the air controllers signalled the beginning of a widespread assault on the strongest sectors of the American working class – where strength is measured in money terms. Along with state sponsored high unemployment, and attacks on welfare designed to cut the floor out from under the wage hierarchy, deregulation – which had been sold with the rationale of 'getting the government off our backs' – played a key role in private efforts to drive down wages and benefits. It not only directly reduced costs to business that had been driven up by workers' struggles (e.g. for work place safety, for environmental improvements) but it made it possible for business to reorganize itself at both the corporate and industrial level. Chapter 11 was used to force concessionary cuts in wages and benefits and increased ease of entry into a variety of industries, such as the airlines, made it easier for capital to reorganize itself in new companies free of unions – and thus free of the old Keynesian formal collective bargaining. Where the unions had proved incapable of containing workers within limits compatible with profits, unions were avoided and the threat of unemployment wielded to hold down wages and benefits.

At the same time, many corporations took increasing advantage of falling wages in the Third World, also imposed by monetary terrorism (in these cases managed by the IMF), to pit lower waged workers against higher paid workers by threatening to move and by actually moving production operations abroad, e.g. American firms moving into Mexico, Northern European firms moving into the Mediterranean area, Japanese and South Korean firms moving into Southeast Asia. As factories were closed, and once highly paid workers thrown down from their place in the wage hierarchy, in Detroit, Liverpool, Lille, Hamburg, Kyoto and Seoul, new factories were opened in Mexico City, Spain, Bangkok and Singapore where considerably less money, or any other form of income, had to be conceded to the working class in exchange for harder, more dangerous work for longer hours.

Efforts to facilitate such multinational decomposition of the global structure of class power involved efforts to reduce obstacles to trade (both merchandise and services) and money flows (both portfolio and direct investment). Necessary for the success of corporate geographical reorganization, these reductions were partially achieved through IMF pressure on national governments facing the need for debt rescheduling. Along with the budget cuts, devaluations, and privatizations mentioned earlier, they were also forced to abandoned various protectionist measures which had been used to support domestic industries and constraints on capital movements designed to limit the repatriation of foreign investment profits. In short, freedom for capital to redeploy money in ways which would allow it to regain control over the working class required 'free markets' of all kinds.[46] This freedom has also been sought through the Uruguay Round of GATT negotiations and the American push for a North American Free Trade Agreement (NAFTA) as a first step toward a hemispheric common market.[47] In both cases the most important obstacle to be overcome – the one that lay behind the conflicting negotiating positions of the various nation states – was the opposition mounted by various groups of workers, from rice farmers in Japan and South Korea, through farmers in Europe and widespread resistance by industrial workers, environmentalists and even peasants[48] throughout North America who clearly understood the threat of workers being pitted against each other through international trade.[49]

At this point, I want to turn from the various efforts to withdraw money and income from the working class to the efforts of the capitalist class to redirect it into accumulation. Part of this story has been necessarily mentioned already: the efforts to convert higher oil prices into investment capital which largely failed, the cross-border geographical relocation of investment which has largely succeeded and the industrial reorganizations which have had mixed results. But beyond these particular efforts there is the broader question of the degree to which capital has been sucessful in using money in such a way as to found a broad-based, new cycle of accumulation, comparable, though perhaps differently managed, to the one organized by the Keynesian state.

The answer to this question, I believe, must be largely negative. Not only was the long recovery (1983–9) from Reagan's monetarist depression weak, not only did the Fed's single-minded pursuit of a repressive 'zero-inflation' anti-wage policy produce a new depression on the eve of the Gulf War in 1990, but the whole attempt to found a new cycle of accumulation was undermined by two phenomena, one old, one new.

The old phenonema were the persistant struggles of the working class, both defensive and offensive, both within the United States and in other parts of the world. I have already discussed the stalwart, and fairly successful, resistance formed against Reagan–Bush efforts to cut social programmes which limited the reductions actually achieved, thus keeping billions of dollars in the hands of the working class. But we must also recognize that besides trying to maintain a standard of living already gained in earlier years (and in real terms this was in fact beaten down), the working class has also ploughed considerable amounts of its money into the pursuit of its own ends. During the 1980s these included, notably, the achievement of black working class autonomy in South Africa, the spread and defence of revolution in Central America, the struggle for Palestinian liberation, the pursuit of an ecological agenda that requires (whether eveyone participating sees it or not) the overthrow of capitalism, the expansion of women's power, the expansion of the rights of minorities and indigenous peoples, cultural innovation and so on. All of this represented a continuing, and in many directions expanding subversion of money away from capitalist purposes and into struggle. Throughout this period the repeated failures of capital to manage the debt crisis in such a way as to regain sufficient control for accumulation measured the strength of working class resistance. Where economic means failed, military intervention – especially the Gulf War in 1991 – provided a vehicle for both direct and indirect attacks on working class power: direct in the case of the oil-producing proletariat which saw their shop floor militarized and a vast process of decomposition inflicted through death, prisons and forced deportations, indirect as the 'crisis' was used to rationalize renewed attacks on working class income (higher oil prices) and its qualitative gains (reduced environmental controls, renewed push for nuclear energy, increased racism in shaping harsher policies for controling immigrant workers).

The new phenomenon was the enormous diversion of money away

from the contested terrain of production and onto the terrain of speculation, suddenly and vastly expanded as a result of financial deregulation that removed many of the constraints put in place during the Keynesian era. That deregulation, which began under Carter, accelerated under Reagan and has not been reversed under Bush or Clinton, made possible the rapid development of a wide array of new financial practices, many well adapted to speculative purposes (e.g. junk bonds). When combined with a new White House ethos (widely publicised by the media) of wealth and greed, the result was an explosion of speculative activity not seen since the 1920s. Instead of being ploughed into investments that might resolve the long-standing class antagonisms, vast resources of money, human talent and organisational effort were redirected into the quickest and most lucrative profit gimmicks available. With rates of return to paper investments sky-high, in part because of the Fed's tight money policies supporting high rates of interest, and industrial rates of return as low as ever under the pressure of depression, the invitable occurred. Money 'capital' flowed into paper and speculative investments fuelling the long bull stock market and an ever deeper participation of banks and Savings & Loan Associations in an equally speculative booming real estate market. The results, as we now know, have included the stock market crash in 1987, the widespread collapse of Savings & Loan Associations and the current crisis in American banking. All those fantastic manias and panics which had fascinated Marx in the 1850s, but whose study had completely disappeared from both neoclassical and Marxist economics during the Keynesian era, were suddenly reborn in what *Business Week* did not hesitate to label, with considerable dismay, a 'casino economy'.[50]

This re-emergence in the late twentieth century of the very fetishistic pursuit of money to the neglect of the management of class relations has undoubtedly hindered the resolution of the crisis of those relations which capital has sought for the last twenty years. By factilitating the diversion of massive amounts of resources away from more serious experiments with the restructuring of the class composition, Reaganomics undercut the very 'supply-side' revolution it sought to bring about. The Reaganauts rejected the arguments of more Keynesian supply-siders, such as Lester Thurow, who wanted a federal 'industrial policy' to accelerate restructuring, in favor of 'leaving investment decisions in the hands of the private sector'. But while part of the private sector was deeply engaged in a debate about alternative managerial models of controlling working class subjectivity (e.g.

the debate over the 'Japanese model'), a much larger part was content to accelerate the concentration of money in its own hands at the expense of workers. The seriousness of the way in which these policies subverted more constructive attempts to cope with the crisis can be measured only partly by looking at the amount of money diverted. More important is to recognize and study the substantive efforts on the part of capital to re-deploy its money in the direction of real accumulation.

Such efforts have included substantial investments in the development and utilization of new technologies that raise the organic composition of capital and allow a reorganization of production and the decomposition of working class power. The most widely recognized of such investments have been those transforming Fordist mass production, such as manufacturing mechanization in the form of computer-controlled robotization which has allowed the replacement of assembly line production with flexible, just-in-time, small batch production managed by a new kind of worker.[51] Such new technologies are now being introduced not only in old, high waged plants that are enabled to lay off redundant workers, but also in the new, displaced manufacturing plants in the Third World, where a much lower waged labour force is proving itself quite able to manage such production processes. Less traditional but of growing importance is the reorganization of information flows (including those involved in the genesis of science and technology itself) through increasingly decentralized but complex webs of computer linked communication.[52] Such 'post-Fordist' approaches to the organization of work have included attempts to relink private industry and public education as a means to relaunch the growth of productivity (i.e. by harnessing the new abilities of working class subjectivity).[53] Both of these directions of capitalist investment come together in decentralized networks of largely self-managed, highly flexible production in which both the products and the technology of their production are being constantly modified by the workers themselves. Nowhere is this more obvious than in the software industry which has grown so dramatically in recent years.[54] Such new developments are creative responses to the emergence of the powerful and diverse working class subjectivity which threw the Keynesian form of capital into crisis. Their spread and development require considerable resources, many of which have and continue to be wasted by business people who have forgotten that the business of business is not just profit but the organization of society through the imposition and management of work.

CONCLUSION

Within the context of the persistence of crisis, and the failures of past policy measures to achieve a solution, the most successful capitalist roles of money have been repressive rather than creative. The victories of monetary terrorism, in the central capitalist countries as in the Third World, have not been matched by a redirection of money into a restructuring of class relationships capable of restabilizing capitalist power and relaunching a new cycle of accumulation. The complex fabric of monetary relationships established within the context of the Keynesian social factory, and ruptured by the struggles of unwaged and waged workers, has not been repaired and no new, coherent tissue of such monetary relations has been woven.

While there are a variety of new approaches and experiments which attempt to harness the emerging new characteristics of working class subjectivity, they have neither been implemented on a broad enough scale, nor produced stable enough results to constitute a successful response to the crisis in class relations that began over twenty years ago. At the level of international monetary relations, the failure of dirty floats has been followed by the failures of the EMS.[55] At the level of production, we have, perhaps, already witnessed the first crisis of incipient 'post-Fordism'.[56] At the level of reproduction, women and students continue to resist the restructuring of their self-activity to be productive of labor power.[57]

The persistence of the crisis, including the crisis in the capitalist use of money, has been such as to allow us to raise a series of far-reaching questions. Will the end result of the crisis be some kind of restabilization of the social relations of capitalism or will we be able to act as subjects whose unchainable self-activities finally achieve the historical culmination of capitalist history and the crafting of new post-capitalist worlds? All around the world, from the streets of Los Angeles to those of Eastern Europe, from Brixton, in London to Tepito in Mexico City, the future of money is up in the air. Can it be converted into capital? We have seen the difficulties. Can it be used by the working class to accentuate the crisis and widen alternatives? We have seen some of the ways. And finally, can it be dispensed with along with all the other forms of capital and all the other forms of unidimensional measures in favour of a world where we judge ourselves and each other by a constantly reinvented set of values in a diversity of free cultural settings knit together by a new kind of democratic politics?

Notes

1. On the role of money in the 'civilizing' of the Scottish Highlands after the rising of 1745 and David Hume's contribution to it, see Caffentzis (1992).
2. Linebaugh (1992).
3. Marx (1977), Chap. 31.
4. Such avoidance of work may take the form of regular weekly absenteeism from waged work, such as that which was rampant in the late 1960s, or it may take the form of only periodical waged employment when enough money can be earned to support a subsequent period free of the labor market. Within the traditional family, where some (usually men) work for a wage and others (usually women and children) do not, those doing the unwaged work of reproduction in the home may be able to channel enough of the wage into labour saving uses (from washing machines to eating out) as to free themselves at least partially from such work. Similar phenomena exist with other forms of income besides the wage including the market income of peasants and unemployment insurance – both of which may be sufficient to allow considerable periods away from work for capital.
5. Such projects of self-valorization, by their very otherness to capital, also involve its negation. The point here is to differentiate those projects of struggle which simple resist or attack capitalist domination from those which seek to establish new bases for social development beyond it.
6. Marx's analysis of these developments can be found in various articles on the English financial problems published in the period 1857 to 1858 and in Chap. 2, Part C of his *'Contribution to the Critique of Political Economy'* (1859).
7. Linebaugh (1992), pp. 210–13. Hume's solution to such problems, as Caffentzis (1992) shows, was the imposition of a unique and metallic monetary standard – not out of any gold fetishism but as a means to enforce monetary discipline.
8. This history is reexamined and reinterpreted in class terms by Caffentzis (1989).
9. 'There's nothing more frequent,' Defoe worried, 'than for an Englishman to work until he has got his pocket full of money, and then go and be idle', cited by Linebaugh (1992), p. 54.
10. Marx's account appears in his work *Class Struggles in France* and it has been analyzed at length in Ricciardi (1985).
11. Marx's comments on the role of banks in primitive accumulation appear in *Capital*, Vol. I, Chap. 31 on 'The Genesis of the Industrial Capitalist'. His writings on the Crédit Mobilier consist primarily of a series of newspaper articles written in late 1857, most of which appear in Vol. 15 of Marx and Engels, *Collected Works*. Their importance to Marx's analysis of capitalist finance has been highlighted in Ricciardi (1985), Chap. 5; See also Bologna (1993).
12. The reference is to Marx's 1865 speech to working men which was crafted as a response to the arguments of the Owenite John Weston

against wage struggles. See Marx, 'Value, Price and Profit', in Marx and Engels, *Collected Works*, Vol. 20, pp. 101–49.

13.   Marx, *Capital*, Vol. II, Chap. 1.

14.   Besides his comments in 'Value, Price and Profit', there is also his discussion in Vol. I, Chap. 25 of *Capital*, where he discusses wages in the context of the business cycle.

15.   See Marx's discussion in the chapter on Money of the *Grundrisse*. In the light of the character of Marx's argument against Weston, he might have been more generous in his treatment of Proudhon – and if he hadn't been so involved in a political struggle against him. While increased working class access to credit would no more bring down capitalism than increased wages, Marx might well have recognized how more credit, like more wages, and how the struggle for credit, like the struggle for wages, might play a useful role in the development of the power of the working class if pursued in non-utopian fashion.

16.   That generation was the one of the 1960s and 1970s in Italy that developed within the struggles of mass workers and then spread beyond them to unwaged and partially waged students, housewives and peasants. Theoretically speaking the Marxist articulation of the theory of the wage grew from a preoccupation with the political autonomy of working class demands to a recognition of the projects of practical self-valorization 'financed' with money increasingly separated from capitalist work.

17.   The seminal work in this interpretation is Negri (1968).

18.   This shift was heralded by socialist economists Baran and Sweezy as the coming of age of corporate 'monopoly capital' and ending the earlier era of 'finance capital'. See Baran and Sweezy (1964), which spelled out an analysis more based on neoclassical firm theory and Keynesian macroeconomics than Marxist theory.

19.   The concentration of money in capitalist hands via public debt and taxation which Marx had observed in the period of primitive accumulation had long since become an integral part of ongoing patterns of accumulation. The newly created Fed had facilitated this process during the First World War and continued to do so in the Keynesian era.

20.   The critique of such collaboration between unions and capitalist development although sanctioned by powerful communist or labour parties, was carried on for years in the oppositional culture of the Marxist extraparliamentary Left. Some examples in the United States can be found in the writings of the Johnson–Forest Tendency in the 1950s (e.g. C.L.R. James (Johnson) and Raya Dunayevskaya (Forest)) and in Italy in those of the New Left in the 1960s (e.g. Raniero Panzieri, Mario Tronti).

21.   The recognition of the integrative function of such managed expenditure has been clear in most critical discourses on 'consumerism' – even when these have lacked a class analysis. Note that the emphasis here is the reverse of the usual perspective on consumerism: instead of work being viewed as displaced by the organization of life around consumption, the argument is that 'consumerism' meant the structuring

of consumption in ways which led to more work. Being suckered into buying the latest model, meant being suckered into working more to earn the money necessary (or to pay off credit obligations). Indeed, as we will see below, where workers actually did begin to separate the use of money from work, it meant a crisis for capital.

22. For a Marxist reading of such 'human capital' investments see Caffentzis (1975).

23. The concept of the 'social factory' originates in the work of Mario Tronti in the early 1960s in Italy and was given an American articulation by the Cleveland group 'Modern Times' in 1974 and by *Zerowork* in 1975. See Tronti (1973, 1976).

24. And thus, indirectly, by the expansion of the imposition of work that produced the commodities and which is being financed by investment. As we will see shortly the crisis of dollar liquidity which so came to preoccupy western policy makers was a manifestation of the underlying crisis of class relations.

It is true that the basing of the post-Second World War international monetary order on the dollar, made possible a growth of money in excess of that required for the growth of trade and capital transactions, and that this possibility would be increasingly realized from the late 1960s on. What is interesting, however, is how the 'liquidity' issue was conceptualized and managed for so many years – such that the money supply grew with the needs of the international economy without generating either deflation or disruptive inflation.

25. See the Introduction to *Zerowork*, 1 (1975) and Moulier (1986).

26. See Romano and Stone (1947) Facing Reality (1964), Georgakis and Surkin (1975) and Georgakis (1981).

27. See Carpignano (1975) and Fox Piven and Cloward (1977).

28. Clearly much of the money paid to the military-industrial complex for war machinery financed investment and employment in war industries, and much has been made of this aspect of the 'permanent arms economy' as a feature of Keynesian state capitalism. However, in retrospect, not only was much of the war money spent on wasteful use values rather than investment, but the diversion of investment from civilian to war industries helped undermine the ability of American capitalists to respond to rising wage demands by raising productivity.

29. On these struggles of public sector workers and their relationship to conflicts in the private sphere as well as in the streets, see O'Connor (1973) Demac and Mattera (1977) and Lichten (1988).

30. For an interesting meditation on the implications of this weakening tie see Nicolas-Le Strat (1992).

31. The growing need of non-financial corporations to borrow from outside financial institutions shows just how little Baran and Sweezy's self-financing 'monopoly capital' was based on monopoly *per se* and how much on the particular composition of class relations characteristic of Keynesianism. With the crisis of the latter came the crisis of the former. Not surprisingly the growth of corporate debt spurred a new interest in Hilferding's work among some Marxists and a new pre-occupation with a supposed renaissance of 'finance capital'. See

the articles by Fitch and Fitch and Oppenheimer in *Socialist Revolution* in 1970 and O'Connor and Sweezy's responses. This whole debate, by separating the analysis of the relations among sectors of capital from that of the crisis in class relations, provided little help in understanding the new roles of money in the crisis.

32.   De Gaulle's Minister of Finance, Jacques Rueff, was a major spokesman for the yearnings of a certain part of the capitalist class for a restoration of the centrality of gold as an international money in reaction to the inability of the United States government to limit the supply of the dollar to amounts compatible with stable prices. Partly this was a certain gold fetishism and partly the same kind of preoccupation with monetary discipline that motivated Hume in the eighteenth century (see above) and would return again with the Reagan Gold Bugs in the 1980s in the wake of the inflation of the 1970s. There is an interesting parallel in the history of Marxist economics which has had its share of gold fetishists, totally convinced that the capitalist system is doomed because it has abandoned 'real' money!

33.   A useful overview, from a capitalist point of view, of these developments is contained in De Vries (1976). A Marxist analysis is certained in Marazzi, 'Money in the Wars Crisis', published in this volume.

34.   For a discussion of these policies in class terms see Cleaver (1977), pp. 35–40.

35.   This 'Sraffian' strategy of value transfer via inflation in basic goods prices was analyzed in Midnight Notes, *The Work/Energy Crisis and the Apocolypse*, 1981, now available in Midnight Notes, *Midnight Oil* (Boston: Autonomedia, 1992).

36.   For a class analysis of an early example of the kind of anti-working class monetarist restrictionism which would later be imposed on the world by the United States, see Berti (1975).

37.   Triffin (1978/1979).

38.   The successful resistance to those attacks on the Food Stamp Program are documented in Reynolds (1980).

39.   Those boards included the Municipal Assistance Corporation and the Emergency Finanial Control Board which made it possible to displace control over city finances to the state and federal level. For the story of the New York City fiscal crisis in class terms see Demac and Mattera (1977) and Lichten (1986).

40.   See Cleaver (1989).

41.   As opposed to the earlier case of Italy, cited above, the adoption of this strategy by the American Fed imposed higher interest rates on the world as a whole as other monetary authorities were forced to follow suit to avoid massive outflows of capital towards higher rates in the United States Despite such efforts by other central banks, as we will see, the United States was able to finance much its massive budgetary deficits with foreign money even in the depths of the subsequent Reagan Depression.

42.   It is beyond the scope of this chapter to discuss them all, but we should note that 'monetarism' narrowly defined was only one element of the 'New Classical' attack on Keynesian theory and policies which

has rationalized a whole series of 'market-oriented' policy shifts in this period, from deregulation to free trade.

43. For one account of the decision to attack consumer credit directly see: Greider (1987), pp. 181–7. According to Greider the impetus came from the President rather than Volcker. It was certainly consistent with Carter's then recent attacks on 'self-indulgence and consumption' and his calls for self-denial and sacrifice. See the text of his famous 15 July speech in the *New York Times* 16 July 1979.

44. For an analysis of the class content of 'supply-side' economics see Cleaver (1981). So obviously was the working class the central enemy of the Reagan administration, despite all its anti-Soviet rhetoric, that Fox Piven and Cloward denounced its policies, see Fox Piven and Cloward (1982).

45. See Cleaver (1986) and Palazzini (1992), which focuses on the battles over food stamps and social security.

46. The obvious exception to this pursuit of international 'free markets' has been the market in labour power. Whereas every effort has been taken to reduce constraints on the movement of commodity and money capital, workers have been subjected to the exact opposite: increasingly severe constraints on immigration and refugee mobility both through official policies (e.g. border controls) and through unofficial anti-immigrant racism. The presence of these controls is vivid testimony to the autonomy of working class mobility and the threat it has posed to capitalist power. If workers went, willy nilly, only where they were desired as labor power, no such controls would be needed. On constraints in Europe in reaction to immigrant autonomy see Moulier-Butang and Ewenzyck (1978). On the constraints of undocumented mobility in North America see Flores (1977).

47. The parallels with eighteenth and nineteenth century classical political economic arguments for free trade would seem to be obvious. Unfortunately those earlier arguments have usually been seen by Marxists as expressions of British imperialism rather than as responses to working class pressures. An exception is the work by Ricardo Salvatore on late eighteenth and early nineteenth century trade between Argentina, England and the United States which he analyzes in terms of the dynamics of class struggle in each country and the way in which trade itself transmits and circulates class antagonisms. See Salvatore (1987).

48. The participation by peasants in the anti-NAFTA movement in North America took a radical leap forward during the period in which this chapter was being edited for publication. On 1 January 1994, the day NAFTA was to go into effect in Mexico, the Indians of Chiapas launched surprise attacks on government control of four different cities and declared revolutionary war on the Mexican state. While their battle cries included age-old demands, such as the return of their lands and the end of oppression, they also quite explicitly linked their struggle to NAFTA. In a statement which was soon flashed around the world through both the mass media and oppositional cyberspace, one of the spokespersons of the Indian forces which invaded San Cristóbal de las Casas declared: 'The free trade agreement is a death certificate for the

Indian peoples of Mexico.' The amazingly rapid and widespread mo-
bilisation of support for the Indian struggle, both in Mexico and around
the world brought the Mexican government's counter-offensive to a
halt. The ability of such a localized and small-scale movement to trigger
such a vast movement of opposition would seem to indicate a maturity
of international working class resistance much greater than many have
realized. The threat to capital's international strategies of class decomposition was understood immediately by the North American business
press, which warned the Mexican government that any substantial
concession to the Indians would jeopardize planned increases in
capitalist investment. See, for example, *Business Week* (January 1994).

49.   Opposition to these trade pacts has obviously also come from various
      groups of capitalists who stand to lose from the reduction of various
      kinds of protection. This mixture of class interests in the opposition
      movement has made it succeptible to various kinds of populist ideol-
      ogy. What has been interesting, however, has been the spontaneous
      and widespread growth of a very sophisticated grassroots opposition
      – increasingly knit together internationally through flows of informa-
      tion and discussion facilitated by the use of international computer
      communications systems.

50.   Few were those among either mainstream economics or Marxism who
      paid any attention to the issue of speculative booms and busts before
      the 1980s. A notable exception was Hyman Minsky. The few others
      were mostly interested in 'financial fragility' as an historical issue, e.g.
      Kindleberger (1978).

51.   See Coriat (1990). On the debate over these patterns of post-Fordist
      capitalist restructuring see Coco and Vercellone (1990) and Bonefeld
      and Holloway (ed) (1991).

52.   See Lazzarato and Negri (1991) and Virno (1992).

53.   The degree of state involvement in such efforts to solve the 'crisis of
      education' has varied enormously from country to country, from
      countries like Japan and Germany where the state plays a key role to
      those like the United States where, in the absence of a coherent federal
      policy, the role of the state has been mostly limited to local govern-
      ments prostituting their school systems to the private sector in a com-
      petitive effort to attract an increased share of investment, jobs and
      taxes.

54.   Despite the existence of large-scale corporate management of parts of
      the software industry, more striking has been the role of autonomous,
      decentralized programming as well as similarly unmanaged circulation,
      modification and utilization. The difficulties of capitalist control of this
      kind of productive activity, however, have been clear from the beginning
      as most members of this growing community of 'workers' have insisted
      on their own independence – to the point of refusing to allow their
      'products' to be turned into commodities and adopting an ideology of
      free access to information.

55.   In September 1992, a few months after this chapter was originally
      written, these failures became dramatically obvious as Britain, then
      Italy and Ireland dropped out of the system and allowed their currencies

to depreciate far below the System's pemitted fluctuations. The refusal of several European governments to accept the Bundesbank's dictation of higher interest rates (the bank pushed its discount rate to a record 8.75% during July) and higher unemployment (the EC was predicting an increase to 9.5% for 1992 and 9.7% in 1993) must be understood as a failure to impose these anti-wage, anti-working class measures on their own workers. The summer of 1992 saw a whole cycle of strikes (local and general) throughout Europe against the attacks on both private and social wages (reductions in unemployment benefits, etc.) that culminated in the breakdown of the European ERM and threw into question the ability of European capital to impose an EMU as scheduled for 1997.

56. Negri (1993), pp. 11–15.
57. Despite the 1980s and 1990s 'backlash' against the women's movement, there has been neither a reversal of the gains made nor any clear-cut success in integrating new forms of the family within capital. Within education, the difficulties of transforming young people into malleable labour power continue. Despite the massive shift of resources from liberal arts to the professional schools in the 1970s and 1980s, the latest evidence suggests a 'perverse' (from the point of view of capital) flow of university students back into less job-oriented academic disciplines.

References

Baran, P. and Sweezy, P. (1964) *Monopoly Capital* (New York: Monthly Review Press).
Berti, L. (1975) 'Inflazione e recessione. La politica della Banca d'Italia (1969–1974)', *Primo Maggio*, 5 (Spring).
Bologna, S. (1993) 'Money and Crisis: Marx as Correspondent of the New York Daily Tribune, 1856–1857', *Common Sense*, 12 and 14.
Bonefeld, W. and Holloway, J. (1991) *Post-Fordism and Social Form: A Marxist Debate on the Post-Fordist State* (London: Macmillan).
Caffentzis, G. (1975) 'Throwing Away the Ladder: The Crisis in Higher Education', *Zerowork*, 1.
Caffentzis, G. (1989) *Clipped Coins, Abused Words and Civil Government: John Locke's Philosophy of Money* (New York: Autonomedia).
Caffentzis, G. (1992) 'Hume, Money and Civilization, or, Why was Hume a Metallist?', TS, University of South Maine, Portland.
Carpignano, P. (1975) 'US Class Composition in the 1960s', *Zerowork*, 1.
Cleaver, H. (1977) 'Food, Famine and International Crisis', *Zerowork*, 2.
Cleaver, H. (1981) 'Supply-side Economics: Splendori e miserie', *Metropoli*, 7(3) (December) (An English Language version is available from the author.)
Cleaver, H. (1986) 'Reaganisme et rapports de classe aux États-Unis', in Marie-Blanche Tahon and André Corten (eds), *L'Italie: Le Philosophe et le Gendarme* (Montreal: Éditeur VLB).
Cleaver, H. (1989) 'Close the IMF, Abolish Debt and End Development: a class analysis of the international debt crisis', *Capital & Class*, 36 (Winter).

Coco, G. and Vercellone, C. (1990) 'Les paradigmes sociaux du post-fordisme', *Futur Antérieur*, 4 (Winter).

Coriat, B. (1990) *L'atelier et le robot: essai sur le fordisme et la production de masse à l'âge de l'électronique* (Paris: Christian Bourgois).

Demac, D. and Mattera, P. (1977) 'Developing and Underdeveloping New York: The "Fiscal Crisis" and the Imposition of Austerity', *Zerowork*, 2.

De Vries, T. (1976) 'Jamaica, or the Non-Reform of the International Monetary System', *Foreign Affairs* (April).

Facing Reality (1964) *Negro Americans Take the Lead* (Detroit: Facing Reality).

Fitch, R. (1972) 'Sweezy and Corporate Fetishism', *Socialist Revolution*, 12, Vol. 2, No. 6 (November–December).

Fitch, R. and Oppenheimer, M. (1970a) 'Who Rules the Corporations? Part 1', *Socialist Revolution*, 4, Vol. 1, No. 4 (July–August).

Fitch, R. and Oppenheimer, M. (1970b) 'Who Rules the Corporations? Part 2', *Socialist Revolution*, 5, Vol. 1, No. 5 (September–October).

Fitch, R. and Oppenheimer, M. (1970c) 'Who Rules the Corporations? Part 3', *Socialist Revolution*, 6, Vol. 1, No. 6 (November–December).

Flores, E. (1977) *A Call to Action: An Analysis of Our Struggles and Alternatives to Carter's Immigration Program*, pamphlet, 28–30 October.

Fox Piven, F. and Cloward, R.A. (1977) *Poor Peoples' Movements* (New York: Panteon Books).

Fox Piven, F. and Cloward, R.A. (1982) *The New Class War: Reagan's Attack on the Welfare State and Its Consequences* (New York: Pantheon Books).

Georgakis, D. (1981) 'Young Detroit Radicals, 1955–1965', *Urgent Tasks*, 12 (Summer).

Georgakis, D. and Surkin, M. (1975) *Detroit: I Do Mind Dying, A Study in Urban Revolution* (New York: St Martin's Press).

Greider, W. (1987) *Secrets of the Temple: How the Federal Reserve Runs the Country* (New York: Simon & Schuster).

Kindleberger, C. (1978) *Manias, Panics and Crashes: A History of Financial Crises* (New York: Basic Books).

Lazzarato, M. and Negri, A. (1991) 'Travail immatériel et subjectivité', *Futur Antérieur*, 6 (Summer).

Lichten, E. (1986) *Class, Power and Austerity: The New York City Fiscal Crisis* (South Hadley: Bergin & Garvey).

Linebaugh, P. (1992) *The London Hanged* (Cambridge: Cambridge University Press).

Marx, K. (1859) *Contribution to the Critique of Political Economy* (London: Lawrence & Wishart).

Marx, K. (1967) *Capital*, Vol. II (International Publishers: New York).

Marx, K. (1973) *Grundrisse* (Penguin Books: Harmondsworth).

Marx, K. (1977) *Capital*, Vol. 1 (New York: Vintage).

Marx, K. and Engels, F. (1975–) *Collected Works* (London: Lawrence & Wishart).

Moulier, Y. (1986) 'L'Opéraisme Italien: Organisation-Representation-Idéologie, ou la Composition de Classe Revisitée', in Marie-Blanche Tahon and André Corten (eds), *L'Italie: Le Philosophe et Le Gendarme* (Montreal: Éditeur VLB).

Moulier-Butang, Y. and Ewenzyck, P. (1978) 'Immigration: The Blockage of Mobility in the Mediterranean Basin' (English typescript), originally in French in *Critique de l'Economie Politique*, Nouvelle Serie, 3(4), September.

Negri, A. (1968) 'John M. Keynes e la teoria capitalistica dello stato nel '29', *Contropiano*, 1; reprinted in S. Bologna *et al.*, *Operai e stato: Lotte operaie e riforma dello stato capitalistico tra rivoluzione d'Ottobre e New Deal* (Milano: Feltrinelli 1972); available in English as 'John M. Keynes and the Capitalist Theory of the State in 1929', in Negri, *Revolution Retrieved: Selected Writings on Marx, Keynes, Capitalist Crisis and New Social Subjects, 1967–83* (London: Red Notes 1988), pp. 9–42.

Negri, A. (1993) 'La premiére crise du postfordisme', *Futur Antérieur*, 16.

Nicolas-Le Strat, P. (1992) 'La monétarisation des rapports sociaux', *Future Antérieur*, 9.

O'Connor, J. (1971) 'Question: Who Rules the Corporations? Answer: The Ruling Class', 'Reply', *Socialist Revolution*, 7, Vol. 2, No. 1 (January–February).

O'Connor, J. (1973) *The Fiscal Crisis of the State* (New York: St Martin's Press).

O'Connor, J. and Fitch, R. (1971) 'Reply', *Socialist Revolution*, 7, Vol. 2, No. 1 (January–February).

Palazzini, K. (1992) 'Supply Side Economics, A Successful Counterattack?' (typescript) (April).

Reynolds, T. (1980) *The Food Stamp Explosion*, M.A. dissertation, University of Texas, Chapter 3.

Ricciardi, J. (1985) *Essays on the Role of Money and Finance in Economic Development*, Ph.D. thesis, University of Texas, Chapter 4.

Romano, P. and Stone, R. (1947) *The American Worker* (Detroit: Bewick).

Salvatore, R. (1987) *Class Struggle and International Trade: Rio de la Plata's Commerce and the Atlantic Proletariat, 1790–1850*, Ph.D. thesis, University of Texas at Austin, 1987.

Sweezy, P. (1971) 'The Resurgence of Financial Control: Fact or Fancy?' *Monthly Review*, Vol. 23, No. 6 (November).

Triffin, R. (1978/1979) 'The International Role of the Dollar', *Foreign Affairs* (Winter).

Tronti, M. (1973) 'Social Capital', *Telos*, 17 (Fall).

Tronti, M. (1976) 'The Social Factory', *Falling Wall Review*, 5.

Virno, P. (1992) 'Quelques notes à propos du general intellect', *Futur Antérieur*, 10.

8 Money, Equality and Exploitation: An Interpretation of Marx's Treatment of Money

Werner Bonefeld[1]

INTRODUCTION

Since the deregulation of the international money markets in 1971 and 1973, money has emerged as a central axis of class conflict. Throughout the world, governments have responded to the shift from fixed to flexible exchange rates with policies of tight money. However, beginning with the recession of the early 1980s, developing through the 'debt crisis' of the 1980s, the recession of the early 1990s signals the failure of a politics of state austerity. Although the crash of 1987 and the recession of the early 1990s bear comparison with the inter-war period, it does not necessarily follow that the outcome of this crisis will match that of the 1930s. But can parallells be dismissed so easily?

One of the major difficulties in analysing the current capitalist crisis lies in seeing how changes in the international monetary system fit in with the capitalist imposition of work. To approach this question we must grasp the self-contradictory mode of existence of 'money'. The purpose of this chapter is to contribute to this understanding by reworking Marx's writing on money. Marx offers many remarkable insights which need to be made productive. The aim is to interpret Marx's conceptualisation of money with a view to theorising money as a self-contradictory phenomenon of human relations.

The understanding of money as a self-contradictory form of human relations raises the fundamental theoretical question of the constitution of social existence and thus the constitution of categories. As indicated by Reichelt (1993, p. 74), 'if one wishes to treat dialectics seriously as a method of the critique of political economy, one has to put the idea of constitution into the context of value as a permanently moving form of existence'. In other words, the category of money cannot be grasped simply in terms of 'economic theory' – whether 'Marxist' or not (cf. Marazzi's 'Money in the World Crisis', Chapter 4 in this volume). The constitutive contradiction of capitalist social reproduction is not that between financial and productive capital, but between capital and labour. Most of Marxist writing on 'money' is remarkably sterile, particularly when contrasted with Marx's own writings. This is because it has focused on a merely formal understanding of 'money', neglecting the fundamental question posed by Marx, namely, why do human relations exist in the form of a relationship amongst things.[2] The conceptualisation of this question supplies an understanding of money as a self-contradictory phenomenon of human relations. Such a view is in contrast to approaches which 'define' money according to its institutionally specified determinations (Aglietta, 1979; Coakley and Harris, 1983) and to those which stress the necessity of money and derive 'money' in merely formal terms from Marx's presentation (De Brunhoff, 1976; Reuten, 1988; Hall, 1992). In all of these approaches social reality is construed in terms of a formal system of rules and laws. Although there are differences between the authors, they share the same problem: they understand capital fetishistically in terms of a logical system.[3] Rather than conceptualising the contradictory constitution of a capitalist world, these approaches emphasise the role and contradictions of 'money'. The understanding of labour as the substance, and of the labourer as the creator, of value, and hence of surplus value, is, by implication, seen as something existing outside the contradictory role of money itself.

The chapter starts with Marx's notion of 'value' as a form of human practice. There then follows a conceptualisation of 'money' which interprets the pertinent themes of Marx's treatment of money. Money will then be discussed as the elementary and meaningless form of the existence of labour in capitalism. The next section supplies a conceptualisation of the relationship of the state to money. This section emphasises the 'state' as a political form through which the 'social power of money' subsists. The final section summarises the argument.

VALUE AND HUMAN PRACTICE

Labour was seen by Marx (1973, p. 361) as the 'living, form-giving fire; it is transitoriness of things, their temporality, as their formation by living time'. Human beings produce themselves through labour. Labour is a general precondition of human existence regardless of the concrete historical form of social existence. Labour is understood, by Marx, as the appropriation of nature, as social, sensual, critical – purposive activity. 'But the so-called general preconditions of all production are nothing more than these abstract moments with which no real historical state of production can be grasped' (Marx, 1973, p. 88). The determination of labour as human activity in general needs to be specified in its historically specific form.[4] The labour process is the production of human relations in and through the 'appropriation of nature on the part of an individual within and through a specific form of society' (Marx, 1973, p. 87).

While in every society human beings play the role of producers, the simplest category, i.e. labour, transforms, in capitalist society, into a mystifying character because the material elements of wealth transform from products of labour into properties of commodities and still more pronouncedly they transform the production relation itself into a thing. The productive power of social labour appears in the 'perverted' form of value.[5] The 'objective', or factual, existence of 'capital' can thus not be taken as a conceptual starting point, as in those approaches mentioned above. This is because that which asserts itself to the economic mind as 'objectivity', or 'objective logic', or 'objective being' is, in Marx, understood as 'alienated subjectivity' (as specified by Backhaus, 1992). Any conceptualisation of money which focuses on its institutional determination or its formal logic or functional role, disregards the distinctiveness of Marx's theory and tends to espouse, instead, the reified world of capitalism as the object and purpose of theory. The distinctiveness of Marx's theory lay in the understanding of the essential social relation, of the 'movement of labour in capitalist society' (Psychopedis, 1984).

According to Marx, the best points in his critique of political economy are: '(1) the twofold character of labour, according to whether it is expressed in use-value or exchange-value. (All understanding of the facts depends upon this.) It is emphasised immediately, in the first chapter; (2) the treatment of surplus value independently of its particular forms as profit, interest, ground rent, etc.' (Marx, 1867, quoted in McLellan, 1977, p. 525). Marx thus determined (*bestimmte*) the concept of 'value' qualitatively: as a general equivalent (exchange value) it must be a use value and vice versa. The Marxian revolution is the critique of value as a fetish which seems to possess extra-human powers. The critique of political economy shows 'value' as a social relation, as a mode of existence of labour in capitalism. The critique of fetishism supplies an understanding of 'value' *ad hominem.*[6] That is, it shows that the so-called 'economic forms' are, in fact, forms of human practice. Thus, the critique of political economy amounts to a 'conceptualised practice' (*begriffene Praxis*, cf. Schmidt, 1974), that is, an understanding of the totality of human practice which constitutes, suffuses and contradicts the perverted world of capitalism.

Marx understood labour, in capitalist society, as specified by abstract labour. Individual labour is abstract labour in the sense that it is part of the labour of the whole society and, moreover, derives its significance from this fact. The category of abstract labour exists through the exchange of commodities. The historical specificity of labour concerns the contradictory unity of exchange and production, that is, the exchange of commodities through which concrete labours are reduced to their common substance as abstract labour. The 'surplus-value extorted by capital in the actual production process . . . must first be realised in the circulation process' (Marx, 1966, p. 827). Capitalist social relations are distinguished by the 'integration of the value form with abstract labour as the substance of value, and of the labour process with the valorisation of capital, as the appropriation and distribution of surplus labour is achieved through the exchange of commodities' (Clarke, 1989, p. 136; see also Clarke, 1980; Elson, 1979). The substance of value is living labour commanded by capital for the purpose of exploitation. Labour is the presupposition of social existence as a whole, a presupposition from which capital cannot autonomise itself. Capital is dependent upon labour. Capital lives by turning labour against itself on the basis of the fetishistic existence of wage labour, that is of a value-creating commodity.

MONEY AND LABOUR

Money is treated, by Marx, as premise and result of the social process of value, integrating value and money theory as moments which presuppose and which are the result of each other (Backhaus, 1974, 1986). Individual labour attains its social character through the exchange with money in circulation. Money is the 'physical medium into which exchange values are dipped' (Marx, 1973, p. 167). In its role of universal equivalent, money shows that all commodities do in fact have a common property: they are all products of 'labour's social productive force' (Marx, 1966, p. 827). As the medium of circulation, money acts as this common property. It is in and through money that the particular individual concrete labour asserts itself as social, as abstract, labour. 'That is to say it is the medium through which concrete labour becomes abstract labour. In a word it is money that is the form of existence of abstract labour' (Kay, 1979, p. 58). The difference-in-unity of production and circulation is achieved through money at the same time as it is obscured by money. It is obscured because, in money, labour's productive force confronts labour as an independent 'thing'. In money, the social presupposition of 'value', i.e. purposive human activity, is displaced[7] to abstract labour *sans phrase*. 'Considered as value, all commodities are qualitatively equal and differ only quantitatively' (Marx, 1973, p. 141). In sum, in money, labour's social productive force asserts itself against itself inasmuch as the 'interchange with nature' (Marx, 1966, p. 815) exists in the form of seemingly extra-human system properties: The 'direct coalescence of the material production relations with their historical and social determination . . . is an enchanted, perverted, topsy turvy world, in which Monsieur le Capital and Madame la Terre do their ghost-walking as social characters and at the same time directly as mere things' (Marx, 1966, p. 830). The substance of value confronts its formal existence in the form of the monetary authority of capital. However, this authority exists only through labour, this latter being the substance of value. In sum, labour's social productive power asserts itself against itself inasmuch as labour's productive activity means nothing for as long as it is not expressed in money.

Money is the 'elementary' form of the capitalist organisation of exchange and, within exchange, of exploitation. It is an expression of 'capital's ability to impose work (abstract labour) through the commodity form (exchange value)' (cf. Marazzi's 'Money in the World Crisis', Chapter 4 in this volume). The imposition of work through the commodity form entails a constitution of labour in the form of 'wage labour', defined primarily by the source of its income and as an equal and free exchange relation on the market (Marx, 1983, Chap. 6; Marx, 1966, Chap. 48). Labour assumes an existence in terms of wage labour, an existence upon which exploitation rests while it, at the same time, 'eliminates' (Marx, 1966, p. 814) the specific character of surplus value production. The constitution of social relations on the basis of formal equality, liberty and private property treats social relations and the power of money as equal. Money is the form in and through which liberty, equality, property and Bentham obtain. As a relation of formal liberty, money signals non-coerced exchanges between equals on the market. As a relation of formal equality, money signals the inequality of property relations. It does so, however, by representing exploitative relations as relations of formal equality: everybody is equal before money. As a relation of property, money signals the relationship of each individual to society. As a relation of Bentham, money signals the pursuit of individual happiness. Monetary equivalence in circulation denies a content which is a content of inequality, a content of social reproduction as domination. The relations of exploitation are the content of equality expressed in 'money' as the form through which the contradiction, between formal equality and exploitation, moves. However, the displacement of labour to wage labour does not 'sweep away' the contradictory mode of existence of capital. Rather than being an accomplished fact, the displacement of labour to wage labour presupposes 'labour as value creating' (Marx, 1966, p. 823). As indicated by Psychopedis (1991), taking 'wage labour' as the starting point (as, for example, in the Regulation Approach and the Profit Squeeze[8]) entails conceptualising 'capital' as a fetishised form, i.e. as an economic relation. Such a conceptualisation does not permit an understanding of the social constitution of this form. This is because labour is merely seen as a value-producing commodity which capital sets to work.

As was reported above, 'labour's social productive force' (Marx, 1966, p. 827) becomes a very mystical being in the form of capital. As the 'universal form of labour' (Marx, 1971, p. 98), money negates social relations as human relations and affirms, instead, social relations as relations of things. Money, thus, negates its own contents, that is labour's purposive productive activity. 'Capital' assumes thus an existence as an 'automatic subject' (see Marx, 1979 p. 169).[9] This characterisation does not mean that capital has a logic independent of labour.[10] Such an understanding would fail to raise the fundamental question of the social constitution of value and thus of the critique of fetishism. The productive power of labour exists in the form of abstract labour within the circuit of social capital as a whole. The circuit of social capital is the movement of abstract labour. In other words, that which proceeds behind the back of the subjects is the movement of the social totality of value (see Backhaus, 1992) or, in other words, the abstract category of labour in action. Capitalist reproduction is social reproduction in perverted form: private production in a social context. Since the social character of private production is not a matter of the conscious decision of society, and since the latter exists only in the inverted form of private fragmentation (commodity production), the social existence of private production confronts individual producers as an external and independent thing which, as argued by Marx (1974, p. 909), is their condition of existing as private individuals in a social context. The perversion of social labour into capital as an 'automatic subject' connotes the existence of labour as an abstraction in action which capital needs to contain within the limits of its form.[11]

Capitalist production is not just use-value production, but value production which, in turn, is surplus-value production (Negri, 1984), and not only surplus-value production but the social reproduction of the social relations of production (Clarke, 1982). Living labour attains social form as abstract labour within the circuit of social capital as a whole.[12] 'Capital extorts surplus labour by compulsion exerted upon labour-power and realises the products of labour as abstract value in the sphere of circulation' (Marx, 1966, p. 823). This sphere mediates the restless appropriation of labour:

> If we take all three forms [money, commodity, productive capital] together, then all the premises of the process appear as its result, as premises produced by the process itself. Each moment appears as a point of departure, of transit, and of return. The total process presents itself as the unity of the process of production and the process of circulation; the production process is the mediator of the circulation process, and vice versa (Marx, 1978, p. 180).

The displacement of exploitation into circulation, and conversely, the displacement of circulation into exploitation entails that the movement of a particular form of capital is itself only a moment of the generality of its form. Capital 'circulates in the shape of a constant change of form, its existence is process, it is the unity of its form, it is the constant change between the form of generality and the form of particularity, of money and of commodity' (Reichelt, 1978, p. 48). The self-contradictory unity of surplus-value production comprises different forms of capital which exist only as distinct-in-unity, i.e. the continuum of forms of abstract labour in action. Money and commodity 'represent only different modes of existence of value itself, the money its general mode, and the commodity its particular, or, so to say, disguised form' (Marx, 1983, p. 152). Value cannot be grasped as a static thing. Considering value as a mere abstraction, is to 'forget that the movement of industrial capital is this abstraction in action' (Marx, 1978, p. 185). This abstraction in action connotes labour's constitutive power: the interchange with nature exists, contradictorily, in the form of a relationship between the things themselves. 'Circulation is the movement in which the general alienation appears as general appropriation and general appropriation as general alienation' (Marx, 1973, p. 196). The general alienation of human relations as relations between things is the general appropriation of labour's social productive force measured in money.

Different forms of capital relate differently to labour. The movement of value exists in the form of a dialectical continuum as production *sans phrase* (i.e. the objectification of capital in machinery and hence as immobilised) and, at the same time, as mobility *sans phrase* (i.e. capital in the form of money as social incarnation of abstract wealth). This dialectical continuum exists as a process of contradiction within which different forms of value coexist and within which particular capitals transform in a successive movement from one to the other value form. Productive, commodity, and money capital are forms that value assumes in its restless process of expansion. Their distinctiveness exists only as unity-in-difference, and hence as a contradictory movement. This contradictory movement is not constituted by the competition between different capital fractions or capital 'logics'[13] but, rather, by the contradictory integration of abstract labour with the value form. 'The money relation is itself a relation of production if production is looked at in its totality' (Marx, 1973, p. 214). Capitalist exploitation of labour is not external to the money relation. Rather, it is constitutive of the money relation itself. The social character of labour appears as the money existence of commodities, and thus as a thing external to actual production. This 'externality' is a mode of existence of labour in capitalism. 'Money does not create these antitheses and contradictions; it is, rather, the development of these contradictions and antitheses which creates the seemingly transcendental power of money' (Marx, 1973, p. 146). The notion that 'money is labour time in the form of a general object' (Marx, 1973, p. 168) entails labour as the constitutive power of wealth. That is to say that the reified generality of money exists only in and through labour. The integration of social production with capitalist reproduction is thus not achieved by money as a mere economic measure but, rather, by money as a form of social command which constitutes the unity between production and circulation 'by force' (Marx, 1973, p. 150). The inner nature between sale and purchase is 'established through a violent explosion' (Marx, 1973 p. 198), an explosion which shows the contradictory character of capitalist appropriation of labour's products 'through and by means of divestiture [*Entäusserung*] and alienation [*Veräusserung*]' (Marx, 1973, p. 196). Money is not external to production because circulation manifests itself as a 'process of production, as a real metabolism. And thus money is itself stamped as a particular moment of this process of production' (Marx, 1973, p. 217). The productive existence of money is the imposition of work through the commodity form. Money is a universal in movement – it is in 'constant flux, proceeding more or less over the entire surface of society; a system of acts of exchange' (Marx, 1973, p. 188), and, thus, a system of imposed work.

The transformation of value from one form to the other integrates production and circulation as different moments of one process. Each moment is a result and a presupposition of the other in and through the exploitation of labour. Circulation and production are distinct in unity, the common interest of which is the 'valorization of value as the determining purpose, the driving motive' (Marx, 1978, p. 180). The social validation of appropriated labour in circulation implies the social comparison (*Vergleichung*) of particular capitals in terms of *socially* necessary labour time as expressed in money. Socially necessary labour time constrains individual capitals in the form of an average rate of profit. The 'equalisation process of capitals . . . divorces the relative average price of the commodities from their values, as well as the average profits in the various spheres of production . . . from the actual exploitation of labour by the particular capitals' (Marx, 1966, p. 828). As 'profit seems to be determined only secondarily by the direct exploitation of labour . . . , normal average profits themselves seem immanent in capital and independent of exploitation' (Marx, 1966, p. 829). In sum, capital appears as a value-creating thing. This relationship 'between the things amongst themselves' (Marx, 1976, p. 145) obscures the internal connection between 'value' and its social constitution. The sphere of circulation, in which the products of labour are realised as abstract value, is 'dominated by chance' where the 'inner law' of the class struggle over exploitation prevails in an 'invisible and unintelligible' form concerning 'the individual agents in production' (Marx, 1966, p. 828). Everything appears to be contingent. The production relations appear independent of one another and profits 'seem to issue from the womb of capital itself' (Marx, 1966, p. 827). Profit manifests itself in circulation as a source of the revenue of capital, a source in which the category of surplus labour is eliminated. 'Still more does all connection vanish no sooner the formula is transformed into "capital-interest" ' (Marx, 1966, p. 823). While the connection might have vanished, the reified generality of money exists only in and through the abstract category of labour.

Capital exists as individual capital only within the historically dynamic and changing composition of the social process of value. Particular capitals are only moments of this process, the mobility of which is imposed upon them through the fluidity of money capital. The circuit of money capital is, according to Marx (1978, p. 140), the 'most striking and characteristic form of appearance of the circuit of industrial capital'. Money is the material representative of general abstract wealth, of general labour, i.e. of the labour of all individuals (see Marx, 1973, p. 224). As the representative of abstract labour, money is the universal power: it is a means 'for creating the true generality' (Marx, 1973, p. 225) of a social existence in which 'capital pumps the surplus-labour, which is represented by surplus value and surplus-product, directly out of the labourers' (Marx, 1966, p. 821). The social character of individual labour is manifested to particular capitals through the money form.

Money capital is the rational expression of equality, productivity, repression and thinghood (*Dinglichkeit*) that characterises the determination of wealth as a social process of abstract labour. It is not only the true generality of abstract labour, it is, also, and because of this, the elementary form of capitalist social command. The 'money-subject' (Marx, 1973, p. 144) entails the imposition of work through the commodity form, that is through the formal equality and the formal freedom which characterise capitalist exchange relations. 'The general interest is precisely the generality of self-seeking interests. Therefore, when the economic form, exchange, posits the all-sided equality of its subjects, then the content, the individual as well as the objective material which strives towards the exchange, is *freedom*. Equality and freedom are thus not only respected in exchange based on exchange values, but, also, the exchange of exchange values is the productive, real basis of all *equality* and *freedom*' (Marx, 1973, p. 245). Money represents the standardisation of individuals as abstract citizens. Money treats exploitative relations and citizenry as equal. All individual market agents are equal before money. As 'reification, reified relation, reified exchange value' (Marx, 1973, p. 160), money 'represents the universal terrain within which all subjects are reduced to subjects of exchange' (Bologna, 1993b, p. 67). Money is thus the incarnation of liberty, of private property. It represents the liberty of individualised property owners, their equality and freedom. As an expression of equality, money serves as a moment of exchange that perverts human activity into a commodity: wage labour. 'If money is an equivalent, if it has the nature of an equivalent, it is above all the *equivalence of a social inequality*' (Negri, 1984, p. 26). The abstract citizen of bourgeois society, and the suppression of human emancipation in favour of political emancipation (see Bonefeld, 1992), is the other side of money as the reified generality of human activity, if liberty, freedom and equality are looked at in their totality. The 'republic of the market' (Pashukanis, 1979) is the other side of the imposition of work through 'non-coerced', and hence free and equal, market relations. Money expresses the abstract average and formal equality of capitalist domination as it measures capital's capacity to impose work in a repressive and oppressive, but nevertheless contradictory, way.

The separation-in-unity of formal equality and exploitation indicates the contradictory power of money, expressing equality as a mode of existence of domination.[14] 'Money has the advantage of presenting me immediately the lurid face of social relations of value; it shows me value right away as exchange, commanded and organised for exploitation' (Negri, 1984, p. 23).[15] Whether money serves as measure, medium of exchange or capital, it presents exploitative social relations in the form of equality and freedom. The concept of money, displaced from the contradictions of surplus-value production and, at the same time, the ultimate expression and suppression of these contradictions, is a concrete representation of the social reality of class antagonism. Money is the elementary form of the self-contradictory existence of the category of abstract labour. 'The precondition of commodity circulation is that they [commodities] be produced as *exchange values*, not as *immediate use values*, but as mediated through exchange value' (Marx, 1973, p. 196). In the circuit of money capital, value assumes a form which disregards labour as concrete labour inasmuch as money is disconnected from the production of use value and becomes a distinct thing. 'Money has a power which no right, no positive norm, can touch' (Bologna, 1993b, p. 67). It does not know a right to employment, housing, welfare, and education, etc. It is a disinterested power which only acknowledges its own 'rule': accumulate, accumulate! It negates social reproduction in and through the representation of capital as a value-creating thing: money presents itself as 'the' form of property. The contradictory character of 'capital' lies in its negation of labour's purposive productive activity at the same time as capital exists only through it. 'Money' is collective and abstract. It is collective because of the generality of its form. It is abstract because it represents 'form' without 'content'. Money is the 'meaningless' and most 'elementary' form (cf. Marx, 1966, Chap. 24) of the abstract category of labour, its incarnation and its self-contradictory negation.

> Capital in general, as *distinct* from the particular real capitals, is itself a *real* existence . . . For example, capital in this *general form*, although belonging to individual capitalists, in its *elementary form* as capital, forms the capital which accumulates in the banks or is distributed through them, and, as Ricardo says, so admirably distributes in accordance with the needs of production (Marx, 1973, p. 449).

Money expresses the abstract average and formal equality of capitalist domination as it measures capital's capacity to impose work in a repressive and oppressive way. Nevertheless, the existence of money as command over labour is contradictory, as each of the world's debtor crises shows.

Money is the meaningless[16] and elementary form of capital because it asserts itself as a thing which has the capacity to expand abstract wealth independently of exploitation. The capacity of money to dissociate itself from exploitation involves money in the form of credit. Credit exists as a lever for expanded reproduction as it realises the internal relation of production and circulation without this internal relation having been performed in real terms. Credit-sustained accumulation, rather than eliminating the contradictory unity of surplus value production, constitutes a mode of existence through which this contradiction can temporarily move without, however, sweeping away the contradiction. The contradiction involved in the coexistence and sequence of different value forms within the circuit of social capital is the potential autonomisation (*Verselbständigung*) of monetary from productive accumulation. Money is thus in danger of losing its capacity of commanding the labour of others. Hence, it becomes meaningless (*begriffslos*) because it loses its grip on labour: it is deprived of meaning. However, the autonomisation of money emphasises also its elementary power as command over labour. The autonomisation of money means that the contradictory unity of surplus-value production is displaced to the constitution of a contradiction between productive and loanable capital or, in other words, of a contradiction 'between the factory and the credit system' (cf. Marazzi in this volume).[17]

In the credit system money functions as capital, 'though not in the hands of its proprietors, but rather of other capitalists at whose disposal it is put' (Marx, 1978, p. 261). In the form of credit, capital accumulates independently from its parent stock. 'The antithetical character of capital assumes an independent form' (Marx, 1966, p. 382) inasmuch as 'capital appears as a mysterious and self-creating source of interest – the source of its own increase' (Marx, 1966, p. 392). Interest bearing capital is capital *par excellence* (Marx, 1976, p. 447) as it manifests the pure form of capital $(M \ldots M')$ and, as such, is an 'obscure thing' ('*Dunkelding*': Marx, 1976). Interest-bearing capital expresses capital as 'the subjectification of objects, the objectification of subjects' (Marx, 1976, p. 484) because it exists as an 'alienated form of the conditions of labour, it is realised in interest' (Marx, 1976). Hence money is the elementary and meaningless form of capital: capital assumes the form of an 'undifferentiated homogeneous form of independent value – money' (Marx, 1966, p. 368). The contradictory unity of surplus value production finds its most elementary mode of existence in the accentuation of abstract labour as money *sans phrase*: money is identified with money. In this 'mystification of capital in its most flagrant form' (Marx, 1966, p. 392), the process of production and the process of circulation appears directly as if it were 'unassisted by the process of production and circulation' (Marx, 1966, p. 392). 'Money' obtains here as an independent category of value in general inasmuch as 'capital assumes its pure fetish form, $M \ldots M'$ being the subject, the saleable thing' (Marx, 1966, p. 393). The productive generality of social labour obtains as money's presupposition, a presupposition which is denied by the money form. 'Capital is now a thing, but as a thing it is capital' (Marx, 1966, p. 393). This displacement of abstract labour reduces capital 'to a meaningless condensation' (Marx, 1966, p. 391) without, however, dissolving the existence of particular capitals. Rather, it imposes upon them the social character of their own existence, while 'eliminating the relation to labour' (Marx, 1976, p. 456). However, money capital exists only in and through labour $(M \ldots P \ldots M')$. The value of money capital is not determined through the value it represents in relation to commodities or, more pronouncedly, in relation to itself, but through the surplus value which it produces for its owner (Marx, 1976). The contradictory unity of surplus value production makes itself felt through money capital's apparently self-valorising capacity. The productive power of labour exists *qua* contradiction in-and-against the form of money.

Capital assumes an apparently 'independent form' in interest as a relation between the owner of money capital and the manager of production. Profit splits into enterprise profit and interest 'as though they generate from essentially different sources' (Marx, 1966, p. 375). In these two forms of profit, the relation to surplus value is eliminated since they are concepts relating to each other as opposites. The differentiation between enterprise profit and interest disguises profit as a property of capital as such, a profit which would have been yielded even if capital had not been applied productively. The choice of investing reproductively or in monetary terms is, however, dependent on labour as substance of value, the contradiction between productive and financial engagement being determined by the class struggle over capitalist command in production. 'Labour must directly produce exchange value, i.e. money' (Marx, 1973, p. 224). The contradictory relation between production and circulation is transformed into a movement in which the contradictory unity of surplus value production reasserts itself in M . . . M′ – 'the meaningless form of capital, the perversion and objectification of production relations in their highest degree, the interest-bearing form, the simple form of capital, in which it antecedes its own process of reproduction' (Marx, 1966, p. 392). While the 'social relation is consummated in the relation of a thing, of money, to itself' (Marx, 1966, p. 392), 'interest is only a portion of the profit, i.e. of the surplus-value, which the functioning capitalist squeezes out of the labourer' (Marx, 1966, p. 392). In sum, while capital, in the form of money, assumes the form of an 'automatic fetish' (Marx, 1966, p. 392), it appropriates unpaid labour; and it is such power because it 'commands the labour of others bestowing a claim to appropriate the labour of others, and therefore represents self-expanding values' (Marx, 1966, p. 355). Although we see, in interest-bearing capital, 'only form without content' (Marx, 1966, p. 392), money must command labour so as to sustain itself as the universal of abstract labour. It cannot forget 'the slow pace, the daily struggle for the extortion of surplus value' (Bologna, 1993b, p. 83). And yet, it is this 'forgetfulness' which characterises money as the elementary and meaningless form of capital.

Credit-sustained exploitation of labour is more than just a lever for expanded reproduction of capital. The contradiction involved here is that credit posits itself as the incarnation of wealth: 'value in process, money in process, and, as such capital' (Marx, 1983, p. 153). Although, in credit, the relation to labour as substance of value is seemingly eliminated, credit asserts itself as 'claim of ownership upon labour' (Marx, 1966, p. 476), i.e. as a claim on a portion of future surplus value. Credit represents abstract labour in the form of a claim on the future exploitation of labour. This claim exists in the form of the elementary and meaningless form of money. Credit attains social existence as command to exploit labour effectively. The constitution of the circuit of social capital on the basis of a crisis-ridden auto-nomisation of money capital from exploitation involves the assertion of 'private property' in its most abstract form. Credit-sustained accumulation implies a gamble with the future. The exploitation of labour presents itself as a mortgage on the future. This is because, in money, the abstract category of labour attains its most rational and at the same time meaningless mode of existence (M . . . M'). While money asserts itself as the source of its own self-valorisation, M . . . M' exists only in and through the ability of capital to harness labour as the variable component of exploitation. M . . . M' exists only in and through the ability of capital to exploit labour effectively, i.e. to harness labour as the variable component of capitalist command for exploitation.

During a crisis,[18] the expansion of credit increasingly spills over into unproductive and speculative channels. This spill-over appears as a disproportionte relation between the production of goods and market relations. In turn, this disproportion appears to be deter-mined by contingent factors (e.g. erratic monetary policies), the eradi-cation of which looks like a simple readjusting exercise so as to restore proportionality between supply and demand on the market. Accord-ing to monetarist ideology, all that is here required is a consistent monetary and fiscal policy, which curtails economic activity. The notion that, if there is inflation, then the money supply needs to be deflated, is basically correct. However, it is correct only in terms of the monetary decomposition of class relations through the subordi-nation of social relations to the abstract equality of money.[19] This is because of the inner connection between different value forms. The disproportion between production and circulation cannot be explained by reference to the autonomisation of one form from the other, an autonomisation which can be resolved through a simple exercise of economic readjustment. A policy of state austerity does not relate directly to the crisis of surplus value production, but to the constitu-tion of this same crisis in the form of money capital accumulating independently of the exploitation of labour while, at the same time, existing only in and through it.

The contradiction is not that between production and circulation; it is between capital and labour. The contradictory relation between the unfettered development of labour's productive power and the limits of the capitalist form of social reproduction imposes the compression of necessary labour so as to multiply the productive power of labour. The compulsion upon each individual capital not only to produce, but to increase relative surplus value in the course of accumulation, forces each capital to decrease necessary labour to the utmost. This process relates to the '*relation between necessary labour and surplus labour* that is . . . the relation between the constitutive parts of the working day and the class relation which constitutes it' (Negri, 1984, p. 72). Capital exists only in antithesis to living labour at the same time as capital exists only in and through the imposition of necessary labour. Capital depends on labour. Capital cannot autonomise itself from labour. Living labour is the substance of value. Individual capitals exist only as a moment of social capital and, as such, only in and through each other, and not only in and through each other, but only in and through the exploitation of labour. The strength of the link between money and exploitation depends on the imposition of work through the form of this imposition, that is exchange.

The capitalist crisis asserts itself in the form of unemployed capital. Unemployed capital does not simply cease to perform as capital. Unlike excess capital in production, unemployed capital exists in the general form of capital and, at the same time, in its elementary form; that is, money:

> The so-called plethora of capital always applies essentially to a plethora of the capital for which the fall in the rate of profit is not compensated through the mass of profit – this is always true of newly developing fresh offshoots of capital – or to a plethora which places capitals incapable of action on their own at the disposal of the managers of large enterprises in the form of credit (Marx, 1966, p. 251).

This development is a moment of the overaccumulation of capital as money capital itself can no longer be converted into reproductive activity. In other words, money capital cannot be converted into expanded command over living labour. Hence, 'unemployed capital at one pole and unemployed workers at the other' (Marx, 1966, p. 251) – different poles of a continuum constituted by the existence of labour in-and-against capital. The sustaining of overaccumulation through credit constitutes the circuit of social capital on the basis of a speculative deferral of mass devaluation of capital. This deferral entails the possibility of an accumulation of debt. Money accumulates in the form of a potentially worthless claim on surplus value. The solidity and very existence of money capital is endangered insofar as a progressive deterioration of the relation between credit and exploitation renders capital, in its elementary form of money, increasingly meaningless. At the same time all social relations rest on the maintenance of formal exchange equality. All social relations depend thus on the stability of credit as a claim on future exploitation. The safeguarding of 'credit' or, in other words, of the formal exchange equality of the 'transcendental power of money', depends on how effectively capital can exploit labour, and of how effectively labour resists exploitation (see Holloway, 1990).

The sustaining of the exploitation of labour through unemployed capital is fictitious. This is because the exploitation of labour is sustained through an accumulation of claims on surplus value still to be pumped out of the worker. Unemployed capital has to be transformed into 'employed capital' if a general devaluation of social capital through hyperinflation and an accumulation of worthless debt and, ultimately, general bankruptcy of capital through the default of money, is to be avoided. The only way for this to happen is through the transformation of money into truly productive capital, a transformation which presupposes the recomposition of the relation between necessary and surplus labour. In order to keep up with interest payments and to transform credit into means of payment, capital needs to exploit labour more effectively so as to increase the surplus value already represented in the money supply but not yet produced by the workers. The stability of money divorced from productive accumulation is feasible only on the expectation of some future surplus value. This would require future profits that must not only be adequate to the further demands of accumulation but, in addition, large enough to replace the money capital which sustained accumulation through, in fact, unemployed capital. The more accumulation is sustained by credit, the more effectively capital needs to exploit labour so as to increase profitability, which is the only way of keeping up with debt. However, this is easier said than done since money is unemployed because it failed to impose expanded exploitation on labour. Further, the development of labour's productive power makes the exploitation of labour more and more expensive. The investment required to set labour in motion in production increases the cost price of production which, even under conditions of a rising rate of exploitation, tends to decrease the rate of profit. This is so because of the rising value of constant capital (means of production) relative to variable capital (labour power).[20] Overaccumulation is thus 'the false name which is given to overexploitation' (Bologna, 1993a, p. 51). Additionally, capital has to overcome the disruptive power of labour which resists an exploitation beyond certain limits and below a certain wage. In other words, money is unemployed because it cannot command labour in the present and seeks, instead, to invest in the future exploitation of labour. It seeks redemption in the future. However, without a mass devaluation of money, the destruction of productive capacity, the scrapping of labour power, the liquidation of excess capital, widespread bankruptcy, worsening conditions, and intensification of work, this future remains fictitious. But capital has to prolong the present into the future in order to avoid a breakdown. The sustaining of production through debt, and its recycling, only intensifies the speculative dimension of capitalist command over labour, and with it, the fictitious integration of labour into the capital relation itself: capital's inability to exploit labour effectively threatens insolvency and liquidation for productive and money capital alike through the failure of one of the extreme poles of the contradictory unity of productive and money capital. Monetary panic and industrial crash are two sides of the same coin.

In the course of a crisis, which is itself stimulated by credit, reproductive capital's demand for means of payment increases. This demand can only be satisfied by credit. Consequently, credit becomes more expensive as demand rises, while depressed 'economic activity' and the effects of 'deflationary inflation' (cf. Mattick, 1980) threaten to turn debt into insolvency and bankruptcy of reproductive capital. Banks themselves face the threat of insolvency as credit defaults, threatening a collapse of the circuit of social capital based on speculation and debt-financing of reproduction. The tension between different value forms is signposted by the autonomisation of the meaningless, but elementary, form of value from exploitation. The safeguarding of the elementary form of money depends on exploitation which, itself, is sustained by 'unemployed' capital. In order to sustain the most elementary, and meaningless, form of capital, labour and productive capital need to be sacrificed so as to make it possible for banks to absorb heavy losses without default. However, the sacrificing of surplus value production on the altar of money destroys the basis through which the 'meaningless' form of capital exists. The default of productive activity threatens to bring about a collapse of the credit relations upon which all social relations rest. The sacrificing of surplus value production on the altar of money destroys the basis through which the money power of capital subsists. The unity of monetary and productive accumulation asserts itself in and through its destructive separation. The supremacy of money displaces, as a form of class struggle, the contradictory existence of the production process into a contradiction between credit and functioning capital. This displacement of the contradictory unity of surplus value production is abstract in terms of social command as its form of wealth is meaningless in content in terms of use-value production; it is none other than the dissociation of the valorisation from the labour process (see Marx, 1983, p. 48). All depends on the strength of the relation between money and exploitation. Credit has to command labour. It has to do so by integrating labour into the capital relation on the basis of the supremacy of the valorisation process rather than an accumulation of monetary claims upon the future exploitation of labour. Productive accumulation has to succeed in order for money capital to be sustained. Failure to turn credit into effective command over labour involves insolvency and bankruptcy for capital as a whole. Crisis shows what money is.

MONEY AND THE STATE

Basic to the development of the state is social conflict over the imposition of the value form upon social relations. The state is not an *agent* of capital. Each capital exists only in and through each other as moments of one process; their difference-in-unity is constituted through the abstract category of labour in action. For capitalist reproduction to take on the form of overaccumulation and crisis, each individual capital must be involved as a moment of the social process of value in terms of negation (devaluation) and affirmation (average rate of profit). The continuous transformation of value between particularity and universality (Reichelt, 1978) is mediated and composed within the circuit of social capital (see Marx, 1978, Chaps 1–4). One cannot derive the historical development of the state from the specific interests served by particular policies.[21] Rather the form of the state needs to be seen as a mode of existence of the class relation which constitutes and suffuses the circuit of capital. Consequently, the form of the state attains existence as the political mode of existence of the abstract category of labour in action.[22]

The most developed form of the category of abstract labour in action is the global relations of exploitation. The world market is a presupposition and a premise of the whole process of capitalist reproduction. The world market 'is directly given in the concept of capital itself' (Marx, 1973, p. 163) as it constitutes the presupposition of capitalist reproduction 'as well as its substratum' (Marx, 1973, p. 228). This is because in the form of the world market 'production is posited as a totality together with all its moments, but within which, at the same time, all contradictions come into play' (Marx, 1973, p. 227). Accordingly, the utmost expansion of the process of abstract wealth founded on exploitation comprises also the expansion of the money form. The global movement of money 'acquires to the full extent the character of the commodity whose bodily form is also the immediate social incarnation of human labour in the abstract' (Marx, 1983, p. 141). Social relations subsist in and through the equality, repression, and thinghood represented by the global 'terrorism of money' (cf. Marazzi's 'Money in the World Crisis', Chapter 4 in this volume). Global relations of exploitation are the premise of the imposition of work within national boundaries. 'Although the state is constituted politically on a national basis, its class character is not defined in national terms, the capitalist law of property and contract transcending national legal systems, and world money transcending national currencies' (Clarke, 1992, p. 136). Nation states are not only in competition with each other, as each tries to divert the flow of money capital into its particular territory. They exist also as particular nodes within the global flow of capital. The nation state exists through the global relations of exploitation and is confined 'within limits imposed by the contradictory form of the accumulation of capital on a world scale' (Clarke, 1992, p. 136)[22].

In a crisis, the overexpansion of credit appears in the form of a growing drain on the reserves of the central banks. The reserve funds of the national banks are pivotal for the functioning of the credit system and, as such, for sustaining the exploitation of labour. The reserves guarantee the existence of credit in terms of the convertibility of bills of exchange to 'real' money. The limit to sustained accumulation appears in the form of a limited supply of official reserves with which to support the exchange rate in the face of a drain on reserves. This limitation appears to be related to the inflationary expansion of money and not to the crisis of containing labour's productive power within the limits of the capitalist form of reproduction. For the state, the drain on reserves manifests itself in the form of balance of payments deficits, over-ridden by a claim on tax revenue by creditors, and in the form of a threat to the convertibility of currency in commodities on the world market, over-ridden by speculative pressure on the exchange rate.[24] The integration of national currency on the world market is backed by the ability of the central bank to meet a drain on reserves and to convert bills of exchange into means of payment. This ability of the central bank is supported by the revenue of the state. It is the revenue of the state which supports the reserves through the guarantee of credit as claim on taxation. The convertibility of national currency in commodities on the world market depends on the acceptability of national currency as legal tender on the world market. Such acceptability depends on the acceptance of credit as claim on tax revenue by financial markets, endowed with the ultimate sanction of speculative pressure against currency in case of 'domestic mismanagement'. The convertibility of credit depends on the ability of the state to restrict the expansion of credit as banks will fuel overaccumulation of capital by investing their capital in interest bearing ventures.[25] 'It is ultimately through the monetary policies of the state, mediated through the banking system, that the "interests" of capital-in-general are imposed on particular capitals, as the expansion of production is confined within the limits of its capitalist form' (Clarke, 1988b, pp. 9–10). Restrictive monetary policies involve not so much a quest for sustaining capital in its most elementary form of money but, rather, a quest to sustain the existence of capital as a social form of reproduction. A default of the global credit relations endangers not only the abstract process of wealth in the meaningless form of money capital but, also, the elementary form of capital upon which all social relations rest. Money is the elementary form of abstract labour.

The speculative character of credit-sustained accumulation comes to the fore when the pseudovalidation of surplus value production through credit expansion asserts itself in an accumulation of (possibly) worthless paper. With the demand for means of payment rising, the ability of the central bank to act as lender of last resort becomes increasingly difficult. In order to maintain formal exchange equality on the world market, the political control of the money supply means a cutback on credit so as to sustain financial stability. In other words, it involves a policy of state austerity. However, an imposition of tight money is fraught with contradictions. Productive accumulation has to succeed in order for money capital to be sustained. The failure to turn credit into effective exploitation of labour reasserts, for productive capital, the crisis of exploiting labour effectively in the form of insolvency and bankruptcy, precipitating a default of credit as a claim on future surplus value.

In order to understand this working of 'money', one has to descend 'from the monetary image of crisis to an analysis of the crisis of social relations, from the crisis of circulation to the crisis of the relation between necessary and surplus labour' (Negri, 1984, p. 25). The substance of money is labour, the acceptability of money as legal tender being guaranteed by the effective exploitation of labour. The 'illusory community' of the formal equality of money subsists only through its command of 'alien labour'. The movement of the contradiction between productive capital and the credit system is determined by the class struggle over the imposition of valorisation upon the labour process. This struggle is constituted in the form of monetary pressures which are mediated through the state. In this crisis-ridden process, the state attains generality as a self-contradictory moment of the social power of money. The dissociation of money from exploitation impresses itself upon the state through the money power of capital ($M \ldots M'$), a power in which the precondition of its existence, i.e. the expansive reproduction of capitalist exploitation of labour ($M \ldots P \ldots M'$), is seemingly eliminated. The contradictory unity of surplus value production impinges on the state as the contradiction between functioning and money capital. Because of the contradictory unity of surplus value production, the state rather than resolving the contradictions of capital, reproduces these contradictions in a political form.

A *Keynesian* policy of easy credit does not resolve overaccumulation, nor does the growth of the market which it stimulates (Mattick, 1980). Rather, it tends to fuel overaccumulation through the integration of the working class by guarantees of full employment and through the underwriting of profits by the creation of demand. Increase in the money supply, through the extension of credit and state loans, provides the guarantee that price increases can be realised, permitting accumulation and the maintenance of full employment in an ever-growing inflationary spiral. While depreciation charges might be absorbed through credit expansion and while unemployment is postponed, the tendency to overaccumulation accelerates, expressing itself in the form of price increases, budget difficulties, speculative pressure on currency and growing devaluation of money capital through inflation, erosion of confidence in the domestic organisation of money, threat to formal exchange equality of national currency on the world market, and, ultimately, a possible collapse of global credit relations. Credit-sustained overaccumulation teeters on the edge of collapse, the manifestation of which will be ever the more severe the more accumulation is sustained by credit. Credit expansion and growing state expenditure, domestically and internationally, eventually only exacerbates the very tendencies which these policies sought to regulate in the first place (Mattick, 1980).

A *monetarist* credit policy seeks to rectify overaccumulation through a restrictive monetary policy, politically reinforcing devaluation and liquidation of capital as well as unemployment. A policy of tight money and high interest rates makes it expensive for reproductive capital to draw additional means of payment required to sustain productive activity and employment, while high interest rates accelerate capital insolvency and liquidation. Although high interest rates make it possible for banks to absorb heavy losses without defaulting, a policy of tight money threatens to undermine the whole process upon which accumulation rests. Productive activity cannot be sacrificed because money exists only in and through labour as the substance of value. The attempt to impose the capitalist form of social reproduction through high interest rate policies reinforces the slump in productive activity as credit for outside financing gets scarce and costly and as debt service becomes more expensive. The credit system teeters on the edge of collapse as the claim on future surplus value defaults, precipitated by the inconvertibility of money into command over labour for the purpose of exploitation.

Both monetarism and Keynesianism are political phenomena of the contradictory unity of the abstract category of labour and the value form, that is to say, they are distinct moments of the dialectical continuum of the unity-in-separation of production and circulation. Keynesianism seeks to sustain unity by establishing demand which sustains overaccumulation through debt and inflationary pressure on profits, discriminating against the elementary form of money capital. Monetarism seeks to rectify disunity between production and circulation by sacrificing reproductive accumulation and labour on the altar of money. Such a restriction on the ambitions of reproductive capital threatens expansive production of surplus value and the credit system itself. Although Keynesian and monetarist policies can, to a certain degree, moderate the disunity between production and circulation, neither offers a resolution of the contradictions of capitalist reproduction. They seek to rectify the disruptive tension between distinct moments of social capital (i.e. productive and money capital) from different extremes, threatening to intensify the tension by sacrificing one moment in favour of the other.

The difference between monetarism and Keynesianism is political by virtue of the way in which the productive power of labour is subordinated to value production. Containment of social relations on the basis of tight monetary control entails the guarantee of credit through deteriorating living standards, and thus through the enforcement of debt on social relations. For example, during the 1980s, the monetarist attempt to re-tie money to work through a control of the money supply was abandoned shortly after this policy's inception. However, monetarism's short-lived political achievement was the decomposition of class relations on the basis of the individualising and fragmenting form of debt.[26] The state attained generality as the political form of money-in-command: i.e. the organisation of labour power on the basis of the planning and control of social conflict and of the anticipation of the political behaviour of the working class. The 'enforcement of debt' or, in other words, monetarism's aim at making social relations pay capital's gamble with the the future, went hand-in-hand with a state prepared to resort to provocation and the use of force. The assertion of the face of equality in the form of debt amounts to the disciplining of labour to the power of money through the state. The political imposition of the disinterested rule of money involved the imposition of formal equality and formal freedom, an imposition which treated citizenry and debt as equal. In other words, the 'republic of the market' transformed into a 'republic of debt'. It is debt enforcement which holds the system together. This involved the recognition of the working class so far as property ownership was concerned.

The imposition of money involves the imposition of market equality on the basis of law and money. For example, the monetarist ideology of the New Right articulated the crisis of surplus value production in terms of the relationship between money and the state. It rejected the conception of the Keynesian interventionist state which was criticised as creating dependency and as sapping responsibility and self-respect. The monetarist attempt to regain financial stability through the imposition of non-coerced exchanges on the market aimed, thus, at reducing people's dependence on the state in favour of their subordination to the unfettered rule of exchange relations, of money. This subordination entails the imposition upon social relations of the abstract equality of money. According to monetarist ideology, the imposition of 'self-responsibility' is identical with the unfettered market freedom. This freedom restrains those who are not alert to the messages of the market: an attachment to any values other than those of material gain is ruthlessly penalised. As was reported above, in capitalism, money reduces all 'subjects to subjects of exchange' (Bologna, 1993b, p. 67). Every individual is equal before money. For those who possess money, it is a means to freedom and prosperity. For those who do not have it, their lack of money defines not only their poverty, but also their existence as a labouring commodity. 'The power which each individual exercises over the activity of others or over social wealth exists in him as the owner of *exchange values*, of *money*. The individual carries his social power, as well as his bond with society, in his pocket' (Marx, 1973, pp. 156–7). The monetarist articulation of the limits of the market involved not only the monetary decomposition of class relations on the basis of the individual market agent. It involved, also, the attempt to impose work on the basis of the use of force: accommodate to market forces – or else! The coercive use of power manifests the right of property to secure private property against debt default. Monetarism's 'preemptive counterrevolution' (cf. Agnoli, 1975) entailed the use of force to secure debt as a claim on future exploitation in the present.

By imposing upon social relations the elementary form of capital, i.e. money, the state is involved in safeguarding the guarantee of money through coercion, binding the present to the future in an attempt to make certain the turn over of monetary claims on the future exploitation of labour. In this process, the self-contradictory form of the state attains generality as the 'harmonies' last refuge' (Marx, 1973, p. 886) – harmonies of formal equality and formal freedom upon which exploitation rests. The state as the harmonies' last refuge represents thus 'communal interest' (cf. Marx and Engels, 1982), imposing formal exchange equality through the sacrificing of social relations to the meaningless form of money. The imposition of money involves the political safeguarding of economic freedom as the abstract average of equality, the incarnation of which is money. The state attains existence as the collective representative of money in command: i.e. the subordination of social relations to monetary scarcity, involving law and order control as its preconditions, premise and result. The imposition of the value form involves not only the subordination of social relations to monetary scarcity but, more fundamentally, the monetary decomposition of class relations on the basis of the wage relation. Capital has to contain labour as the condition of its own existence. The antagonistic tendency of abstract labour involves, as already reported, the contradiction that labour must directly produce exchange value, i.e. money, at the same time as abstract labour, in the form of money, contradicts its capitalist form. The other side of labour's productive power is the potentially irredeemable accumulation of unemployed capital, of debt. Marx (1966, p. 438) characterised this situation as 'the abolition of the capitalist mode of production within the capitalist mode of production itself'. Within capitalist society, this contradiction can be contained only through force (*Gewalt*) including not only the destruction of productive capacities, unemployment, worsening conditions, and widespread poverty, but also the destruction of human life through war and starvation.[27] 'Force' is as meaningless and elementary as money. Labour's antagonism to capital is the other side of money's 'transcendental power'. 'Money is now pregnant' (Marx, 1966, p. 393) with a future which threatens to push it into the museum of history. Money is the circuit of happiness which goes forward as total horror. 'One must entice the ossified social relations to dance by singing their own melody to them' (Marx).

CONCLUSION

This chapter has argued that the category of money is a self-contradictory form of labour's constituting power. It is neither a regulative mechanism for capitalist production nor does it exist merely as the incarnation of abstract wealth. And yet it is both. However, the question is not that of the function of money, but that of the explanation of its contradictory existence as a social power. As indicated by Clarke (1988a, pp. 13–14) money is 'the most abstract form of capitalist property' and so is 'the supreme social power through which social reproduction is subordinated to capitalist reproduction'. As this supreme social power, money asserts in meaningless and elementary form the dependence of capital upon labour. In money, the social usefulness of production appears as a mere thing (interest), inasmuch as the connection of money to labour is seemingly eliminated.

However, it is the failure to contain labour's productive power within the concept of profitability which lies behind the crisis-ridden dissociation of money from exploitation. At the same time, the stability of credit depends on the capacity of capital to exploit labour effectively. It has to exploit labour effectively because capital has not only to generate surplus value sufficiently to allow accumulation but also to satisfy its creditors.

The potential autonomisation of money capital is constituted in and through the productive and disruptive power of labour. Money is the form in which capital flees from working class resistance in the factory. As Bologna (1993a, p. 52) indicates in his commentary on Marx's work between 1856 and 1857, 'the historical significance of monetary speculation resides precisely in the fact that it avoids a direct relationship with the working class'. At the same time, however, capital's attempt to suppress the 'law of value' by making money out of money rather than by exploiting labour, emphasises that capital lives beyond its means in a desperate attempt to prolong the present into the future. For capital, crisis is evidence of 'its loss of control over the working class' (Bell and Cleaver, 1982, p. 258). This loss emphasises the meaningless form of money as an aggressive force which seeks to ensure the alienation of the present to the future.

Against the background of the contemporary crisis, the continued expansion of credit indicates that capital has not succeeded in imposing a restructuring of the relations of exploitation adequate to its needs. Since the late 1960s capital has tried to impose a controlled deflation and has succeeded in a continued and unprecedented expansion of credit on a global scale. The debt crisis is a false name which is given to the crisis of money. Capital cannot redeem itself by making money out of debt. It has to face the working class. It cannot escape the class struggle by avoiding a direct confrontation with labour in production. It can only redeem its command over labour by imposing, with ruthless force, the relation between necessary and surplus labour on a global scale. Contemporary proposals by reformed socialists that 'government must make money its servant, not its master' (Mitchell, 1989, p. 61) are not just a delusion. The understanding of money as a 'medium which must be put to work for growth and jobs rather than the selfish purposes of the merchants of greed' (Mitchell, 1989, p. 61) proposes, in fact, that money must manage and organise the exploitation of labour. This chapter has shown what that means.

Notes

1. Many people have provided helpful comments on the chapter: my particular thanks to Peter Burnham, John Holloway and Richard Gunn.
2. See Marx's (1983) critique of commodity fetishism.
3. For a critique of such an understanding, see Holloway (1992); Bonefeld (1994).
4. On the dialectics of human presuppositions (general abstractions) and social form (real abstraction) see Psychopedis (1992), Gunn (1992), and Holloway (1991).
5. In the German edition of *Capital*, Marx speaks about 'verrückte Formen'. In German, 'verrückt' has two meanings: verrückt (mad) and ver-rückt (displaced). Thus, the notion of 'perverted forms' means that these forms are both mad and displaced. In other words, the forms are the modes of existence of labour, in which 'subject and object do not statically oppose each other, but rather are caught up in an "ongoing process" of the "inversion of subjectivity into objectivity, and vice versa"' (Backhaus, 1992, p. 60, referring to Kofler).
6. A similar argument is made by Psychopedis (1992). His reconstruction of dialectical theory shows the contradictory integration of social presuppositions with capitalism's fetishistic and destructive perversion of human relations into relations of 'things'. See also Backhaus (1992), Holloway (1992) and Bonefeld (1994), as well as Schmidt (1974) who argues that Marx's critique of political economy is characterised by the primacy of 'practice'.
7. 'Displaced' (ver-rückt) means here, and in the subsequent discussion, the constitution of labour's existence in and through perverted forms. These forms, using our earlier argument, are both mad and displaced. They are forms which are permanently in movement and cannot be presupposed as statically existing forms. In *Capital* Marx emphasised this by talking about *prozessuale Existenzformen*. 'Displaced' thus indicates the constitution, and hence self-contradictory mode of existence, of alienated subjectivity.
8. The classic expression of these approaches is Aglietta (1979) and Glyn and Sutcliff (1972), respectively.
9. In the German edition of *Capital*, Marx uses the phrase 'automatisches Subjekt'. In the English edition, this phrase is translated as 'automatically active character' (Marx, 1983, p. 152).
10. See, for example, Jessop (1991) whose approach depends on this misunderstanding.
11. I use the term 'abstraction in action' as indicating the circumstance that value is not static but permanently moving. 'Action' connotes the idea of the transformation of objectivity (the objectivity of labour as purposeful activity) into subjectivity (the subjectivity of things), and conversely, the transformation of subjectivity into objectivity (objectivity of social existence). 'Abstraction' connotes the notion that that which moves is, in fact, a constituted self-contradiction, namely labour's constitutive power which exists against itself in the perverted form of

value. 'Abstraction' and 'action' exist as moments of one process, that is, 'alienated subjectivity'.

12. Were one to adopt the notion of capital having a logic independent from labour, the contradictory unity of surplus value production would only obtain as a conflict between different 'fractions' of capital, i.e. between productive and money capital. What these different fractions of capital are competing about remains unexplored inasmuch as the social constitution of value is not conceptualised.

13. See Jessop (1985): for a critique see Bonefeld (1993a).

14. On the term 'mode of existence' see Gunn (1987, 1992).

15. This is not to endorse Negri's view of value as an economic category.

16. In the German edition of *Capital*, Marx talks of 'money' as a *begriffslose* form. In the English edition of *Capital*, *begriffslos* is translated as 'meaningless'. This translation is misleading. I use the term 'meaningless' here and in the subsequent discussion in terms of 'losing its grip' and hence as 'deprived of meaning'. This use of the term is much closer to the German term *begriffslos*.

17. Some authors conceptualise the contradictory relationship between 'credit and the factory' in terms of the banks suppressing productive activity (Fine and Harris, 1985). This view is misleading because it presupposes that capital ought not to make money out of money. The question is not what capital ought to do. Rather, the question is what constitutes the contradictory character of capitalist social relations.

18. Space forbids a systematic conceptualisation of 'capitalist crisis'. On Marx's crisis theory see Bell and Cleaver (1982) and Clarke (1994); see also Bologna (1993a, 1993b); Holloway (1992) and Bonefeld (1988).

19. See Clarke (1988a) and Bonefeld (1993b) on the monetary decomposition of class relations in Britain during the 1980s.

20. On this see Rosdolsky (1977, Chap. 33).

21. Such an understanding can be found in the work of Poulantzas (1973); Van der Pijl (1984); Ingham (1984); Fine and Harris (1985) and Anderson (1987); for a critique, see Clarke (1978, 1988b).

22. See Bonefeld (1992) for a systematic conceptualisation of the form of the state as a mode of existence of labour in capitalism.

23. See also Holloway's 'Global Capital and the National State', Chapter 6 in this volume and Burnham's 'Capital, Crisis and the International State System', Chapter 5 in this volume. See also Burnham (1990, 1993) and Bonefeld (1992).

24. See also Clarke (1988a).

25. In its historical development the state arrogated to itself powers to restrain the inflationary expansion of money. These powers provide the basis for the state's monetary and financial policies (see Marx, 1966, on the Bank Act of 1844).

26. See Bonefeld (1993b), Clarke (1988a); and Cleaver's, 'The Subversion of Money-as-Command in the Current Crisis', Chapter 7 in this volume.

27. See, for example, Barratt Brown (1993) on the war in the former Yugoslavia, Cleaver (1977) on 'Famine and Crisis', Postone (1986) on the political economy of 'Anti-Semitism', as well as Aly and Heim (1991) on 'population policies' under Nazism. See also Bonefeld (1988).

References

Aglietta, M. (1979) *A Theory of Capitalist Regulation: The US Experience* (London: Verso).

Agnoli, J. (1975) *Überlegungen zum bürgerlichen Staat* (Berlin: Wagenbach).

Aly, G. and Heim, S. (1991) 'The Economics of the Final Solution', *Common Sense*, 11, trans. Norma von Ragenfeld-Feldman, first published in English in *Simon Wiesenthal Centre Annual*, 5, Krau International (1988).

Anderson, P. (1987) 'The Figure of Dissent', *New Left Review*, 161.

Backhaus, H.-G. (1974) 'Materialien zur Rekonstruktion der Marxschen Werttheorie', *Gesellschaft*, 1 (Frankfurt: Suhrkamp).

Backhaus, H.-G. (1986) 'Zum Problem des Geldes als Konstituens oder Apriori der ökonomischen Gegenständlichkeit', *Prokla*, 63.

Backhaus, H.-G. (1992) 'Between Philosophy and Science: Marxian Social Economy as Critical Theory', in W. Bonefeld, R. Gunn and K. Psychopedis (eds) *Open Marxism Vol. I. History and Dialectics.*

Barratt Brown, M. (1993) 'The War in Yugoslavia and the Debt Burden', *Capital & Class*, 50.

Bell, P. and Cleaver, H. (1982) 'Marx's Crisis Theory as a Theory of Class Struggle', *Research in Political Economy*, 5.

Bologna, S. (1993a) 'Money and Crisis: Marx as Correspondent of the New York Daily Tribune, 1856–57', Part I, *Common Sense*, 13, trans. Ed Emery and John Merrington.

Bologna, S. (1993b) 'Money and Crisis: Marx as Correspondent of the New York Daily Tribune, 1856–57', Part II, *Common Sense*, 14, transl. Ed Emery

Bonefeld, W. (1988) 'Class Struggle and the Permanence of Primitive Accumulation', *Common Sense*, 6.

Bonefeld, W. (1992) 'Social Constitution and the Form of the Capitalist State', in W. Bonefeld, R. Gunn and K. Psychopedis (eds) *Open Marxism Vol. I. History and Dialictics.*

Bonefeld, W. (1993a) 'Crisis of Theory', *Capital & Class*, 50.

Bonefeld, W. (1993b) *The Recomposition of the British State During the 1980s* (Aldershot: Dartmouth).

Bonefeld, W. (1994) 'Capital As Subject and the Existence of Labour', forthcoming in Bonefeld *et al.* (eds) *Open Marxism Vol. III: Emancipating Marx.*

Bonefeld, W. and Holloway, J. (eds) (1991) *Post-Fordism and Social Form* (London: Macmillan).

Bonefeld, W., Gunn, R. and Psychopedis, K. (eds) (1992a) *Open Marxism Vol. I: History and Dialectics* (London: Pluto Press).

Bonefeld, W., Gunn, R. and Psychopedis, K. (eds) (1992b) *Open Marxism Vol. II: Theory and Practice* (London: Pluto Press).

Bonefeld, W., Gunn, R., Holloway, J. and Psychopedis, K. (eds) (1994) *Open Marxism Vol. III: Emancipating Marx* (London: Pluto Press).

Burnham, P. (1990) *The Political Economy of Postwar Reconstruction* (London: Macmillan).

Burnham, P. (1993) 'Marxism, Neo-Realism and International Relations', *Common Sense*, 14.

Clarke, S. (1978) 'Capital, Fractions of Capital and the State', *Capital & Class*, 5.

Clarke, S. (1980) 'The Value of Value: Rereading Capital', *Capital & Class*, 10.

Clarke, S. (1982) *Marx, Marginalism and Modern Sociology* (London: Macmillan).

Clarke, S. (1988a) *Keynesianism, Monetarism, and the Crisis of the State* (Aldershot: Edward Elgar).

Clarke, S. (1998b) 'Configuration of Dissent: Fractions of Capital, Class Struggle and the Decline of Britain', unpublished paper, *University of Warwick*.

Clarke, S. (1989) 'Review Article on M. Itoh's "Basic Understanding of Capitalism"', *Capital & Class*, 37.

Clarke, S. (1992) 'The Global Accumulation of Capital and the Periodisation of the Capitalist State Form', in W. Bonefeld, R. Gunn and K. Psychopedis (eds) *Open Marxism Vol. I: History and Dialectics*.

Clarke, S. (1994) *Marx's Theory of Crisis* (London: Macmillan).

Cleaver, H. (1977) 'Food, Famine and the International Crisis', *Zerowork*, 2.

Coakley, J. and Harris, L. (1983), *City of Capital* (Oxford: Basil Blackwell).

De Brunhoff, S. (1976) *Marx on Money* (London: Pluto Press).

Elson, D. (1979) 'The Value Theory of Labour', in D. Elson (ed.) (1979) *Value: The Representation of Labour in Capitalism* (London: CSE Books).

Fine, B and Harris, L. (1985) *The Peculiarities of British Capitalism* (London: Lawrence & Wishart).

Glyn, A. and Sutcliff, B. (1972) *Workers, British Capitalism and the Profit Squeeze* (Harmondsworth: Penguin).

Gunn, R. (1987) 'Marxism and Mediation', *Common Sense*, 2.

Gunn, R. (1992) 'Against Historical Materialism', in W. Bonefeld, R. Gunn and K. Psychopedis (eds) *Open Marxism Vol. I: History and Dialectics*.

Hall, M. (1992) 'On the Creation of Money and the Accumulation of Bank-Capital', *Capital & Class*, 48.

Holloway, J. (1990) 'The Politics of Debt', *Common Sense*, 9.

Holloway, J. (1991) 'In the Beginning was the Scream', *Common Sense*, 11.

Holloway, J. (1992) 'Crisis, Fetishism, Class Composition', in W. Bonefeld, R. Gunn and K. Psychopedis (eds) *Open Marxism Vol. I: History and Dialectics*.

Ingham, G. (1984) *Capitalism Divided* (London: Macmillan).

Kay, G. (1979) 'Why Labour is the Starting Point of Capital', in D. Elson (ed.) *Value: The Representation of Labour in Capitalism* (London: CSE Books).

Jessop, B. (1985) *Nicos Poulantzas: Marxist Theory and Strategy* (London: Macmillan).

Jessop, B. (1991) 'Polar Bears and Class Struggle: Much Less than a Self-Criticism', in W. Bonefeld and J. Holloway (eds) *Post-Fordism and Social Form* (London: Macmillan).

Marx, K. (1867) 'Letter to Engels, 24. Aug. 1867', in D. McLellan (1977), *Selected Writings of Marx and Engels* (Oxford: Oxford University Press).

Marx, K. (1966) *Capital*, Vol. III (London: Lawrence & Wishart).

Marx, K. (1971) *A Contribution to the Critique of Political Economy* (London: Lawrence & Wishart).

Marx, K. (1973) *Grundrisse* (Harmondsworth: Penguin).

Marx, K. (1974) *Grundrisse*, German edn (Berlin: Dietz Verlag).

Marx, K. (1976) *Theorien über den Mehrwert* (MEW) 26.3 (Berlin: Dietz Verlag).

Marx, K. (1978) *Capital*, Vol. II (Harmondsworth: Penguin).

Marx, K. (1979) *Das Kapital*, Vol. I, German edn (MEW) 23 (Berlin: Dietz Verlag).

Marx, K. (1983) *Capital*, Vol. I (London: Lawrence & Wishart).

Marx, K. and Engels, F. (1982) *The German Ideology*, ed. and introd. by Chris Arthur (London: Lawrence & Wishart).

Mattick, P. (1980) *Economics, Politics, and the Age of Inflation* (London: Merlin Press).

McLellan, D. (1977) *Selected Writings of Marx and Engels* (Oxford: Oxford University Press).

Mitchell, A. (1989) *Competitive Socialism* (London: Unwin).

Negri, A. (1984) *Marx Beyond Marx* (Cambridge, Mass.: Bergin & Garving).

Pashukanis, E. (1979) *Law and Marxism* (London: Pluto Press).

Postone, M. (1986) 'Anti-Semitism and National Socialism', in A. Rabinbach and J. Zipes (eds), *Germans and Jews Since the Holocaust* (New York: Homer & Meier).

Poulantzas, N. (1973) *Political Power and Social Classes* (London: NLB).

Psychopedis, K. (1984) *Geschichte und Methode* (Frankfurt and New York: Campus).

Psychopedis, K. (1991) 'Crisis of Theory in the Contemporary Social Sciences', in W. Bonefeld and J. Holloway (eds) *Post-Fordism and Social Form* (London: Macmillan).

Psychopedis, K. (1992) 'Reconstruction of Dialectical Theory', in W. Bonefeld, R. Gunn and K. Psychopedis (eds) *Open Marxism Vol. I: History and Dialectics*.

Reichelt, H. (1978) 'Some Remarks on Flatow and Huisken's Essay "On the Problem of the Derivation of the Bourgeois State" ', in J. Holloway and S. Picciotto (eds), *State and Capital: A Marxist Debate* (London: Edward Arnold).

Reichelt, H. (1993) 'Some Notes on Jacques Bidet's Structuralist Interpretation of Marx's Capital', *Common Sense*, 13.

Reuten, G. (1988) 'The Money Expression of Value and the Credit System: a value form theoretic outline', *Capital & Class*, 35.

Rosdolsky, R. (1977) *The Making of Marx's Capital* (London: Pluto Press).

Schmidt, A. (1974) 'Praxis', in *Gesellschaft: Beiträge zur Marxschen Theorie 2* (Frankfurt: Suhrkamp).

Van der Pijl, K. (1984) *The Making of the Altantic Ruling Class* (London: Verso).

9 Conclusion: Money and Class Struggle

Werner Bonefeld and John Holloway

INTRODUCTION

> It can't be defended except as mob rule. Maybe the country doesn't know it yet, but I think we may find that we've been in a revolution more drastic than the French Revolution. The crowd has seized the seat of government and is trying to seize the wealth. Respect for law and order is gone (Bernard Baruch's comment on Roosevelt's abandonment of the Gold Standard in 1933, quoted in Schlesinger, 1959, p. 202).

Few statements express more forcefully the inner connection between money and class struggle which has been the principal theme of this book. Baruch's reaction to the abandonment of the Gold Standard is very far from being the wild exaggeration that it at first appears to be. The abandonment of gold did indeed carry 'mob rule', the insubordination of labour, right to the very core of capitalism, where it was transformed into credit expansion and monetary instability. The inner connection is, however, two-sided: Baruch's the statement can be read backwards as well as forwards. The logical Keynesian response to Baruch's monetarist anxieties would have been: 'Yes, respect for law and order has gone, the crowd has seized the seat of government and this revolution is more drastic than the French Revolution, but the country doesn't know it yet. Credit expansion is our only hope, as long as the country doesn't know what is happening, the monetary trick will help us to restore respect for law and order, throw the crowd out of government and bring about a restoration before anyone has even realised that there has been a revolution.'

The inner connection between money and class struggle is a complex one: at the same time as money (as credit) gives recognition to the power of labour, its movement and changing configuration both

210

disarm and fragment that power. The monetary response to the power of labour is at the same time a re-shaping, or re-composition of the antagonism between labour and capital. In other words, the history of money can be seen as the movement of the composition, decomposition and recomposition of class relations.

CREDIT EXPANSION AND CLASS STRUGGLE

Credit always plays an important role in the reproduction of capitalist social relations. It always involves an element of risk, a gamble on the future. If a capitalist asks a bank for a loan, he is in effect saying: 'I need money; I do not have enough money at the moment because the exploitation of my workers has not given me enough surplus-value. But I shall exploit them sufficiently in the future to allow me to repay the debt with interest.' Credit always involves a gamble on the future, a bet which creates a fiction: the future exploitation of labour is treated as though it were present exploitation. If the capitalist succeeds in exploiting the workers sufficiently in the future, he wins his bet; if not, both he and the banker lose.

The same can be said at the level of capitalism in general: the expansion of credit is an admission that the present subordination of labour is not sufficient for the expansion of capital, that is for capital to exist as capital, as self-expanding value. The historical tendency is for capital to gamble and to bet on the future subordination of labour.[1] Credit is a means of integrating the exploitation of labour with the realistion of value in circulation. This credit-based integration is always precarious. It presents a claim on the future subordination of labour and thus a speculative integration of labour into the capital relation. In other words, credit expansion which is not matched by a corresponding expansion of the exploitation of labour substitutes a fictitious subordination of labour for the present lack of subordination, and it always involves a gamble on future subordination: if capital loses the bet, there is a financial collapse.

Credit expansion is not the cyclical phenomenon that economic theory presents it to be. Rather, for capital, it is a way of escaping the present insubordination of labour. This insubordination is concealed and dressed up as an economic problem. As the economic expression of the insubordination of labour, credit expansion has become an apparently ineradicable cancer at the very core of capitalism. This is not the result of policy errors, as monetarists would claim, but reflects the dependence of capital on a force which it does not control: labour.

The great wave of revolutionary struggle at the start of this century which found its most intense expression in the October revolution of 1917, was overcome partly by violence, but partly by the expansion of credit in the 1920s, which led eventually to the Crash of 1929. The expansion of credit which preceded the Crash was the other face of the open insubordination of the October Revolution, a bet on future subordination.

After the trauma of 1917 and its echo in 1929, the expansion of credit was raised to a central principle of capitalist rule. The importance of Keynes as a theorist was that he provided underpinning for a process already taking place, the acceptance that the state could maintain order only through accepting and promoting the expansion of credit. After the Second World War, the labour question was controlled crucially through the expansion of credit. As Burnham indicates, the purpose of the Marshall plan 'was the raising of living standards "to resist the lure of Communism" ' (Burnham, 1990, p. 100, quoting Gifford, Advisor to the US Department of Commerce). The insubordination of labour was translated into an economic problem, into monetary instability.[2]

The expansion of credit was double-edged. On the one hand, it provided a means of integrating the exploitation of labour with the realisation of surplus value in circulation. On the other hand, the acceptance of credit expansion as a principle of rule meant acceptance of a tendency towards the inflationary dissociation of money from production. In these circumstances 'book-keeping' on a global scale became one of the most important 'mechanisms' of control. The prevention of a separation of money from production was based on the recognition of the dollar as a world currency and the subordination of other currencies to the dollar within pre-determined margins. 'Book-keeping' took the form of an alternation between deflationary pressure on and inflationary support of 'domestic accumulation'. In Britain, the so-called 'stop–go cycles' gave an economic name to the containment of labour on the basis of global demand management. Credit expansion provided a means of containing conflict, of taking the sharp edge off the open class battles that dominated the early part of the century and that had reappeared after the Second World War when the mood was decisively socialist.[3] But the price paid was the loosening of the crucial nexus between the monetary system and the rate of productivity.

1970S AND 1980S: CREDIT AND DECOMPOSITION–RECOMPOSITION.

The second great wave of struggle this century, that associated with 1968, gave a renewed impulse to the expansion of credit. The revolt of those years, as in the early part of the century, was contained in part through violent suppression, but to a much greater extent through the expansion of credit. For this reason, the consequences of '1968' (the accumulated wave of struggle that showed its crest in 1968) were less dramatic but in some ways even more profound than the up-heavals of the earlier part of the century. The precarious relation between the monetary system and the rate of productivity was ruptured even more fundamentally, as reflected in the breakdown of the Bretton Woods system in 1971.

The struggles of the late 1960s meant that capital could no longer count on direct control of labour power in the factory. The exploitation of labour's productive power was confronted with depressed rates of profits. The exploitation of labour had become much too expensive at the same time as capital's ability to impose necessary labour upon social labour power was severely restricted. Further, the disruptive power of labour made itself felt in the late 1960s in resistance against the intensification of work and attempts to reduce wages (incomes policies). In other words, the working class made it clear that it would no longer permit itself to be exploited beyond certain limits.

Capital responded by fleeing the factory. The dramatic and un-precedented increase in global money capital was not matched by the reduction of necessary labour, the constitutive side of surplus labour. In other words, capital started to accumulate wealth in the money form without a corresponding exploitation of labour power in the factory. It seemed that capital had 'forgotten' the slow pace and dirty place of production. Capital tried to become clean: profits could be yielded much more easily in financial investment, and the extortion of 'interest' was promoted by the state through fiscal and anti-inflationary policies. Capital's attempt to 'liberate' itself from the contested terrain of exploitation and to go beyond itself by asserting itself in its most 'rational' form of money capital indicates the power of labour's insubordination. It indicates also the fictitious character of the containment of labour: the monetary accumulation was in fact an accumulation of 'unemployed' capital, of capital which had fled the factory and made money from betting on the future exploitation of labour. In other words, the speculative dimension of accumulation and the power of labour's insubordination are two parts of the same walnut.

Capital's flight from the factory into the fantastic world of the self-expansion of money recomposed the global relations of exploitation and struggle. The world market became a market in money. Capital's attempt to avoid the factory and to make money out of money created a much more fragile capitalism on a global scale. Without capital's global search for profit in money it would have been unthinkable for the Mexican debt crisis of 1982 to have had such an immediate knock-on effect on 'western' banks and through them on the global circuit of capital. In other words, capital's inability to impose expanding valorisation upon the productive power of labour was matched by a much stronger assertion of labour's disruptive power. The effects of the inability of the Mexican government to contain the social conflict over debt repayment which forced it to threaten default, made it clear that conflicts which would once have seemed small and marginal now had a disastrous effect on the stability of the capitalist world as a whole. The dissociation of money from exploitation provided a new unity to the international struggle against capitalism. This unity has its concrete materiality in the struggle against austerity.

The Mexican debt crisis of 1982 made clear that the formidable attempt at containing labour on a global scale within the capital relation through a policy of tight money had reached an impasse. The 'crisis of 1982' indicated a tremendous recomposition of the class relation. Seemingly 'marginal' pockets of resistance to the imposition of money-in-command threatened to transform the attempt to make money out of poverty into a severe global financial crisis. The de-regulation of global credit relations not only undermined the corporatist integration of big labour. It also presented an opening of political spaces. 'Mexico 1982' signalled that 'money' does not only subjugate all social relations to relations of exchange. It signalled also that 'money' supplies a global unity to struggles against 'debt enforcement'. In other words, the global debt crisis indicated the recomposition of labour as the antagonist to the terrorism of money on a global scale.

'Mexico 1982' showed the disruptive power of labour on a global scale. In fact, the homogeneity of labour's resistance to the imposition of global debt enforcement reached its peak. The 'cycle' which had begun in 1971 with the detachment of the dollar from gold, and which had developed through the recession of 1974–5 and the Italian crisis of 1976, the pound sterling crisis of 1976 and the dollar crisis of 1977[4] came to a crunching halt during the recession of the early 1980s.

The initial response to the upheavals of 1968–1971–1974, the attempt to impose austerity by consent, had been abandoned by the late 1970s–early 1980s against the background of the so-called crisis of social democracy. The discrediting of a policy that sought to implement austerity by consent made itself felt in various ways, such as the 'winter of discontent' in the UK, the rise of new social movements in Germany, and Italy's movement of 1977.[5] The deregulation of global credit relations had undermined the attempt to contain the labour question through policies of social reform and to integrate labour into the capital relation through selective corporatist policies.

Resistance to austerity by consent gave the political significance to the monetarism of the New Right and its strategy of imposing tight money without prior agreement and endorsement from the trade union movement. The financial crises of 1976–7 expressed labour's insubordination in economic terms. They signalled not only the end of a policy of class decomposition associated with corporatist forms of integration and exclusion but, also, a shift to a much more direct and indiscriminate attempt to deflate the 'economy' and to 'increase productivity'. The ascendancy of neo-liberal policies entailed a forceful and much more direct confrontation with the 'labour question'. The 'currency' crises of the 1970s paved the way for monetarism's indiscriminate attempt to tie money to exploitation.

The Mexican crisis of 1982 was a response to this attempt. The insubordination of labour which constituted both the 'currency crisis' and 'Mexico 1982' are thus closely connected. There was a new homogeneity of resistance directed against a policy of debt enforcement, a homogeneity which sprang from the undermining of the corporatist integration of big labour and the indiscriminate attack on social labour through tight money. This indiscriminate monetarist attack opened up tremendous political spaces. These spaces were integrated through, and defined by, money. Thus, the events of the 1970s reappeared in a much more forceful way in 1982. This is why, in 1982, the breakdown of control through tight money spread through the capitalist world with lightning pace.

The crisis of 1982 was not a crisis at the margins of the capitalist world. Rather it was a crisis at the very heart of capitalist reproduction. The monetarist project of using money as a means of disciplining labour power through debt and its enforcement, and through unemployment and devaluation of capital on a massive scale in the early 1980s, acknowledged the force required to reimpose capitalist command over labour for exploitation. However, it could reimpose command only by threatening the stability of the credit relations upon which existing social relations rested.

AFTER 1982: DECOMPOSITION THROUGH CREDIT

The indiscriminate imposition of money failed to redeem money and was thus hastily abandoned. The rapid shift from a policy of tight credit to a policy of credit expansion meant that capital, rather than confronting the working class directly at the place of production, embarked upon the socialisation, rather than the eradication, of debt. This response acknowlegded labour's insubordination and sought to contain it by decomposing class relations through the encouragement of debt. Credit expansion helped to decompose the homogeneity of resistance to austerity on a global scale. It integrated the working class into the capital relation through a credit-sustained boom.

The boom of the 1980s acted as a neutralising agent as it helped to coopt parts of the working class to the project of prosperity. The unity of opposition to the imposition of money in command was thus broken. The credit-sustained boom of the 1980s, which built on the continuous transfers from the so-called debtor countries to the so-called metropolitan countries, acknowledged the fact that sustained accumulation is the best guarantee for the fragmentation or decomposition of class relations. This decomposition involved not just a fragmentation of unity as between the metropolitan countries and 'debtor countries'. It involved crucially the decomposition of class relations within each country. Capital brought to bear its monetary destruction on every point of the social unification of labour as the antagonist to debt enforcement. Poverty, unemployment and marginalisation of superfluous labour power coincided with prosperity. The boom vindicated the monetarist imposition of market equality. The decomposition of resistance to austerity was based on poverty, a poverty which was the mirror image of a credit-driven prosperity. In the face of poverty, prosperity broke the homogeneity of resistance against austerity.

The significance of credit expansion as a central principle of capitalist rule reasserted itself. The policy of deregulation and the assault of the global decomposition of labour's antagonism to money went hand-in-hand. As Negri (1989, p. 134) puts it, the 'reconstruction of the market means giving a free hand to the individualistic pillage of social cooperation; it means to promote the ignoble legend of competition ... At the head of the reconstruction of the market, capitalist ideology places the objective of *segmenting the labour market*.' (1989, p. 134). Thus, credit expansion not only sustained the exploitation of labour in an increasingly fictitious dimension. It also helped to promote the notion of the market and thus to counter working class solidarity through the impartial imposition of abstract equality, i.e. the equality of money. The policy of market freedom equated citizenship with the power of money. Everybody is equal before money. This was a formidable attempt to 'establish conditions of separation and detachment, and effective obstacles to the cooperative process' (1989, p. 134). The decomposition of class relations through the market-based pluralism of the New Right depended on the continuous reproduction of '*the dual society*' (1989, p. 134). Against the background of a continuous dissociation of money from exploitation, the 'dual society' was not an end in itself but rather the condition of capitalist reproduction, a condition which had itself to be reproduced: the decomposition of class relationships on the basis of market equality had to be durable in order to prevent the recomposition of labour as the antagonist to money's disinterested and increasingly violent rule.

The monetary decomposition of class relations through the encouragement of private ownership involved, as its presupposition, the equally individualising enforcement of debt in the courts. The ready extension of credit and the coercion entailed by the collection of debt are two sides of the same state-sponsored coin. The lifeblood of the boom was credit and the price for the control of credit expansion was paid by the working classes in so-called debtor countries, as well as by the unemployed and impoverished. Those fortunate enough to participate in the boom were controlled by the threat of marginalisation. They faced harsh penalities should they fail to respond adequately to the market forces or should they be in disagreement with 'management's right to manage'. The sack, or lost wages due to strikes, meant that contractual agreements on interest payments might be disrupted. The threat of unemployment was reinforced by the threat of a forcible collection of unpaid debt, eviction and thus homelessness and poverty.[6] The disciplining power of debt and precarious work cannot be overestimated. The incentive not to endanger the bases of life, such as housing, education, health, clothing, heating, and so forth, undermined solidarity with those whose poverty stood as a constant warning.

The decomposition of class relations rested on the benefits generated by the boom, the tight control over that part of public spending that supported the working class, the enforcement of law and order, the encouragement of property ownership and the encouragement of personal debt. The pacification of the class struggle through a credit-sustained boom and a policy of state austerity belonged together. The overt face of the credit-sustained imposition of the wage relation was the use of the welfare state as a means of making people work for their benefits and of supervising social relations on the basis of poverty.

The reconstitution of the circuit of social capital on the basis of credit expansion and monetary attack on the working class extended the non-resolution to labour's insubordination into an increasingly fictitious dimension. The Keynesianism of the New Right speculated on the future subordination of labour by diverting surplus capital into financing the growing mountain of public and consumer debt on a global scale. Credit-sustained accumulation reproduced the speculative dimension of accumulation, while the rise in productivity rested on the scrapping of unproductive plant, the shedding of labour, and the intensification of work. At the same time, the credit-sustained accumulation made possible the fragmentation of the working class on the basis of a divisive imposition of the wage relation through the conceding of wage rises to some and the destruction of the relation between public spending and wages.

The last decade did not represent a frontal assault on the working class. Sections of the working class enjoyed a growth in living standards, even if they paid the price of intensification of labour. The use of public expenditure focused on the disorganisation of class premised on the divisive orientation of collective welfare provision to the market through, for example, contracting out of services, deregulation of wage protection, integration of employment and social policies and encouragement of property ownership. The decomposition of class relationships in terms of property owner and citizen involved the use of repressive means of political domination. The monetary expansion which responded to the homogeneity of labour's antagonism to the enforcement of debt in 1982, was overtly repressive in form. The decomposition of class relations through the imposition of the abstract equality of money meant that the positive rights and entitlements associated with the Keynesian era were pushed aside:

the right to welfare was attacked; the right to employment disappeared; the right to housing was delegated to market forces, the right to health care became more and more selective; the right to education was eroded; the right to enjoy values other than material gains was restricted to those financially able to entertain a happy life. Rights were redefined: instead of the right to employment, the right to go in search of employment ('get on your bike') was proclaimed. Other rights either disappeared or were severely restricted: the right to campaign for higher wages, health and safety standards, for example, became more and more restricted, if not abolished altogether,[7] during the 1980s. The erosion of 'rights' coincided with the privatisation of services, deregulation of wage protection and the encouragement of private insurance against risks, such as ill-health.

Money is a great 'equaliser'. It showed its true potential to push aside 'rights and entitlements' which were associated with the institutionalisation of labour's political power after the Second World War. Money knows no special privileges. It treats poor and rich as equals. Money does not know the 'value' of health care, it only knows the cost of health care and the profit which can be gained from it. The attack on the welfare state involved the injection not only of commercial criteria but also the attempt to impose the spirit of inequality, i.e. the inequality of the private market individual. The imposition of the abstract equality of money involved the imposition of inequality because 'the power which each individual exercises over the activity of others or over social wealth exists in him as the owner of *exchange values*, of *money*' (Marx, 1973, p. 157). The decomposition of labour on the basis of 'equality' negated and disrupted the socialisation of labour's antagonism in favour of the reconstitution of social relations on the basis of financial ability; the equality of the market individual before the power of money. The attack on collective provision in favour of market freedom and choice encouraged individualistic forms of social cooperation as amply expressed in the encouragement of greed associated with the modern personification of the erstwhile clerk: i.e. the yuppy. The abdication of public responsibility for private provision and the erosion of those provisions that remained in public responsibility revolved around the market-led recomposition of class relations on the basis of the distinction between the strong and able and those who are not. The market-led reconstitution of social relations involved the imposition of formal equality through selective access to hierarchical values. All this involved the imposition of the lurid face of equality which is characteristic of an organisation of work based on capitalist exchange relations. The imposition of poverty, hierarchical values and individualistic forms of social cooperation were used as a means of countering solidarity on the part of insubordinate labour.

The great institution of civilisation, money, supported itself by making those whom capital found it difficult to exploit pay for the promiscuous and incestuous speculation of money with itself. The containment of labour in the form of capital took on the forms of credit and fiscal expansion (permitting a containment of labour's productive power in ever-more speculative forms), on the one hand and, on the other, the expansion of pacification costs designed to decompose class relations and to destroy the Keynesian nexus between public expenditure and wages. The monetary decomposition of class relations involved a repressive use of public expenditure, conferring on those upon whose passivity the stability of a policy of state austerity rested the generosity of the market (wage increases, shareholding, owner occupation), while imposing poverty, work, and repressive bureaucratic supervision upon those pushed to the margins of the labour market.[8]

During the 1980s, the welfare state was progressively transformed from an institution designed to maintain workers for capitalist exploitation into an institution not only of controlling those pushed to the margins of social life but also of imposing poverty and of trapping and forcing people into low paid employment. However, this transformation of the welfare state was expensive and proved difficult to implement, as can be seen by the uneven development in the reconstruction of the welfare state. The attack concentrated on those sections of the working class, such as women, young workers, the unemployed and 'racial' minorities, which could be separated from the organised labour movement much more easily than others. On a global scale, the attack focused on those hardest hit by the recession of the early 1980s. The antagonism to a control through debt was thus decomposed on the basis of what Hirsch (1985/1991) refers to as the 'southafricanisation' of metropolitan countries. This characterisation is shared by Negri (1989, p. 97) who argues that the 'ideal of modern-day capitalism is apartheid'. However, and as Negri insists, unlike Hirsch, apartheid is the ideal but not the reality. The reality was insubordinate labour and its containment through the decomposition of class relations. The aim has been to avoid, even at the cost of unrestricted credit expansion, any overt form of working class insubordination.

The decomposition of labour along the lines of a 'dual society' imposed upon the class conflict a pluralist conflict over status and position in society. Hierarchies and pluralist conflicts were imposed and reinforced. These run counter to class relations and channelled class conflict into forms which divided social relations according to wage differentials, according to gender, according to 'race', according to 'region', according to religion, according to skill, according to 'nation' (bloodiest of all) and according to rich and poor countries.

Divisions increased the conflict amongst the 'segments'. As Cleaver (1993, p. 37) puts it in discussing the United States, 'counterattacks against particular sectors, expecially those whose demands and struggles cut transversally across numerous other conflicts (e.g. the women's movement, "minority" movements, and immigrant self-mobilisation) have involved fuelling the most vitriolic ideologies of human division – sexism, racism and ethnic jingoism'. Instead of the abstract equality of money being confronted with the demand for social self-determination, the decomposition of class relations resulted all too often in a conflict which balanced society: the political response to already ghettoized 'minority populations' supported 'juridical and legislative attacks on gender rights' and 'racial rights as well as welfare state cuts' (see Cleaver, 1993, p. 38). The decomposition of class relations helped, thus, to make 'conflicts' constructive for capital and capable of being exploited for the removal of 'protective rights'. However, a constructive conflict is always precarious and does not lack its destructive potential.[9] The war in the former Yugoslavia stands as a warning.

The imposition of tight money rested on a systematic exercise of state power that defined social activity on the basis of the market – poverty is not unfreedom. The shift in emphasis of the meaning of consensus to unquestioned obedience and the crushing of 'disobedience' through a repressive display of state power reaffirms negatively the difficulty capital faced in securing the subordination of social relations to the abstract equality of exchange relations and, within exchange, of exploitation.

The decomposition of class on the basis of the categories of property owner and citizen was made possible by sustained accumulation and an array of state violence, stretching from the repressive use of the welfare state to the paramilitary suppression of dissent and the legal and monetary disciplining of trade unions to police their members without leaving them in exchange even a semblance of political involvement. The highly differentiated mixture of attack and conciliation involved the policing of social relations by a state that was prepared to resort to provocation and highly differentiated use of force.

AND YET...

The destruction of the conditions of homogeneity of the class struggle against the imposition of money-in-command went hand-in-hand with a continuous dissociation of money from exploitation. The monetary and legal decomposition of class relations and the attempt to recompose social relations on the basis of the individualising and fragmenting form of the wage relation was based on credit-sustained accumulation. During the 1980s, speculation was not a sign of a lean and fit capitalism but an expression of insubordinate labour. Insubordinate labour was not only contained through speculation: it existed through speculation. Monetarism's control through book-keeping was never successful, however painful the results of its attempt.

The very intensity of the attack against labour underlines the depth of the crisis of capital. In spite of all the hardship, all the misery, all the cost-cutting, all the poverty, all the intensification and restructuring of labour, capital is still incapable of reproducing itself other than by credit expansion, other than by committing more and more of the surplus value not yet produced. In spite of all the triumphs of capital, it seems incapable of ridding itself of the insubordination which has entered into it like a chronic disease.

During the 1980s, the speculative dimension of accumulation expressed the speculative containment of insubordinate labour. The unregulated expansion of credit and the abrasive attack on the working class are closely interconnected. The more the dependence of capital on labour was sustained by credit, the more the state had to guarantee credit through the eradication of public deficits. The more the state cut back on welfare spending, on housing, health and social security, the more people were forced into debt in order to maintain a tolerable standard of living. The more the whole existence of capital was based on credit, the more capital needed to push through changes in working practices, changes in technology and intensification of work as well as reductions in state expenditure in order to sustain the validity of credit. The more the state sought to reduce its social expenditure, the more private debt became a means either of securing the newly-won property rights or of sustaining basic subsistence levels, such as housing. Besides, the growth of credit increased inflationary pressure and speculative attacks on currency. High interest rates helped to control inflationary pressure and to liquidate some money as personal bankruptcies and repossessions increased. The disciplinary force of the socialisation of 'bad debt' is enormous. The inability of capital to control social relations through a policy of state austerity is oppressive in terms of individualising private debt and its enforcement. However, the attempt to decompose the homogeneity of resistance to money had a contradictory result in that the fragmenting attack on social relations involved the reconstitution of class relations on the basis of debt. The republic of individualised property owners turned, by the 1990s, into a republic of debt. The inflation of credit is the most powerful expression of the fragility of capital's containment of labour.

By the late 1980s, it became clear that the expansion of credit was not matched by an integration of labour with an expansion of capitalist accumulation. The attempt to deflate the money supply, and thus to guarantee credit through taxation, by a policy of state austerity was successful in containing class struggle through a monetary and legal decomposition of class relations. However, it failed to decompose the working class into a profitable labour force. The credit boom of the 1980s turned into a credit crisis. The integration of abstract labour with the value form is based on bad debt. The attempt to guarantee credit growth through poverty, increased job insecurity, and an attack on trade unions which sought to hinder a collective response by limiting the scope for trade union organisation and action, has failed. Capital has to face labour in the contested terrain of production. It cannot run away forever because the rising ratio of debt to surplus value will make it increasingly difficult to make money out of debt.

Over a period of two decades money has emerged as a central axis of class conflict. By the 1990s, the weakness of productive activity and the instability of the financial system presents the failure of neoliberalism to secure the future exploitation of labour in the present. Debt calls into question the monetarist attempt to recompose class in terms of the categories of property owner and citizen. The individualising monetary decomposition of class relations comes to the fore in its most violent form: the exhaustion of the illusion of prosperity and the transformation of prosperity into debt and bankruptcy. Far from stimulating investment, employment and output, the result of credit expansion in a tight monetary framework was the deterioration of conditions and mass unemployment. There was no breakthrough in investment. Credit expansion was used for speculation rather than for the generation of surplus value. The use of debt as an instrument of control, and the failure of this control in the form of a speculative boom, shows the strength of labour, even at the moment of defeat, to resist the recomposition between necessary and surplus labour. The result of this resistance was an integration of labour into the capital relation on the basis of an iredeemable expansion of credit.

The reconstitution of the circuit of social capital does not just require, as during the 1980s, a divisive and fragmenting decomposition of class relations in terms of the property owner and citizen. Rather, it involves the imposition of valorisation upon the labour process. Such an imposition implies not just the intensification of work and the repressive exclusion from production of those whom capital is forced to disregard as being inessential. It entails the transformation of money into truly productive capital. This transformation presupposes the subordination of labour to an expanded extortion of surplus value. In other words, money, rather than betting on future exploitation, has to be transformed into an effective command over labour in the present. This means that the exploitation of labour has to deliver rates of profit adequate to redeem debt and to allow for expanded capitalist accumulation. This exploitation of labour presupposes the recomposition of the relation between necessary and surplus labour. The recomposition of this relation is still beyond the horizon. There is no surer indication than the ballooning of bad debt that capital has not succeeded in imposing a recomposition of the relations of exploitation adequate to the accumulated claims upon surplus value.

The experience of the last twenty years suggests that the transformation of money into truly productive capital is both essential and impossible. Capital cannot run from labour for ever, yet the experience of the last twenty years suggests that it is also incapable of confronting labour on the terrain of production in a way that would restore a sound basis for capital accumulation. For the last twenty years, everything possible has been done to avoid a repeat of 1929, not for humanitarian reasons, but because a comparable destruction of fictitious capital would now be not at all comparable in its magnitude and its implications: it would shake capitalism to its very foundations. When a repeat performance of the Crash of 1929 threatened in October 1987, even the most fierce monetarists advocated expansion – anything to avoid the catastrophe, and confrontation, that a slump would bring.

There seems to be no way forward, for capital or for labour. Yet this is not the first time. Writing in 1934, Paul Mattick suggested that capitalism had entered an age of permanent crisis:

> The periodicity of crisis is in practice nothing other than the recurrent reorganisation of the process of accumulation on a new level of value and price which again secures the accumulation of capital. If that is not possible, then neither is it possible to confirm accumulation; the same crisis that up to now had presented itself chaotically and could be overcome becomes permanent crisis (1934/1978, p. 94).

In contrast to previous crises of capitalism, which had always led to a restructuring of capital and to a renewed period of accumulation, the crisis of the 1930s appeared to be so profound and prolonged as to be incapable of solution. Crisis, Mattick suggested, had ceased to be a periodically recurring phenomenon and had become an endemic feature of capitalism.

Mattick's suggestion, pessimistic though it was, turned out to be far too optimistic. Capital *did* resolve its crisis, in blood. Capital *was* restructured and the basis for a new period of accumulation created. This 'golden age' of post-war capitalism is now a memory and once again it would seem that we are in a situation of permanent crisis. It is possible that the crisis will be permanent, with a progressive 'southafricanisation' or 'brazilianisation' of the world, a gradual increase in inequality, violence, famine, war. It is possible too that the crisis will not be permanent, that it will in fact be resolved: what the resolution of 'permanent crisis' can mean stands behind us as a warning of a possibly nightmarish future.

The argument proposed here suggest also another possible future. The crisis of capital is the crisis of capital's dependence upon labour. The 'permanence' of the crisis is not only a warning but a message of hope. The hope is that, if capital, for all the intensity of its struggle, has not yet achieved the decomposition of the working class into a profitable labour force, it is because of the enormous power of insubordinate labour. Currency crisis, debt crisis, recession and so forth, are false names for the crisis of the capitalist exploitation of labour. 'Capital' cannot be blamed for its crisis. Rather, credit should be given to whom credit is due: the insubordinate existence of labour. Theoretically and practically, this power must be made manifest.

226   *Conclusion*

Notes

1. See also Bologna's (1993) intriguing commentary on Marx's writing on money between 1856 and 1987.
2. On the politics of post-war reconstruction, see Burnham (1990).
3. Of course money was not the only element. Rearmament and Mc-Carthyism also played an important part. McCarthyism is merely the US–American expression of virulent anti-communism which was supported on a global scale by the theory of totalitarianism which equated fascism with communism. This equation destroyed any connection between fascism and capitalism. Totalitarian theory worked like a washing powder: capitalism cleaned itself from fascism, war and destruction, and reappeared as the true and only lover of humanity. The Cold War was the lover's honeymoon.
4. See Bonefeld's 'Monetarism and Crisis', Chapter 3 in this volume. See also Marazzi's, 'Money in the World Crisis', Chapter 4 in this volume.
5. See Bonefeld (1993), Hirsch (1980) and Lotringer and Marazzi (1980), respectively.
6. See Ford (1988) on debt and individualisation.
7. For example, in the United Kingdom, the young unemployed on government training schemes are not regarded as employed by the Department of Health and Social Security. This means that they are not entitled to industrial injury benefits.
8. The dispersion between high and low paid workers increased dramatically. According to S. Brittan (*Financial Times*, 6 January 1994) it 'has increased to levels greater than anything since the 1940s'. See also Mitter (1986).
9. On the dialectical continuum between contructive and destructive conflicts, see Agnoli (1992).

References

Agnoli, J. (1992) 'Destruction as the Determination of the Scholar in Miserable Times', *Common Sense*, 12.
Bologna, S. (1993) 'Money and Crisis: Marx as Correspondent of the New York Daily Tribune, 1856–1857', *Common Sense*, 13 and 14.
Bonefeld, W. (1993) *The Recomposition of the British State During the 1980s* (Aldershot: Dartmouth).
Burnham, P. (1990) *The Political Economy of Post-War Reconstruction* (London: Macmillan).
Cleaver, H. (1993) 'Marxian Categories, The Crisis of Capital and the Constitution of Social Subjectivity Today',*Common Sense*, 14.
Ford, J. (1988) *The Indebted Society: Credit and Default in the 1980s* (London: Routledge).
Hirsch, J. (1980) *Der Sicherheitsstaat* (Frankfurt: Europäische Verlagsanstalt).
Hirsch, J. (1985/1991) 'Fordism and Post-Fordism', in W. Bonefeld and J. Holloway (eds), *Post-Fordism and Social Form* (London: Macmillan).
Lotringer, S. and Ch. Marazzi (eds) (1980) *Italy: Autonomia – Post-Political Politics* (New York: Semiotext(e)).

Marx, K. (1973) *Grundrisse* (Harmondsworth: Penguin).

Mattick, P. (1934/1978) 'Zur Marxschen Akkumulations- und Zusammen-bruchstheorie', *Rätekorrespondenz*, 4 (1934); reprinted in Spanish in K. Korsch, P. Mattick and A. Pannekoek, 'Derrumbe del Copitalismo o Sujeto Revolucionario?', *Cuadernos del Pasado y Presente*, 78, Siglo XXI, Mexico City (1978).

Mitter, S. (1986) *Common Fate Common Bond* (London: Pluto Press).

Negri, A. (1989) *The Politics of Subversion* (Cambridge: Polity Press).

Schlesinger, A. (1959) *The Coming of the New Deal* (Boston: Houghton Mifflin) (Vol. II of *The Age of Roosevelt*).

Index of Names